Electronic Communication Interception

Technologies and Issues of Power

Series Editor
Daniel Ventre

Electronic Communication Interception Technologies and Issues of Power

Daniel Ventre

Philippe Guillot

WILEY

First published 2023 in Great Britain and the United States by ISTE Ltd and John Wiley & Sons, Inc.

ISTE Ltd
27-37 St George's Road
London SW19 4EU
UK

www.iste.co.uk

John Wiley & Sons, Inc.
111 River Street
Hoboken, NJ 07030
USA

www.wiley.com

Any opinions, findings, and conclusions or recommendations expressed in this material are those of the author(s), contributor(s) or editor(s) and do not necessarily reflect the views of ISTE Group.

Library of Congress Control Number: 2023936114

British Library Cataloguing-in-Publication Data
A CIP record for this book is available from the British Library
ISBN 978-1-78630-802-3

Contents

Introduction

For several decades, the practices surrounding the interception of communications have steadily occupied a prominent place in the news, giving rise to societal, political, legal and sociological debates. The risks of the democratic states' abuse of practices reminiscent from totalitarian regimes have been repeatedly pointed out by the advocates of freedom in the western world. The further the communication technologies evolve, the more communication spaces are deployed, and the stronger the temptations to control what is said and written seem. Alongside targeted interceptions – aiming at one or a few individuals in particular – the possibilities for bulk interception have multiplied. These two practices have quite a long history. But the advent of the Internet society ("cyberspace") has undoubtedly marked a turning point in the practices and ambitions of those who resort to interceptions. Despite requiring technically complex operations, the very architecture of cyberspace – a planetary network of continuous flows – facilitates the exploitation of these masses of data, which simultaneously provide information about individuals, observable one by one, and human groups. While communication technologies have multiplied and extended, interception technologies have also done so, be it for security, surveillance or control purposes, for economic, political or military espionage, or for other applications. The practice seems unabashed: all states practice legal interceptions. There are many who practice interceptions outside the legal framework, or have failed to define a proper set of rules. Interceptions seem to be practiced all around, with many reasons legitimizing their use. They also benefit from a panoply of technologies which allegedly have no limits. Such commercial products are capable of intercepting almost every communication, by wire or wireless, regardless of the protocols or the media the communication infrastructures pass through (land, air, sea). The debates over the past decade have emphasized the erosion of trust between allied countries that have never ceased to spy on each other, intercepting the communications of their political or industrial leaders; debates have also insisted on the weakening of the rights and freedoms of citizens all over the world. While the responsibility of the actors deciding on the implementation of interceptions is essential, the role of technology is also relevant. Because, beyond the law itself, technology determines what can actually be done. The role of inventors, researchers, engineers, developers, industrialists and merchants is just as crucial as that of the customers who benefit from such technologies, even if the latter are not always totally aware of how technology works, nor the effects it may produce. Not only do the end users of interception depend on technologies they cannot master, but also on the designers, technicians and engineers who certainly master their technical side, but who sometimes remain distant from the social and political implications of their work. There are many who navigate in a universe of misunderstanding, ignorance, beliefs and even the unthought-of.

Definitions of interception (and some associated notions)

Let us start by clarifying the terms of our study.

If we refer to the definition proposed by the *Centre national de ressources textuelles et lexicales*[1] (CNRTL, National Center of Textual and Lexical Resources), interception denotes at least two categories of action. The first category involves detaining the object or message so that it does not reach its recipient, whereas the second one refers to the act of reading a message intended for a third party. Interrupting the progress of the message can also result in its destruction. These two facets of interception are broken down as follows by the CNRTL:

> The action of taking something in passing, of diverting it from its destination; the action of becoming aware of a conversation, of a message intended for others; the action of hindering the spread of something, someone's progress; in the military field, the attempt at destroying an enemy target (ship, plane, missile) in motion.

Interception is also defined in legal technical or political documents. Thus, the ITU (International Telecommunication Union) formulates a definition which insists on the technological dimension of interceptions. It contemplates several practices such as:

> the acquisition, viewing, capture, or copying of the contents or a portion thereof, of any communication, including content data, computer data, traffic data, and/or electronic emissions thereof, whether by wire, wireless, electronic, optical, magnetic, oral, or other means, during

---

1 See: https://www.cnrtl.fr/definition/interception.

transmission through the use of any electronic, mechanical, optical, wave, electromechanical, or other device [INT 12].

Interception refers to a set of practices, which are reserved for specific actors, mainly the state, for intelligence purposes and/or for fighting against crime, terrorism and for the defense of national security: "Interception includes all acts of monitoring, copying, diverting, duplicating and storing communications in the course of their transmission by or for law enforcement or intelligence agencies" [PRI 21].

Interception can be implemented on all communication vectors, and applied to all types of content (voice, image, text). It involves the use of diverse interception means, depending on the media and the targeted content: "The term 'intercept' is defined in 18 U.S.C.§ 2510(4) to mean the aural or other acquisition of the contents of any wire, electronic, or oral communication through the use of any electronic, mechanical, or other device" [DEP 20].

> An "intercept" is the term used to describe the covert interception of a private communication by intelligence services or law enforcement agencies. The interception of telephone calls – e.g. by use of wiretaps, etc. – is perhaps the best-known example. However, under the Regulation of Investigatory Powers Act 2000 ("RIPA"), "intercepted communications" also covers other kinds of communications, including mobile phones, email, fax and ordinary post [JUS 06].

A distinction should also be made between interception and surveillance, even if the two practices are closely related.

For the CNRTL[2], surveillance is:

> The action or act of watching over a person that you are responsible for or interested in; the monitoring of suspicious persons or risky environments by the police, in order to prevent criminal actions and guarantee public security.

According to the CNRTL[3] dictionary, to surveil is to:

> Observe someone with a certain attention to understand their behavior; to watch over a person that you are morally responsibility for or interested in; to observe the actions of potential adversaries, the places where danger may arise from. A sentry surveilling the bridge;

2 See: www.cnrtl.fr/definition/surveillance.

3 See: www.cnrtl.fr/definition/surveiller.

to be kept informed about the activities of people deemed suspicious, the behavior of communities, groups or places at risk, by police means.

Therefore, interception is generally only one component of surveillance. It is possible to monitor individuals without necessarily resorting to the interception of their communications. But when surveillance is exercised over communications, a whole set of practices and techniques take place alongside interception, such as observation, collection, etc., creating a long chain of processes into which interception is inserted:

> Communications surveillance is the monitoring, interception, collection, preservation and retention of information that has been communicated, relayed or generated over communications networks to a group of recipients by a third party [...] In turn, communications surveillance is no longer limited to intercepting a messenger or attaching a 'crocodile clip' to a telephone line. There are now four main methods of communications surveillance: internet monitoring, mobile phone interception, fixed line interception, and intrusion technologies (which are explained in detail below). Surveillance over internet, mobile, and fixed-line networks can take place with or without the cooperation of the network operator... [PRI 18].

> The interception of communications is simply one type of covert surveillance among the many used by law enforcement agencies and intelligence services in order to prevent and detect serious crime (including terrorist activity). However, for reasons that are examined in detail below, UK law has long treated the use of information gained from intercepted communications differently from other forms of surveillance [JUS 06].

Therefore, surveillance cannot be reduced to the sole practice of interceptions.

Interception involves performing an action on the telecommunications system (modifying or tampering with the system or its operations, monitoring transmissions). This should result in the provision of the communication's contents to a person who is not its originally intended recipient. Interception can take place during the transmission of information, or in a deferred manner during its storage, for example, before or after the transmission:

> Interception is the obtaining of the content of a communication – such as a telephone call, email or social media message – in the course of its transmission or while stored on a telecommunications system [HOM 17].

The principle of interception can be summarized in a simple diagram. If we consider two interlocutors, A and B (two individuals, groups or "actors") who exchange one or more messages, interception is the intervention of a third (C) uninvited party the exchange, whose aim is to be able to hear, read or know what is being said or written within this intimate space formed between A and B.

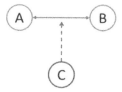

Figure I.1. *Elementary diagram of the interception principle*

This implies that for C, the exchange between A and B contains a certain value, a (real or potential) interest. C hopes to draw some benefit from, or to gain an advantage over A, B, or other parties not directly involved in the exchange between A and B. In the view of A and B, entity C is an intruder who undermines the intimacy space conveyed by communication.

This basic scheme will be further discussed later, as it can be supplemented and made more complex by integrating other actors, in particular, those related to technology.

Let us recall some of the features characterizing the interception of communications:

– The access to the very contents of the exchanges is the main specificity of interception. Does the access to metadata (and not to the content) imply interception, and if so, which legal framework governs this?

– Interception does not appear to be strictly limited to data-in-transit, but can also apply to statically stored data in a storage space or "data-at-rest" (but in that case, what is the difference between interception, access and intrusion?).

– Interception is one of the modalities of surveillance, which it can supplement and accompany.

– Interception is of interest only insofar as the message's sender and receiver are unaware of its existence, and ignore the presence of an indiscreet ear or furtive glance over their communications. But, as will be shown, sender and receiver have learned to adapt, even when their communications are intercepted or threatened with being intercepted. Resistance tactics or strategies have been developed.

The notion of interception is thus broken down into legal, strategic, tactical, bulk, passive and active interception (non-exhaustive list). The distinction between targeted interception and non-targeted or bulk interception is key.

Targeted interceptions are those aimed at one or more distinct individuals, in a specific manner. Targeted interception can be used on UK citizens who are suspected of illegal activity. It can be conducted on a specific person or a specific location by the police, intelligence agencies or the armed forces. The request must be specific as to who or what will be spied on and where. Targeted can also be used in a thematic way. Thematic means groups of people, an area of locations, a number of organisations[4].

> States have access to a number of different techniques and technologies to conduct communications surveillance of a targeted individual's private communications. Real-time interception capabilities allow States to listen to and record the phone calls of any individual using a fixed line or mobile telephone, through the use of interception capabilities for State surveillance that all communications networks are required to build into their systems. An individual's location can be ascertained, and their text messages read and recorded. By placing a tap on an Internet cable relating to a certain location or person, State authorities can also monitor an individual's online activity, including the websites he or she visits [LAR 13].

Bulk interceptions differ from the previous ones both by their target and their technological dimension: capturing data in larger volumes, for example, by exploiting the data flows circulating on the Internet, they are not used in the context of surveys, but rather for intelligence collection: "Bulk interception is a vital tool designed to obtain foreign-focused intelligence and identify individuals, groups and organizations overseas that pose a threat to the UK" [FAC 15]:

> [Bulk interception] is done by tapping internet cables carrying the world's internet traffic. The intelligence agencies now have the lawful power to tap these cables and grab chunks of internet activity. Bulk interception is broad, rarely based on a specific investigation and is used to look for plots, behavior or activity which may potentially be of a criminal or terrorist nature[5].

Interception is the ability to listen in on what someone says or writes. There are two types of interception in the Investigatory Powers Act;

---

4 See: www.bigbrotherwatch.org.uk/wp-content/uploads/2016/03/Interception.pdf.
5 See: www.bigbrotherwatch.org.uk/wp-content/uploads/2016/03/Interception.pdf.

targeted and bulk. Targeted is used when the focus of the investigation is known. Bulk is used when the target is unknown. Bulk interception describes the gathering of large chunks of internet traffic from around the world. Because bulk is used to discover rather than investigate it could be described as a form of pre-crime investigation[6].

Bulk interceptions began long before the recent harshly criticized American intelligence agency programs:

> Mass interception of telegrams, known as "cable censorship", began along with postal censorship on 2nd August 1914, days before the formal outbreak of the First World War. The primary aim in the beginning was to ban enemy diplomatic traffic altogether rather than to selectively intercept it. Censors were installed at London cable offices and in Porthcurno, Cornwall, which had by then become a relay hub for the world's international submarine cables [KEE 17].

The second essential notion is that of "data", which can be classified into several categories. The term "data" does not only refer to the content (the information communicated), but also to traffic data (i.e. its communication), metadata (a category of data that is differentiated from the content[7] itself), computer data, location data, stored communication data ("data-at-rest", "in the cloud", "in storage"), dynamic data ("data-in-transit", "data-in-motion"), personal data, private data, sensitive data, confidential data, secret data, etc.

Dynamic data, or data-in-motion, are the main target of interceptions.

Our definition of the interception of communications: rebalancing an informational asymmetry

Interception creates or reveals power relationships that aim to rebalance an informational asymmetry existing between the parties involved in a communication, and those who are left outside of it.

---

6 See: www.bigbrotherwatch.org.uk/wp-content/uploads/2016/03/Interception.pdf   [Accessed March 1, 2017].

7 "Données techniques nécessaires à l'acheminement d'une communication" [Online]. Available at: www.signal.eu.org/blog/2015/04/20/eu-org-les-metadonnees-et-la-loi-information. "Metadata designate a set of standardized information relating to a file, such as author name, resolution, color space, copyright information, and other keywords applied to it" [Online]. Available at: www.helpx.adobe.com/fr/bridge/using/metadata-adobe-bridge.html.

The communicating parties thus create a confidentiality space, and those who are excluded feel that this situation is prejudicial to them, or that the access to knowledge is essential to them.

The variables at stake are:

– the communication space, the target area of interception attacks, essentially involving communication technologies;

– the defensive dimension: the protection techniques (against interception threats);

– the offensive dimension: interception technologies.

The technological dimension is key. Law itself may seem constrained by the technology whose developments it strives to integrate:

> Section 702 itself is a relatively new amendment to the FISA statute [...] It was written to accommodate prior developments in technology, but also intended to adapt to future changes by remaining technology neutral[8].

> Even the Supreme Court has begun to recognize the limitations on its ability to set out a legal framework that suitably marries Fourth Amendment doctrine with emerging technology[9].

State of the art of recent research on interceptions

CITs (Communication Interception Technologies)[10] and more broadly, electronic surveillance technologies, ignited hot debates in the 1980s [OFF 85, OFF 87], and then specifically at the end of the 1990s, with the reports regarding the Echelon network [WRI 98, BEC 99, CAM 99, SCH 01]. These debates were renewed in the early 2010s, even before Edward Snowden's revelations [HOF 05, DEA 10,

---

8 "Judicial Oversight of Section 702 of the Foreign Intelligence Surveillance Act, Presented to The Robert S. Strauss Center for International Security and Law and The University of Texas School of Law, Austin, Texas", September 14, 2014 [Online]. Available at: www.nsa.gov/DesktopModules/ArticleCS/Print.aspx?PortalId=70&ModuleId=9757& Article=1619167.

9 "Failing to Keep Pace: the Cyber Threat and Its Implications for Our Privacy Laws, Washington", May 23, 2018 [Online]. Available at: www.nsa.gov/news-features/speeches-testimonies/Article/1608850/.

10 We will retain this acronym (CIT) so as not to confuse it with ICT (Information and Communications Technology).

BUT 12, CON 13, BEL 14]. CITs are portrayed as essential "weapons" in the fight against crime, namely as indispensable police intelligence tools. Apart from these few academic references and reports produced over the period, it becomes clear that the volume of works specifically addressing interception technologies in the humanities and social sciences remains relatively low. Legal and ethical debates take the lion's share (interceptions, and more broadly surveillance, motivate debates on the right to privacy), and the theme of the surveillance society or panoptic society has declined in sociological and political works. These debates mainly focus on all kinds of interception and surveillance practices, the effects produced, the organizations that deploy them, their consequences on societies, the international scene or individuals.

Over the past decade, works in the human and social sciences that addressed the phenomenon of interceptions have essentially adopted three types of approach: the legal, the historical or the political/sociological/geopolitical approach.

These works are indicative of the shock wave caused by the Snowden revelations, which manifested through debates on a planetary scale regarding the questions of surveillance, freedoms (of speech, of opinion, etc.), privacy, as well as Internet geopolitics [CLE 14] or governance, digital sovereignty, data protection, security and national defense, the configuration of the balance of power in the international scene, the relationship between economy/industry, citizens and the state.

The legal approach

Legal studies deal with interceptions in several aspects and propose to:

– compare the legal regimes applicable to interception in several countries [GAL 16a] through their particularities or convergences in terms of the distribution of interception powers, the levels and methods for protecting communication secrecy, the conditions for content interception, the access to traffic and user data, the access to stored data [POL 16];

– debate the question of fundamental rights (freedom of expression, respect for the secrecy of correspondence, etc.) in contrast with the evolution of national laws on interception [MAK 11; NGW 17];

– analyze the role of each actor involved in interception procedures from a legal perspective [GAL 16a];

– discuss the limits to weight-of-evidence approaches regarding the data collected during interceptions [GAL 16b];

– consider the conditions for respecting individual rights in the face of illegal interception, or the abuse of legal interception [EIJ 18];

– confront existing law with technological developments and the adaptation of crime to its environment (e.g. when criminal interceptions exploit Wi-Fi communications) [THO 15].

The historical approach

Similarly to the study by David Sherman [SHE 16], which focuses on the Bletchley Park code breakers since the start of World War II, many works explore particular moments in history (interceptions during World War I, World War II, the Cold War, etc.).

On the contrary, the work by Bernard Keenan [KEE 16; KEE 17] on interceptions covers several centuries. It offers a chronology of interceptions in England, which he classifies into three periods: the so-called royal "prerogative" phase, from 1590 (or 1634) to 1984; the "obfuscation" phase from 1985 to 2015; and the so-called "transparency" phase, since 2016.

The first phase (1634–1984) began with the English Royal messenger service opening up to public use, introduced as a means for disseminating knowledge, information and commerce. The centralized control of information paved the way for new intelligence methods, in fields as diverse as the fight against crime and against any form of political conspiracy, whether domestic or foreign. From a legal point of view, since those times, the secrecy of correspondence has been a principle enshrined in law (1657)[11], establishing that mail can only be intercepted and opened with the authorization of a judge. The law makes it possible to sanction anyone who interferes with the Post Office. However, authorizations are not expected to ensure control over state-related power practices, which have been covered by secrecy until the 21st century.

The second period (1985–2015), known as the "obfuscation" phase started with the Malone case, named after a criminally prosecuted dealer who forced the issue in the High Court in 1979, after he found out that the police had been tapping his telephone line. The High Court dismissed Malone, recalling that there is nothing illegal about wiretapping, with the principle of privacy protection not being contemplated by Common Law. Malone then brought the case before the European Court of Human Rights in Strasbourg. The latter considered that Article 8 of the European Convention on Human Rights grants the British people a right to privacy,

---

11 British History (1911). June 1657: An Act for settling the Postage of England, Scotland and Ireland. In *Acts and Ordinances of the Interregnum, 1642–1660*, Firth, C.H. and Rait R.S. (eds). British History, London [Online]. Available at: www.british-history.ac.uk/no-series/acts-ordinances-interregnum/pp1110–1113.

and therefore, that the interception of communications interfere with this right. To make such interceptions legal, several conditions must be met, under Article 8: the country must specify the legal limits to interception, and the legality of interference has to comply with two principles: necessity and proportionality. In 1985, the United Kingdom adopted a law (Interception of Communication Act, 1985), passed by the Thatcher administration, which privatized telecommunications companies and allowed the state to maintain its prerogatives, by retaining its interception power. This law from 1985 was replaced with the RIPA (Regulation of Investigatory Powers Act) in 2000. This text was sufficiently imprecise or general to grant the authorities ample powers, applicable to all kinds of technologies. The text was intended to be technologically neutral: "its high degree of abstraction served to ensure it was 'technology neutral', in that it established general rules applicable across different forms of digital media" [KEE 17].

This method is what Keenan denominates obfuscation[12]. Duncan Campbell's revelations (on the nature of the Echelon network) as well as those by Snowden, confirmed the existence of state practices neglecting citizen's rights, by capturing massive amounts of data from ordinary individuals. The scope of powers related to interception is broad, giving authorities free rein to conduct mass interception programs, share data with third countries, hack systems, impose constraints on operators, etc. The opacity surrounding these practices was such that none of the organizations (Investigative Powers Tribunal, Interception of Communications Commissioner) that were expected to monitor interception practices and formulate opinions or receive complaints from citizens seemed to be fully aware of their extent.

The debates opened by Snowden and some pro-privacy organizations coincided with a growing awareness of the unprecedented ways in which life lived online renders us transparent to both private companies and state actors. This is the third period that Keenan proposes to consider, which he calls the transparency phase, starting in 2016.

According to Keenan, what has changed in recent decades is how the individual is now less central. The individual is no longer the essential "reference point", with surveillance powers having the ability to reach not only individuals, but entire groups; these individuals and groups can be defined according to characteristics suggested by their data. The fact that the states can collect or intercept data on a

---

12 Obfuscation can be defined as a strategy for protecting privacy on the Internet by publishing false or sufficiently inaccurate information so that the true or relevant information is masked (obfuscation is therefore an anonymization, a masking strategy); it can also refer to a technique for making a program unreadable to human beings, while keeping it fully functional. See: https://en.wiktionary.org/wiki/obfuscation.

massive scale creates the conditions for mass surveillance. This does not imply that all individuals in society are subject to specific observation, but rather that the data drawn from each of us can be present in an analysis process.

The political, sociological, geopolitical approach

The UTIC project

The UTIC research project (research project carried out in France, coordinated by Didier Bigo – Science Po Paris – and funded by the French National Research Agency) focused on "the uses of technologies related to the interception of telephone and internet communications by the police and intelligence services, and by their private providers", specifically addressing the case of France in its European environment. The project was carried out over the 2014–2019 period, set within the post-Snowden context, a period of controversy and polemics around state practices in terms of the interception of communications and their consequences on modern societies, democracies and individuals. The project focused on four areas: surveillance logics, the justification discourse, the redefinition of the boundaries of democracy and state sovereignty.

The project analyzed several aspects of interception:

– Thanks to the Internet, states have a greater oversight on companies through the surveillance of their communications. New technical capacities have contributed to establishing its massive character. Has the fact that they are carried out in bulk, without any individual warrants, changed the nature of the interception? How do we define their bulk character? Does it infringe on the privacy of all the individuals whose data are collected in this way?

– Bulk interceptions are justified by various purposes: the fight against crime, terrorism, economic or political intelligence, etc. The justification for the bulk nature of interceptions changes depending on the intelligence services involved within the same country, and from country to country. The project attempted to analyze these relationships.

– The internationalization of security issues, coupled with the global dimension of the Internet, gives a new dimension to interception and surveillance practices. Data collection escapes the national framework, data are exchanged between intelligence services and private operators that are internationally engaged in data collection, retention and processing. The project focused on these hybridizations (public–private, alliances, international cooperation, etc.) and their effects on the definition of security goals, interception practices, the assessment of the risks and effects produced, and in particular, on fundamental rights.

The project resulted in the production of a series of reports, whose main conclusions are summarized as follows:

– The report produced by Guillot and Ventre, "*Capacités d'interception et de surveillance. L'évolution des systèmes techniques*", explores the wide range of technologies or interception techniques available in the era of electronic communications, as well as the means to protect ourselves against these practices and counter them. "Understanding the techniques, technologies, capacities, resources, means used, deployed and developed, is essential [...] Because there can be no sound measurement of what is at stake without a proper assessment or understanding, even if minimum, of what is possible" [GUI 19].

– The first part of the report "*Techniques et contre-mesures techniques*" [SIL 18] specifically addresses the use of deep packet inspection (DPI) in French and European surveillance. For its authors, in terms of bulk interceptions, law is continually evolving in order to adapt to technological developments. It is therefore not so much that the law constrains technological capacities and their uses, but rather that the latter impose themselves over the law. It is the meeting between the economic interests of companies and the states' security goals that seems to dictate the rules of the game. DPI technologies have been misused in several states. "The tacitly accepted limit between the legitimate or illegitimate use of these technologies, depending on whether the state is 'democratic' or not, and those of the purposes, is subtle" [SIL18, p. 77]. The second part of the report analyzes the phenomenon of resistance to surveillance.

– Bonelli and Ragazzi [BON 14] recall that in a highly technical context, intelligence still resorts to traditional collection and information processing techniques, since the practices of security professionals are rooted in institutional habits.

– The contribution by Bigo and Bonelli [BIG 19] also discusses intelligence actors and their practices, stressing the heterogeneity of the world of intelligence, particularly when it comes to surveillance techniques:

> it seems that digital techniques are put to use in two ways. First, they can be used in support of the more traditional framework of conjectural reasoning in order to provide necessary evidence for the judiciary. Second, they can also be used to impose a preventive and predictive reasoning. The logics and mechanisms of reasoning that are specific to each universe and its actors – be it the police, military, or communications – are therefore to be considered more important than the technology itself themselves. In other words, it is not computer technology itself that plays a role, but rather the entry of computer scientists into intelligence circles and the manner in which they frame problems in relation to technology.

– In "Seeing like big tech: security assemblies, technology, and the future of state bureaucracy", Tréguer [TRE 19] depicted the growing power of private companies as a result of their control over data. To exercise power over a digitized world, the state must reason as the Big Data industry does, adapt to its logics and appropriate them. It must surpass the simple public–private partnership and traditional arrangements aimed at regulating telecommunications networks.

– The report written by Laurent and Kheloufi [LAU 18] offers a legal analysis focusing on two categories of standards applicable to the exchange of individual communications: the "secrecy of correspondence" (SC) and "personal data protection" (PDP). According to the authors, the first was replaced by the second in our cybernetic universe. They concluded that despite the adaptation of legislation to enhance personal data protection, "states have not relinquished their right to exercise digital surveillance".

– In *"Les gouvernances mondiales fragmentées de l'Internet"* [LAU 19], the more global issue of Internet governance is discussed. The Internet's power, its network infrastructures, applications, the organization of its architecture, the role of states and the sharing of responsibilities with the private sector, the possibility of imposing its rules, has a tremendous grip over data, deciding on their flow, and possibilities for interception and the control of planetary communications.

The work of Joseph Fitsanakis

Since the 19th century, governments have always made sure to grant access to user communications, legitimized by the fight against crime and national security requirements. They did this without encountering any real resistance from the telecommunications operators. In the 1930s, the arrival of the telephone hardly changed this situation, which is why many states nationalized their telephone systems, considering them sensitive, in the same way as the army or the police. The United States was an exception, with the telephone being privatized, but the state exercised a strict control over it. These historical periods date the closely cooperative relationship between telecommunication companies and the state (its police, intelligence agencies). But in the 1980s, two factors upset this balance. First of all, digitization revolutionized the telecommunication sector, technically authorizing the creation of a wide range of new services, which can be perceived as obstacles to state interception capacities. Second, a political factor threatened these capacities, namely market deregulation and the privatization of companies in the telecommunication sector (during the mandate of Reagan in the United States and of Thatcher in the United Kingdom). This signaled the end of the AT&T monopoly in 1984 (United States) and the privatization of part of British Telecom in 1984 (United Kingdom), inducing a market fragmentation and an increase in the potential number of interlocutors for the state. Interactions between state security agencies and the private sector are becoming more complex.

The technological transition imposes a rapid evolution of interception means and for the governments, this requires guaranteeing the possibility of their implementation. They have pursued this goal via regulations in order to limit the network's technical means to ensure information security. It is to this end that the governments voted for CALEA (1994, United States) and RIPA (2000, United Kingdom). In both cases, the main measure involved compelling telephone operators to adapt their systems and technologies to meet the state's interception needs. Note that these laws do not define technical standards or specific criteria, but simply establish the principle of obligation.

The work also proposes a state-of-the-art of the literature, reaching back to the 1960s in the United States and the United Kingdom. From the works it lists, let us outline a number of key ideas: telecommunication operators responded without any resistance to police requests for interception [DAS 59]; it denounced the practices of an intrusive American government, exercising citizen surveillance by resorting to illicit means (in the 1970s); a mistrust of governments and security authorities then set in, official data on interceptions were called into question, intelligence agencies were suspected of hiding the reality of their practices to escape their responsibilities. Since the Watergate scandal, the criticism of the state only deepened. Interception is one of the most important practices for western security apparatuses, to the point of assuming banned uses, with the excesses being facilitated by the close, intimate relationship between security or intelligence agencies and operators.

The author usefully recalls the taxonomy of interceptions which had been proposed in the United Kingdom in the report by the expert "Smith Group 2000" [SMI 00], which draws a distinction between three types of interception:

– Active: designates software interception, configured by an Internet service provider (ISP) and which is applicable, for example, to email surveillance. Targeted emails are copied and sent to the authorities' server.

– Semi-active: a collection unit is placed on the premises of the intelligence agency (the GCHQ, Government Communications Headquarters) and connected to the network. The communications of persons under surveillance are routed via the collection unit; pre-selected IP addresses are assigned to people under surveillance.

– Passive: a data collection unit is connected to the network. But in this configuration, the unit permanently supervises the traffic. State agencies are here to supply, install and maintain hardware and software, and the unit can intercept without notifying the provider.

In semi-passive and active models, systems are an integral part of telecommunication networks.

The important development in terms of interception practices lies in the transfer of the interception burden to the industry. Contrary to the practices which had prevailed until then, interception operations are now implemented by the operators.

Most of the publications on interceptions focus on the practices and their legal and political dimensions. Apart from the specialized technical literature (computing, telecommunications), only a few works discuss the interception technologies themselves, what they concretely make it possible to achieve, the way in which they operate, the way in which they are designed and by whom (researchers, engineers, industrialists, hackers, etc.), how they are disseminated and by whom (companies, markets, customers), the effects they produce on the tactical, strategic and political levels, and broadly speaking, in terms of power.

In an article published in 2018, Akin Unver [UNV 18] explored the issues raised by digital surveillance in democracies and autocracies, as well as the mechanisms that characterize the Surveillance Industrial Complex (SIC). The place of technology, and more specifically, of the technological race, is at the center of his political analysis of the surveillance-privacy protection dilemma. This author believes that it is not so much the intentions that make surveillance problematic, as its economic model. While the debates centered on the challenges raised by the antagonism between security and privacy protection are not entirely new, the terms have radically changed not only due to the evolution of the technological environment, but also the political scene. The author dates this transition on September 11, 2001:

> Rapidly changing connection technologies create a system where digitized personal information and official data now have multiple points of interception, cannot reliably be deleted, don't expire and can be disseminated across digital platforms at an infinite rate and dizzying speed [UNV 18].

Unver draws a distinction between two categories of techniques or practices: those organized on the basis of surveillance technologies and those bypassing surveillance. These technologies evolve concomitantly and equilibrate the balance of power: "[...] technology itself is neutral and supports all sides of the spectrum in comparable measure" [UNV 18].

Even though by analogy, we may deem the SIC complex to be similar to the notion of "military-industrial complex", its nature is quite different. In the SIC, the relationship is no longer based on mutual benefit, but on a logic of constraint whose "complex" nature is no longer specific to American politics alone. The state acts as the dominant party: intelligence agencies collect the data from private sector databases or communication systems; agencies take advantage of the permanently evolving technology, thus offering the means to bypass restrictive legal frameworks; they make private companies bear the political and economic costs of surveillance.

The historical prism helps to understand the nature of technological developments and their applications. We will be more particularly attentive to the forms of power that make it possible to build, maintain, reinforce or weaken interception technologies used in their multiple contexts.

The questions addressed in this book

This book is organized as follows:

– The first chapter describes the multiple contexts in which the interceptions of communications have taken place and continue to do so. Implemented by belligerents during wars from past to present, their usefulness has never been denied, as they are essential to intelligence, providing key information at the tactical, operational and strategic levels, guiding political and military decisions. But interception is also at the service of political power, in the hands of the prince, who spies on diplomats, as well as on his relatives or political opponents, to better establish his power by mastering secrecy. Interception is also one of the tools used by the police to fight against crime. Undeniably, the intelligence services also use interception, and states do not hesitate to use it to monitor and control. The frameworks for their use are multiple. Technological developments in the field of communications have introduced new modalities to which interception techniques have had to adapt.

– The second chapter focuses on the challenges of encryption. Many interception techniques, methods and technologies exist at present, which make it possible to intercept (virtually) everything. The catalogs of companies commercializing interception technologies at least suggest so. The encryption of communications appears to be one of the means – if not the only means? – to protect communication content. But, regardless of their motivations, those who try to intercept intend to circumvent the encryption barrier. Even if cryptography is not infallible (encryption systems can simply be badly implemented), there are methods to weaken it (such as backdoors, in particular), and others to circumvent it. Encryption is a political issue, around which the debates on state sovereignty crystallize. The liberalization of cryptography in the 1990s undermined this absolute control power of the states over what was then a "war weapon", before becoming a tool accessible to all, and therefore, much more difficult to control. The states have not surrendered of course, and while the interceptions of planetary communications such as those implemented by the NSA seem to only target metadata and not the contents directly, the latter preserve all their strategic value. How to access them despite cryptographic hurdles is an ongoing challenge.

– The last chapter delves into "power" and the relationships that have taken shape between the various stakeholders involved in interception technology, including its creation, design, marketing and various uses. The relationships between citizens, researchers, technology designers, companies and states are analyzed. The focus will be on the special relationship between the state and companies, which oscillates between constraint and cooperation; the states' desired control limits over technologies (so as not to be controlled by them) and the fragility of the foundations of power built on the confidence in encryption.

History and Repertoire of Communication Interception Practices

The interception of correspondence has been ongoing for centuries. However, we will not attempt to date its origin. By focusing on the period closest to the present, it is possible to identify its multiple contexts of use, as well as its civil, military, political, economic and diplomatic applications. On the one hand, the emergence of new modes of communication in the 19th century led to a considerable increase in the volume and distribution speed of correspondence, and to changes in the geographical dimension, on the other hand. It became much easier to correspond with the other side of the world, thanks to the speed of messages reaching their destination and the reduction in communication costs. Communication also diversified its methods: there was a gradual shift from writing to voice transmission with telephony and radio communications.

The principle of the optical telegraph, then called the aerial telegraph so as to differentiate it from the electric telegraph, has been known since antiquity. As early as the second century BC, the Greek general, statesman and historian Polybius described, in Book X, Chapter VII "Fire Signals" of his *General History*, a system "by means of which anyone who cares to do so even though he is at a distance of three, four, or even more days' journey, can be informed"[1]. He describes the process in the following terms:

> Divide the alphabet into five groups of five letters each [...] the signaling party raises first torches on the left to indicate which of the tablets he means. [...] He next raises torches on the right showing in a

---

[1] Polybius, Book X, Chapter VII [Online]. Available at: www.remacle.org/bloodwolf/historiens/polybe/dix1.htm. In English: http://www.perseus.tufts.edu/hopper/text?doc=Perseus:abo:tlg, 0543,001:10.

similar manner by their number which of the letters in the tablet he wishes to indicate to the recipient.

As early as the 18th century, many inventors proposed and experimented with optical devices for remote communication:

– in 1672, the Englishman Robert Hooke (1635–1703) imagined an assembly of three masts equipped with a horizontal girder for encoding cut-out symbols;

– in 1690, the Frenchman Guillaume Amotons (1663–1705) improved the mechanism to transmit alphabetic symbols;

– in 1786, while in the presence of the Prince of Hesse-Cassel, the German Johan Andreas Benignus Bergsträsser (1732–1812), rector of the University of Hanau, experimented with a mast equipped with two pivoting arms, in order to transmit a message made up of numbers;

– in 1788, Charles-François Dupuis, future deputy to the Convention for Seine-et-Oise, carried out a communication between Ménilmontant and Bagneux using an alphabetical telegraph.

But the telegraph would only experience real growth after 1791 with the invention of the optical communication method by Claude Chappe (1763–1805), which bears his name. After numerous demonstrations and improvements, including a rapid transmission experiment on July 12, 1793 covering a 40 km distance, the Convention decided to nationalize the invention on July 26 of the same year and to entrust its administration to Chappe, under the aegis of the Ministry of War. From this followed a considerable development of the invention, which Chappe and his brothers exploited on a large scale.

Its actual construction at the end of the 18th century did not respond to technical innovations, but to a particular need in the context of the French Revolution and its centralized state administration, for which the speed of communication was crucial.

A Chappe telegraph station is a small stone building furnished with a mast carrying three articulated arms, painted black: the central arm is called the regulator and the two side arms are the indicators. Information is conveyed by the relative position of the regulator and the indicators.

A first Paris–Lille line completed in 1795 included 16 stations and made it possible to transmit a 25-word message within an average of 15 minutes, compared to a whole day required by traditional postal services. This first line was followed by others, forming a network which covered not only metropolitan France, but also Algeria and Tunisia.

In 1844, the French territory had 534 towers for connections over more than 5,000 km between the main cities. The telegraph was initially reserved for government communications. In 1824, the network expanded to commerce, and was made available to the general public in 1851, when it began to decline.

As the position of the articulated arms carrying the transmitted information is visible to all, it is necessary to use a confidential code. The code's secrecy is based on a hierarchical organization with pseudo-military discipline. In 1823, the Central Administration was at the top of the structure, with three administrators, a chief and two assistants for four bureaus: dispatches, staff, equipment and accountability. Then there were the directors in charge of a department, who were responsible for coding, decoding and sending dispatches, using a codebook which was kept secret. From 1795 onwards, 92 arms positions were retained, each being identified by a two-digit number. This number referred to the codebook pages and the lines on each page containing a word or a group of words, which resulted in a total of 8,464 meanings. After the code was revised in 1830, increasing the number of arm positions to 184, 33,856 meanings could be conveyed.

The message could only be understood by the directors at the lines' ends, but remained incomprehensible for all the intermediaries.

The directors supervised the activity of the inspectors assigned to a department who were responsible for a line section comprising around 10 stations.

At the bottom of the hierarchy, stationary workers represented 90% of the staff. Each station was staffed by two operators: one was in charge of the telescope observation, while the other manipulated the controls. The stationaries were poorly paid, as much as 1.25 francs per day until 1826, the salary of a daily laborer. This was considered as a side work, since most of the stations were located in rural areas. Due to budgetary reasons, the stationary position was soon to be occupied by only one person.

Its last use was a light, transportable model on the back of a mule, at the service of military operations during the Crimean war (1853–1856), allowing stations to be moved according to military operations.

Having been the first organized telecommunications system, the Chappe telegraph gradually disappeared from 1847 and was definitively replaced by the electric telegraph in 1855. The latter had the advantage of also operating at night and in foggy weather, while its undersea cables made it possible to cross the seas.

As early as 1820, the French mathematician, physicist, chemist and philosopher André-Marie Ampère (1775–1836), known for his works on electromagnetism, proposed to apply these phenomena to a remote communication system. The electric telegraph was later designed by several inventors, including Pavel Schilling (1786–1837), a German-origin diplomat at the service of Russia. Experiments with electric telegraphs began in England in 1832 under the initiative of William Fothergill Cooke (1806–1879) and later in France, Spain and Italy.

In 1838, the physicist and inventor Charles Wheatstone (1802–1875) installed the first electric telegraph line in England between London and Birmingham. This was a private business.

In 1844, the American inventor Samuel Morse (1791–1872) created the code that bears his name, establishing a telegraphic connection between Baltimore and Washington. Originally sensitive to transmission errors, this code was improved by the German author, journalist and musician Friedrich-Clemens Gerke (1801–1888), who was a pioneer of telegraphy and gave it its final shape in 1850.

In 1845, a first electric telegraph line was set up in France between Paris and Rouen, triggering the decline of the Chappe telegraph. In 1851, a first undersea cable was built between England and France. In 1855, the Anglo-American inventor David Edward Hughes (1831–1900) designed the teleprinter, a printing telegraph with a transmission capacity of approximately 1,000 words per hour. In 1866, the first transatlantic cable (whose installation required about 10 years of work), was put into service. Many cables would follow, making up a world-scale telegraphic network at the beginning of the 20th century.

In 1874, Hughes' teleprinter was improved by Émile Baudot (1845–1903), who invented the code that currently bears his name. It is a device for printing text with a typewriter mechanism which accelerates transmissions by means of an electromechanical process, surpassing the capacities of human operators. Baudot's device, capable of transmitting up to 4,000 words per hour, was adopted by the French telegraph administration in 1875. Each character of the alphabet was coded by five binary units. This would result in the passage (or the absence) of an electric current, directly stemming from the typist operator's keystroke on the keyboard. This coding was written onto a perforated paper tape. It was represented by a mark, or a mark's absence, along five positions. The marks were materialized by a hole on the paper tape.

The holes' layout could represent a letter or a number as a function of a code developed by Baudot, and then modified by Donald Murray (1865–1945) in 1901, to acknowledge typewriter writing. A special encoding activated the number mode, while another activated the letter mode.

These teleprinters were widely used until 1980 for communicating the news to press organizations and newspapers. The baud is a signal transmission speed unit still in use today, in homage to Baudot.

In 1879, the Ministry of Posts and Telegraphs was created in France.

The Frenchman Charles Bourseul (1829–1912), agent of the Telegraphs administration, laid the foundations for the telephone in 1854. He published an article entitled "Electrical transmission of speech" in a journal called *L'Illustration*. As it had occurred with the electric telegraph, many inventors were involved in the invention and improvement of the telephone:

– the German Philipp Ress (1834–1874) performed a good quality speech transmission, but of weak intensity in 1863;

– the Italian-American Antonio Meucci (1808–1889) is said to have manufactured several telephone devices between 1849 and 1870, for which he filed a patent in 1870;

– the Americans Graham Bell (1847–1922) and Elisha Gray (1835–1901) filed a similar patent within two hours in 1876, which led to controversy over inventorship. The Bell Laboratories, a private research institute, was founded in 1925.

The telephone began being commercially exploited in the United States in 1877, and in France in 1879.

Wireless telegraphy was inspired in the works of James-Clerk Maxwell (1832–1819). In his 1872 treatise on electricity and magnetism, Maxwell established that magnetic and electric fields can propagate through space under the shape of an electromagnetic wave carrying energy. He laid the theoretical foundations that Herfich Rudolf Hertz (1857–1894) relied on to discover the waves that bear his name. Hertz was able to produce them using an oscillator.

Édouard Branly (1844–1940) became interested in Hertz's works and noted that the conductivity of a metallic powder varies under the influence of electromagnetic radiation, a discovery which was at the origin of the iron filing field detector. This device could be used as a receiver for the Hertz oscillator, paving the way for the transmission of information over a distance.

On May 7, 1875, the Russian Alexandre Popov (1858–1905) performed one of the first radioelectric transmissions from a distance of 2,400 m in front of the Russian society of physics and chemistry. In 1896, he succeeded a wave transmission among various buildings of the University of Saint Petersburg, with vertical antennas to improve reception, as well as the recording of messages on a Morse device.

Other names are associated with the development of radiocommunications: Guglielmo Marconi (1874–1937) in Italy, Eugène Ducretet (1844–1915) in France. General Ferrié (1868–1932) performed a radio broadcast from the Eiffel Tower in 1904 in France.

Amateurs also played an important role in the discovery of shortwave propagation modes. On November 28, 1923, the first bilateral transatlantic medium-wave communication (110 m) took place between the American radio amateur Fred Schnell, callsign 1MO, in Hardford, Connecticut and the French radio amateur Léon Deloy (1894–1969), callsign 8AB, in Nice. This performance, which was previously unthought-of due to the rectilinear propagation of electromagnetic waves, evidenced their reflection on the ionosphere (the upper layer of the Earth's atmosphere), paving the way for transcontinental communications and triggering their use for global communications.

The development of FST could only be achieved thanks to electronics that strongly shaped scientific and technical advances and had a strong impact on society, encouraging the development of radio, television, computers and telecommunications. In 1904, John Fleming (1849–1945) invented the vacuum diode in England, a device enabling the unidirectional flow of an electric current. This invention was followed in 1906 by the triode vacuum tube, by Lee de Forest (1873–1961), which paved the way for the creation and amplification of electric signals. As early as 1902, a patent was filed in the United States by the Indian botanist physicist Jagadish Chandra Bose (1858–1937) on the semiconducting properties of galena (lead sulfide). In 1906, Geeleaf Wittier Pickard (1877–1956) filed a similar patent on silicon for a silicon crystal detector, permitting the demodulation of radio waves. It was not until the invention of the transistor in 1947 that a semiconductor amplification device appeared.

The second half of the 20th century was undoubtedly marked by the Internet. This period gave rise to a variety of technologies and a new impetus to the progress made in the field of telecommunications in the 19th century and during the first half of the 20th century with radio and telephony. Progress was then reflected in terms of increased transmission speed, distance, increase in correspondence volumes and information flows circulating around the world.

The interception of correspondence has adapted to all these developments, accompanying each of the new technological generations.

1.1. Military interceptions during the war

Communication has always played a strategic role in the war. Intercepting communications, either to gain further information or to interrupt its route, is an act as old as war itself. Reading the minds of enemies, knowing their intentions, contributes to the construction of an advantage or a superiority based on the mastery of information, which partially contributes to lifting the fog of war. "The endeavor to learn what is in the opponent's mind and to draw advantage from it has always been very important in the history of mankind in peacetime and particularly in wartime. During thousands of years only the methods have changed" [FLI 53].

In *The Gallic Wars* [RAT 64], Julius Caesar mentions the interception of letters sent by the warlords and which must escape the enemy: "Then he persuaded one of the Gallic troopers with great rewards to deliver a letter to Cicero. The letter he sent written in Greek characters, lest by intercepting it the enemy might get to know of our designs".

1.1.1. *The interception of telegraphic communications*

Strictly speaking, the 19th century marked the entry into the era of modern communications. The optical telegraph, born during the revolutionary period in France, and in many European countries over the same period, quickly spread to other continents, establishing networks across societies. It has settled in diverse landscapes and in the daily lives of societies, offering the possibility of modern, fast communications over long distances. Before being commercial, the first uses of the Chappe telegraph were warfare-related. In the middle of the 19th century, the optical telegraph was succeeded by the electric telegraph, with its thousands of kilometers of cables deployed on land and across the oceans, which would only increase global networking, accelerating communications over ever greater distances, contribute to the development of economies, to the construction of colonial empires, state powers, as well as to the emergence of new private companies which quickly made their fortunes by producing network infrastructure and offering communication services. As will be frequently stressed here, these networks have often played an essential role in wars, not only in tactical, but also in strategic terms. All these new means of communication impacted the way in which the states conceived and practiced the interception of correspondence until that moment.

On every occasion, technological developments gave new life to interceptions, with new capabilities, authorizing new modes of attacks against communications (interceptions are considered an offensive action): "In the middle of the nineteenth century, when the Morse telegraph came into use, soon followed by the telephone, new technical possibilities of attack resulted by switching-in and listening this quickly produced a new situation" [FLI 53].

The development of the state's capabilities to intercept these new modes of communication seems related to the intelligence-gathering culture or history specific to each state:

> There were two countries in Europe in which the espionage service had been especially cultivated for centuries: France and Austria-Hungary. Consequently, these were the two countries which first recognized the importance of technical means of intercepting communications and took corresponding action [FRI 53].

1.1.1.1. *The American Civil War*

The intensive use of the telegraph was essential during the American Civil War (1861–1865).

The technical characteristics of the electric telegraph exposed unencrypted correspondence to any indiscreet ear. Wiretapping possibilities were multiple and few resources had to be mobilized for this. Network architecture and the characteristics of their components made it relatively easy to intercept signals:

> I then discovered, by sheer necessity, that I could read the messages coming, by watching the movement of the armature of the magnet. The vibrations of a telegraph armature are so slight as to be scarcely perceptible to the naked eye, yet a break, or the separating of the points of contact, are necessary to make the proper signals. Further experiences developed the phenomena that when sound and sight failed I could read still by the sense of feeling, by holding my finger-tips gently against the armature and noting its pulsations. I thus became by practice not only proficient, but expert in telegraphy. Telegraphers know, though the general public may not, that messages can be sent by touching together the ends of a cut telegraph wire, and can be received by holding the ends to the tongue [KER 89].

In addition to these interception "attacks", the telegraph infrastructure suffered direct attacks (cutting of cables, destruction of poles, etc.). The network was particularly exposed and vulnerable:

> As soon as the deed had been accomplished in Baltimore, the news was to be telegraphed along the line of the road, and immediately upon the reception of this intelligence the telegraph wires were to be cut, the railroad bridges destroyed and the tracks torn up, in order to

prevent for some time any information being conveyed to the cities of the North, or the passage of any Northern men towards the capital [PIN 84].

Figure 1.1. *"The electric telegraph shocked by the news it was entrusted to transmit for some time", Cham (Amédée Charles de Noé), 1867, CC0 Paris Museums/Carnavalet Museum*[2]

Telegraph workers were one of the essential links in the intelligence-gathering chain. The quality of the results obtained from the collection of telegraphic information depended as much on cleverness and inventiveness, as on technological vulnerabilities. While telegraph spies had access to information that often ended up being without interest, it sometimes occurred that it had a strategic value. Some of these employees could be tempted to keep a copy of this information for themselves and divert it from its primary purpose:

I had thought, while in possession of the official dispatch, what a pleasant gratification it would be to my old friend Covode to be able to show him an intercepted dispatch from Richmond to the commander of the Rebel armies in the field; and as the thought of this

2 See: www.parismuseescollections.paris.fr/sites/default/files/styles/pm_notice/public/atoms/ images/CAR/aze_carg021974-49_rec_001.jpg?itok=sGZbwTrI.

> performance dwelt in my brain as I walked along, I formed a hasty plan, which I believed I could mature and carry into effect – of securing from the files or papers in the telegraph office a number of copies of the most important dispatches, either in the handwriting of Generals Joseph E. Johnston or Beauregard, addressed to Richmond, or at least signed by them officially [KER 89].

The American Civil War intensified the exploitation of the telegraph and electronic warfare operations. The encryption and interception of messages passing through the telegraph are among the key actions of war.

Many stories abound regarding these practices. In the second chapter of his work dedicated to the role of telegraphy in the American Civil War, William R. Plum [PLU 82] describes the many encryption systems used by the belligerents during the conflict. The balance of power was strongly influenced by the quality of encryption and the ability to ensure the secrecy of telegraphic messages. The Confederates seem to have failed to master the encryption of their messages (telegraph, couriers, signals), which earned them many defeats:

> Lincoln took a personal interest in our translation of the enemy's cipher-despatches, intercepted and brought to the War Department for translation, and whenever he saw the three of us with our heads together he knew that we had something on hand of special interest [...] At various other times our troops intercepted despatches, sent from one Confederate general to another, containing important information in cipher. As a rule, we were able to translate these ciphers after more or less labor. They were generally ordinary letter ciphers, the letters of the alphabet being transposed in various ways [BAT 07].

During this war, encryption was a critical element for superiority. George Washington also used deception methods, intentionally transmitting messages containing false information, to be intercepted by the enemy.

Interceptions were only one of the many bricks of this information war, among others: encryption, deception, the physical control of the telegraphic infrastructure, the attacks against the telegraphic communication network, the engagement of individuals (telegraph agents) in correspondence surveillance.

Let us recall to what extent A. Lincoln was attached to this informational dimension of the war, spending whole days near the telegraph post to scrutinize the arrival of new dispatches. We could also mention the role played by these telegraphic communication networks on the disclosure of information to the American and international press during the war.

1.1.1.2. *The civil war in Chile*

From January to September 1891, Chile engaged in a civil war. President Balmaceda's communications (described as a "dictator" in the following quotation) were intercepted. Note the way in which the belligerents exploit communications: they take into account the existing network infrastructure, they position their means of interception at the best places, they decipher the intercepted messages by taking advantage of the weakness of the encryption method used and they finally communicate their own information to several foreign countries thanks to international cable networks. While intercepts cannot probably be considered the only key to the success of the president's opponents, they certainly played a major role. By combining the interception of communications and the use of network communication tools to organize the opposition, the stakeholders in this conflict were already immersed in the modern era of information warfare:

> Given the fact that the Dictator's communications with his agents outside Chile were hindered by means of the Pacific submarine cable, they could only be verified *via* the trans-Andean route. We were thus able to organize a service for intercepting the Dictator's telegraphic correspondence in the Argentine Republic, becoming fully aware of its contents. All the messages in secret ciphers were easily translated, thanks to the bad choice of keywords used by the Ministry of Foreign Affairs. The information thus acquired was immediately communicated to Iquique or to the Revolution agents in Paris, and proved being crucial to prepare the final result. On an illustrative basis, it will suffice to point out that from February 28 to July 28 we sent 12 telegrams to Iquique, 13 to Antofagasta, 1 to Tupiza, 10 to Pulacayo, 60 to Paris, 2 to London, 1 to Bordeaux, 1 to Hamburg, 1 to New York, 3 to Rio Janeiro, 9 to Petrópolis, 14 to Montevideo; apart from an indeterminate number within the Argentine Republic ([BIA 92], translation from Spanish).

1.1.1.3. *The Spanish American war of 1898*

During this brief war, telegraph cables between Spain and its South American colonies (particularly Puerto Rico, Cuba and the Philippines) [WIN 15] were the target of destruction operations by the American army. The choice was in favor of a systematic destruction instead of maintaining networks. The Americans preferred to deprive themselves of the information that interceptions could have delivered. The strategy was to isolate the armed forces and the enemy authorities, depriving them of their long-distance communication means. The two strategies are opposed: on the one hand, the informational isolation of the enemy via the destruction of its communication means; on the other hand, the collection of enemy information by intercepting (and thus preserving) their communications.

1.1.1.4. Telegraph interception at the beginning of the 20th century

At the beginning of the 20th century, the level of organization and integration of interception activities within the military intelligence-gathering services was uneven, depending on the country. Austria seemed to be ahead of Germany on these questions at the beginning of World War I. It would take almost a year for the systematic interceptions of foreign communications to be implemented on the German side. Other nations, like Russia, were rather slow to take stock of the challenges associated with these new methods of communication. Russian transmissions were unencrypted during the war, or poorly encrypted: "The intercepted Russian telegrams constitute a very trustworthy source of information. Of course, the orders were enciphered, but the cipher system was very simple and was rarely changed; consequently it was easy to read the radiograms" [FLI 53].

During World War I, multiple new communication technologies could be used: the radio, the telegraph, the telephone, electronic tubes, etc. The telegraph was by then a mature technology, which had already been used for several decades, especially in other conflicts. But these techniques were often vulnerable, dependent on electricity lines which could be cut, subjected to the terrain's configuration, to climatic conditions, to distance. During the conflict, however, the belligerents maintained their lines of communication far from the theater of war, in order to preserve them. In the war, wired networks such as the telegraph or the telephone were highly vulnerable. While radio communications made it possible to send messages to several recipients at the same time and enabled the mobility of men and vehicles, they were still vulnerable because they could be easily intercepted by enemies, without the need to physically connect to cables. Radio communications appeared at the end of the 19th century and found immediate applications in the military field (getting rid of cables' physical constraints, extending communication distances, reaching several points, disseminating orders more quickly, etc.). Modern communication means were vulnerable in terms of security, jeopardizing the infrastructure, equipment and data when these could not be encrypted, or were imperfectly encrypted (although their communications were regularly decrypted throughout the war, the Germans were convinced of the resistance of their encryption). As they entered the war in 1914, the British cut several undersea cables connecting Germany and the United States. The Germans favored radio communications which the enemies could easily intercept. In order to divert North American forces to other conflicts and dissuade them from entering the war in Europe, the Germans contemplated inciting Mexico to attack the United States. It is in this context that a senior German official, Arthur Zimmerman, transmitted a message to the German ambassador in Mexico City.

From these few insights into World War I, it will be noted that interceptions have a variable importance. The interception of Zimmerman's telegram can be presented as one of the triggers for the United States' decision to enter the war. But that was not the only element. The maritime war launched by the Germans at the same time, deciding to systematically sink all merchant ships – especially American ones – was just as decisive. Throughout the war, German messages were intercepted and decrypted in large volumes. Despite the fact that interceptions provided often strategic information regarding the various battles conducted, we cannot state that the interceptions provided one belligerent or the other with such mastery over the informational space that the war was shortened in time, or made less lethal. While mastering the information from the opposing camp is essential, it is not necessarily a guarantee of victory. The multiple communication techniques acted more as a complement than as competition against each other. The appearance of the radio did not signal the end of wired communications, nor did satellite communications dethrone cable transmissions years later.

1.1.2. *The interception of radio communications*

Wireless communications appeared at the very beginning of the 20th century and were adopted by the armies during World War I.

The appearance of wireless telegraphy opened up new possibilities for interception. Communications were particularly vulnerable during the war, in particular, telegraphy:

> The problem of secrecy does not appear in similar conditions for these two kinds of communications: while the transmission of military telegrams will always risk being disturbed by the enemy, the security of long-distance communications encounter no other difficulties other than those resulting from the nature of things […] High-speed telegraphy […] contributes to secrecy by reducing the time during which interception is possible [PER 11].

The protection of wireless communications caused deep concern at the beginning of the 20th century. No solution seemed to suffice for protecting radiotelegraphic communications in times of war:

> M. Edouard Branly, who is general credited in Paris with having been the real inventor of wireless telegraphy, has just patented an important

improvement by which interception of messages will be rendered impossible, except by a special apparatus. At present, M. Branly states, it is a popular delusion to imagine that wireless telegraphy could render any service in time of war across country or seas held by an enemy. The latter can, with the greatest ease, either intercept messages, or so disturb their transmission as to render them incomprehensible. M. Branly claims that his new apparatus ensures for a given set of electric waves complete immunity from accidental interference of other waves. But at the same time, it will always be possible in time of war to disturb messages willfully, even when sent off by his new appliance. He says that no wireless telegraph system known is a proof against interferences if a special mechanism giving out waves uninterruptedly by used to that end. His conclusion is that for war purposes on land or at sea "the usefulness of wireless telegraphy would be illusory" [THE 06].

Austrian capabilities for intercepting radio communications enabled them to monitor the Italian army operations on a daily basis during the war against Turkey in 1911. On the eve of World War I, France had also developed military capabilities for the interception and cryptanalysis of telegraphic and radio communications, which enabled it to steadily surveil Germany.

Communication technologies multiplied on the eve of World War I. The French and British forces preparing the defense of the Suez Canal in 1914–1915 deployed several infrastructures around centralized networks, as well as the means to defend them: "A comprehensive system of telegraphic, telephonic and wireless telegraphy communications links the various posts with the headquarters. Defenses have been erected to protect the railway, the telegraphic lines and the freshwater canal" [DOU 22].

For Wilhelm F. Flicke [FLI 53], the battle of Tannenberg (August 26–30, 1914) would be one of the first battles, if not the first, during which radio communication interceptions played a key role in the confrontation's outcome. During this battle, marked by the victory of the German army over the Russian army, the Russian generals exchanged detailed operational orders by radio (unencrypted messages), which were intercepted by the Germans. Strengthened by the information that had been gathered for making strategic decisions, the Germans quickly gained advantage. They accessed information about the enemy's intentions, troop movements, organization, battle plan, points of attack. Since this information was transmitted unencrypted by the Russians, the task was relatively easy for the Germans who – once the data were intercepted – only had to translate them and transfer them from the interception stations to the headquarters. However, it would seem that the German military did not give interceptions a major strategic role in this battle, which would eventually be won despite all odds, according to them. The flaws in the organization of the Russian information system were significant: insufficient cables to establish wired communications, no encryption means between the headquarters and the troops for radio communications, which involved unencrypted transmissions.

On the other hand, unencrypted messages were not harmless for those who intercepted them and took them at face value. Armies could deliberately send unencrypted messages so that the enemy intercepted them and read them without any difficulty. Sending unencrypted messages could be a deception maneuver. The Germans used this maneuver against the Russians: "In the forenoon of 7 September, the radio station at Konigsberg sent a radiogram in plain text [...] The radiogram was intercepted by the Russians and the strategy succeeded. This is the first known case of purposely misleading radio traffic during World War I" [FLI 53].

At the beginning of World War I, there was still no real doctrine for the interception of these new modes of communication (radio). The military doctrine had not yet integrated the transformations that the use of radio interceptions implied:

> People were astounded at the technical progress which made possible wireless transmission of information over rather great distances, but they did not yet understand how to make sensible use of this technical advance in order to gain information [...] On the German side the idea was utterly foreign in lower and medium commands that one might be in a position to shape or alter one's own plans on the basis of intercepted traffic. Military thinking tended to consider one's own operation on the basis of the orders issued to be a fixed factor which could in no wise be influenced by any messages which might be intercepted [FLI 53].

The resources allocated to intelligence-gathering and in particular to wiretapping and the interception of communications are unevenly deployed from state to state. Regarding the Japanese abilities during the war against China, an American report observed that, strengthened by its superiority, the Japanese army neglected intelligence-gathering because it did not deem it essential [STR 46]:

> Since the Manchurian incident, a bad habit of neglecting the intelligence service was created among the Japanese forces in North China as they had always fought against weaker enemy forces. The Japanese forces always were confident of winning worth enemy. The Chinese forces were weaker in quality and equipment. Information obtained regarding the Chinese forces was not the deciding factor for the victory of the Japanese forces.

The relative disinterest of the Japanese headquarters for the intelligence gathered from radio interceptions partly explained the deterioration of the Japanese condition during the war against the Chinese Communists: "Here may be traced one of the causes which lead Japanese forces gradually to an unfavorable war situation".

In certain regions of China, the Japanese forces made significant efforts for intercepting enemy communications:

> Value of Information Obtained: Headquarters of the Japanese North China Army achieved quite satisfactory results intercepting radio communications transmitted by Chungking forces as the latter's supervision and control of radio communication was poor. During actual operations the Japanese forces could relatively accurately perceive in advance attempts and movements to be carried out by Chungking forces.

However, the results were not up to par, and the intelligence gathered was of poor quality. Among the various reasons, let us mention the cautious communication mode of the Chinese forces: "Strict supervision and control of the Chinese Communist forces over their radio communication as well as the poor facilities of the Japanese forces for intercepting the enemy radio communication".

Insufficient intelligence-gathering from the multiple fronts seemingly contributed to the loss of Japan in China:

> Japanese forces had no facilities for intercepting radio communications transmitted by the Soviet-Mongolian forces in the Outer Mongolian area, and also it was almost impossible for the Japanese forces to dispatch their secret agents to that area. It is not too much to say, therefore, that no information was obtained regarding the Soviet-Mongolian forces.

1.1.3. *Telephone interception*

The electric telegraph showed its great sensitivity to interception during the American Civil War (see section 1.1.1.1). Shortly after the American Civil War appeared the telephone, which was equally vulnerable to interceptions.

The Engineer's Handbook published in 1931 describes the duties of wartime communication interception:

The organization of transmissions in the defensive differs from what is suitable for an offensive situation, having the following particularities: […] The fixedness of command posts facilitates the organization of transmissions […] The telephone becomes the capital process; it is set to function even when the struggle reaches its maximum intensity. This implies the construction of layers as numerous, dense and less vulnerable as possible. In particular, the telephone is connected until it reaches the battalion, the battery, even the company command posts, and the front line observatories (all precautions being taken to avoid wiretapping by the enemy). […] Part of the transmission processes enable the surveillance and capture of enemy transmissions, thus enabling useful intelligence-gathering for the command. The processes offering the broadest coverage for surveillance purposes are wireless telegraphy (and telephony), only requiring to tune the earphone station with the emission characteristics of the opposing station, with ground telegraphy and wired telephony. One same station cannot normally assure the emission and reception of our own messages and the listening to the enemy transmissions. It is therefore essential to particularly reserve certain stations for listening to the enemy stations. The organization of surveillance is done at the armed forces level, following the general guidelines of the intelligence-gathering plan. It includes listening to (interception of messages) telegraphy and wireless telephony, ground telegraphy, wired telephony; and radiogoniometry (determining the location of transmitters) for wireless telegraphy (and telephony). Depending on the case, it is either performed by the listening sections of the telegraph sapper battalions (wired telephony, ground telegraphy), or by the radiogoniometry and listening sections of the army's radiotelegraphic companies (other processes). Although discharged from the special listening mission, any station which (without deviating from its own mission), overhears a message from the enemy has the duty to record it and to immediately report it. This rule applies to the ground telegraphy stations of the forward units. In view of the small range of action of the ground telegraphy, the organization of listening by the army cannot include a continuous chain of special stations. Listening relates not only to the text itself, but to all the emission's technical particularities. The staff engaged in optical transmissions, and all the qualified staff, in particular those at the observatories, must record the optical signals which can be observed in the enemy zone (nature, points of emission, and, if it corresponds, the text on the telegram) [COL 31].

During World War II, the Nazis had established telephone lines between all the occupied territories and Germany. To make sure there was no wiretapping, they monitored the voltage level on the lines, as any suspicious change could signal an attempted interception. Frenchman Robert Keller ("source K") is said to have managed to achieve a connection without drawing any attention on himself.

1.1.4. *The use of SIGINT capabilities*

SIGINT (Signal Intelligence) designates electromagnetic intelligence-gathering from signal interception. It comprises the following three components:

– ELINT (Electronic INTelligence) is the intelligence-gathering technique based on electromagnetic signals, except for voice and text. For example, it includes the radar;

– the FISINT (Foreign Instrumentation Signal INTelligence) designates the interception of electromagnetic emissions associated with the testing and outdoor operational deployment of aerospace, surface and undersea systems;

– COMINT (COMmunications INTelligence) includes voice and text: "The interception and analysis of the radio communications is the main application of COMINT systems"[3].

> COMINT is intelligence and technical information derived from collecting and processing intercepted foreign communications passed by radio, wire, or other electromagnetic means. COMINT also may include imagery, when pictures or diagrams are encoded by a computer network/radio frequency method for storage and/or transmission. The imagery can be static or streaming [JOI 13].

COMINT can itself be segmented into five domains or fields[4]:

– the interception of HF radio communications (0.5 MHz to 30 MHz);

– the interception of communications in the V/UHF band (20 MHz to 3 or 6 GHz);

– GSM COMINT;

– satellite communications;

– Internet communications.

---

3 See: www.emsopedia.org/entries/communication-intelligence-comint/ [Accessed April 21, 2021].
4 Here, following the segmentation proposed on the site www.emsopedia.org/entries/communi cation-intelligence-comint/ [Accessed April 21, 2021].

The importance of COMINT lies in "its ability to reveal the intercepted source's posture, activity and intent, thanks to the access of data and voice content"[5].

When it entered the war in 1939, Germany had already acquired experience in interceptions during the interwar period and deployed international listening capabilities integrated into intelligence services combining human intelligence and SIGINT. Some countries were prone to systematic interception, using large-scale infrastructures deployed with allied countries: "All cable lines leading out of Czechoslovakia which touched German, Austrian, or Hungarian territory were monitored. For this purpose there was close cooperation between the German, Australian, and Hungarian espionage and cryptanalytic services" [FLI 53].

At the beginning of World War II, the United States was also in possession of advanced COMINT capabilities. For example, in 1930, the US Army created its own SIGINT intelligence service, the SIS (Signal Intelligence Service) (for a thoroughly documented history of SIGINT within the US Army during World War II, see the important work of James L. Gilbert and John P. Finnegan, published in 1993 [GIL 93]). Even though the military intelligence services had developed significant means of interception and decryption, the Pearl Harbor attack came as a shock, which prompted the Americans to adopt a more systematic approach to diplomatic interceptions [GIL 93]. Unsurprisingly, the development of SIGINT capabilities brings to light the competition between the different forces, in this case, the US Army[6] and the US Navy who competed on these goals[7].

At the end of World War II, intelligence-gathering activities continued to be pursued, and the entry into the Cold War provided a new theater of intelligence operations to legitimize the construction of a SIGINT architecture at a global scale. The goal was to detect any offensive maneuver on the part of the USSR as soon as possible, preventing a nuclear attack and protecting the airspace of the United States. The enemy was communism. China was also under the sight of the United States. SIGINT capabilities were deployed to monitor China, Taiwan (then Formosa) and the region as a whole.

---

5 See: www.emsopedia.org/entries/communication-intelligence-comint/ [Accessed April 21, 2021].

6 The United States Army Signal Corps (USASC) was created as a branch of the US Army in June 1860. It then included only one man, Doctor Albert James Meyer, who was also its initiator. The purpose of this service was to provide the army with a communication system by means of visual signals (flags, light signals, etc.). In 1867, the military exploitation of the electric telegraph became one of the responsibilities of the Signal Corps [KAT 94].

7 See: www.nsa.gov/Portals/70/documents/news-features/declassified-documents/cryptologic-quarterly/SIGINT_Goes_to_War.pdf.

At the end of the two great world wars, the benefits of SIGINT seemed unquestionable:

> The value to the Allies of our Signal Intelligence effort during World War II can scarcely be overestimated. Through the reading of high-grade German and Japanese ciphers, we were able to penetrate the enemy lines and enter the headquarters of High Commands, Army Groups, and Armies. On a strategic level, "Special Intelligence" was the unique source of advance knowledge to the enemy's plans for both offensive and defensive operations. It was the timeliest, most complete, and most reliable source of intelligence in his Order of Battle, intentions, and capabilities [NSA 53].

The expression "special intelligence" (in the original text)[8] denotes the intelligence gathered from cryptanalysis, and its successes, against the enemy's encryption systems. This dimension of technology in war was essential for the effectiveness of SIGINT.

The superiority acquired by SIGINT was reflected at all levels, both strategic, tactical and operational:

> On the tactical level, reading the medium and low-grade ciphers, traffic analysis, and direction-finding provided a rapid flow of operational intelligence in the field. The value of operational intelligence from those sources was proved again during the conflict in Korea, and the vital part which COMINT will play in the event of a third world war of reasonably conventional duration cannot now be in any serious doubt [NSA 53].

> COMINT here includes: both the Special Intelligence of World War II and all other intelligence which may be derived from the radio communications activities of a foreign government medium and low-grade cipher messages, plain language transmissions, radio telephone conversations, traffic analysis and direction-finding [NSA 53].

It is in a war context that the states built their SIGINT capabilities. Australia, for example, began its SIGINT activities in 1942 as part of cooperation between its armies and the American defense forces[9].

---

8 "'Special Intelligence' is COMINT derived from decryption of high level cryptographic systems. Potentially, it is the most important and the most reliable source of indicators of hostile intention" [NSA 54].

The SIGINT agencies created at that moment had the mission of intercepting Japanese military communications. At the end of the conflict, the Australian authorities perpetuated these SIGINT activities within the army.

During World War II, COMINT supported a variety of pursuits in multiple theaters of operations. The literature and archives provide abundant illustrations of these uses:

– in the Pacific theater, the United States deployed capabilities to intercept the communications from the Japanese enemy: for example, it was thanks to the COMINT's interceptions of the Japanese command that the warship Yamato was spotted, tracked and sunk in 1945[10];

– in particular, the reader may refer to the following publications: a history of American COMINT during World War II by Robert Louis Benson [BEN 97]; a reflection on the impact of technology on organization in general, and more particularly, of COMINT technologies on the American military organization during World War II [BER 18].

1.1.5. *Wartime interceptions in cyberspace*

The use of cyberspace by armies and intelligence agencies was accompanied by the introduction of new concepts, including those of CYBINT (Cyber Network Intelligence) or DNINT (Digital Network Intelligence), which refer to network intelligence operations. Cyberspace interceptions are one of three forms of offensive actions undertaken in this dimension:

In general, attacks in cyberspace fall into one of three categories – the interception, modification, or denial of information [WOO 06].

CYBINT is the process of explicitly gaining intelligence from available resources on the Internet. CYBINT can be considered as a subset of OSINT [SOO 14].

Cyberintelligence thus makes it possible to have an almost total vision of the cyber structure of a society, an organization or an individual [LEG 16].

---

9 See: www.naa.gov.au/explore-collection/intelligence-and-security/history-australian-intelligence-and-security.

10 Schulz LR, Comint and the Sinking of the Battleship Yamato, NSA Online Archives, [Online]. Available at: www.nsa.gov/Portals/70/documents/news-features/declassified-documents/cryptologic-spectrum/comint_and_the_sinking.pdf.

Under the premise that SIGINT is gathered from signals and HUMINT is gathered from humans, an emergent simple definition of CYBINT is intelligence gathered from cyberspace. [...] The lack of consensus of what comprises cyberspace makes the definition of cyber intelligence equally pervasive [...] with a lack of consensus on the cyberspace definition, information that would commonly be considered a component of other intelligence-gathering disciplines can easily be defined as a CYBINT component. For example, intercepting signaling channels of digital-communications links to capture information in establishing links between systems is traditionally a practice of SIGINT. Using the "interconnected technology" cyberspace definition and the fact that this intelligence was gathered from connecting two (or more) technological systems brings this intelligence into the realm of CYBINT, as it was arguably gathered from cyberspace. Hence, any information gathered from any technical interconnection could now become CYBINT [SEE 18].

The US Department of Defense [JOI 18] considers cyberspace as a "terrain", analogous to the conventional physical realm. The expression used is "key terrain in cyberspace". In this "cyber" territory, the army can isolate spaces, some of which are vulnerable to interceptions:

The military aspects of terrain (obstacles, avenues of approach, cover and concealment, observation and fields of fire, and key terrain) provide a way to visualize and describe a network map. Obstacles in cyberspace may include firewalls and port blocks. Avenues of approach can be analyzed by identifying nodes and links, which connect endpoints to specific sites. Cover and concealment may refer to hidden IP addresses or password protected access. Cyberspace observation and fields of fire refer to areas where network traffic can be monitored, intercepted, or recorded. Examples of potential key terrain in cyberspace include access points to major lines of communications (LOCs), key waypoints for observing incoming threats, launch points for cyberspace attacks, and mission-relevant cyberspace terrain related to critical assets connected to the DODIN [JOI 18].

The notion of MOE (Measure of Effectiveness) is also available there. Adversary systems must be observed in order to detect any changes in enemy practices and to seize the opportunity to conduct interceptions: "MOEs are used to assess changes in targeted system behavior or in the OE[11] […] For example, a MOE for a cyberspace attack action might be a meaningful reduction in the throughput of enemy data traffic or their shift to a more interceptable means of communication" [JOI 18].

1.1.6. *Drones and interceptions*

Drones can act as interception tools or as interception targets, especially in a military context:

– as part of a call for projects published in 2020, the French army planned to use drones equipped with sensors to intercept radio communications at diverse theaters of operations [SEE 20];

– drones could be used to conduct not only physical attacks, but also software attacks: deploying fake Wi-Fi networks in order to intercept smartphone traffic; attacking other drones equipped with communication tools programmed to intercept other drones' communications, etc. [YAA 20];

– in 2009, Iraqi insurgents intercepted live video feeds from US Predator drones using a $26 program available on the Internet [GOR 09].

1.2. The interception of international communications: espionage, surveillance, war

The combination of speed and volume of Internet traffic means most states have limited capability to intercept and monitor cyberspace communications. This limited ability to intercept and monitor traffic through cyberspace is important to maintaining the neutrality of states that are mere intermediaries in information warfare, as in our opening scenario, because the transited state is unlikely to be aware of the transmission [BAR 01].

1.2.1. *The interception of telegrams*

The economic and commercial field has always been a suitable arena for fraudulent practices and espionage. with its extensive and dense communication networks as never before, the 20th century offered a privileged framework for such practices.

---

11 OE: operational environment.

Fraudulent transactions are mentioned in the international press. The daily *The Straits Times* (Singapore) thus evoked on July 21, 1909[12] the complaints of traders who in Calcutta suspect the interception of their telegrams:

> For the past eighteen months complaints have been reaching the Calcutta telegraph office from local merchants of the interception of their market cables from London relating to the prevailing rates of gold, silver, rice, wheat, jute, etc. The Calcutta police arrested three men in the 10th inst. which clear up the mystery. These men were a telegraph peon named Gunga Saran Roy and Durgahi Lal. The two last named opened a small office near Dalhousie Square in a narrow lane where Dwarks and other peons used to take telegrams. These used to be carefully opened by Gunga and copied by Durgahi; and their contents telephoned to various firms and the particular goods mentioned in the cables bought up. Dwarka will be prosecuted for criminal breach of trust, and Gunga and Durgahi for aiding and abetting him, as well as on charges under the Telegraph Act.

1.2.2. *Espionage during the Cold War: satellite, radio, telephone interceptions*

The Cold War was one of the major periods in the history of intelligence-gathering. Spying on, gauging, confronting one another and sometimes clashing in peripheral wars, the great powers deployed considerable means to spy on each other throughout this period (1947–1991).

All along, operations were planned to intercept the enemy's communications. While certain communications, as, for example, those by satellite, could be subject to interception at great distance in function of the geographical location of the facilities, others required approaching the sources as close as possible. Among the latter, we can mention the following operations:

– Silver: conducted by British intelligence services between 1949 and 1955, and whose goal was to tap into landline communications of the Soviet army headquarters in Vienna.

– Gold (Berlin Tunnel Operation Gold for the United States; Operation Stopwatch for the UK), code name PBJOINTLY, or REGAL[13]: conducted jointly by

---

12 See: www.eresources.nlb.gov.sg/newspapers/Digitised/Article/straitstimes19090721-1.2.75?ST=1&AT=search&k=interception%20of%20telegraph&QT=interception,of,telegraph&oref=article.

13 See: www.coldwar.org/articles/50s/berlin_tunnel.asp.

the Americans (CIA) and the British SIS (Secret Intelligence Services), it exploited a tunnel dug in 1954 into the Soviet-occupied zone of Berlin in order to tap into Soviet communications. This was practiced for nearly a year in 1955–1956 and enabled the recording of hundreds of thousands of conversations and millions of telexes, which then had to be translated, requiring the mobilization of colossal resources by the intelligence agencies.

– These two operations to intercept Soviet strategic communications provided Westerners (American and British) with key information regarding the USSR's intentions.

– Technological developments forced intelligence services to get as close as possible to their sources in order to listen to them. Although low-frequency radio broadcasts could be listened to at great distances, the transmission of communications in large volumes and at high frequencies raised new practical problems. The CIA sought to exploit messages transmitted over landlines. The discovery of a vulnerability in an encryption system from the Bell System company paved the way for the interception of unencrypted signals, without the need for decryption (echoes of the unencrypted message were transmitted on the cables at the same time as the encrypted message). The hypothesis was that this flaw in the Bell system could be shared by other communication systems. The choice of Berlin for the tunnel interceptions can also be explained by the position of the city in the architecture of the communication systems from Eastern Europe. Berlin acted as a hub. Every communication from a point in Eastern Europe passed through Berlin [NSA 88].

1.2.3. *The interception of international communications: the Echelon program*

The Echelon[14] network was established by the United States, the United Kingdom, Canada, Australia and New Zealand to intercept communications from commercial satellites. Its origins lie in the 1943 agreement between the United Kingdom and the United States, amidst World War II. It then developed and extended to other partners during the Cold War with the goal of bulk interception and whose existence was disclosed to the public after the 1990s [FOR 05]. It contributed to economic intelligence actions which gave a competitive advantage to American companies. The loss by Thomson-CSF of the call for tenders for a radar system in Brazil to the American Raytheon is attributable to Echelon interceptions.

---

14 See: www.fr.wikipedia.org/wiki/Echelon.

In 1988, Duncan Campbell[15] published an article in the journal *New Statesman*, which brought the Echelon program to the fore. At the end of the 1990s, the European Parliament published reports on the subject: the 1997 STOA (Science and Technology Options Assessment) report, the "Interception Capabilities 2000" report which addresses commercial satellite espionage systems, and especially the Schmid report which is an uncompromising document, presented to the European Parliament [SCH 01]. From the report "Interception Capabilities 2000" written by Duncan Campbell, let us retain the following points:

– Dozens of Silicon Valley companies supply SIGINT technologies to the NSA (companies such as Lockheed Martin, TRW, Raytheon, etc.).

– Some of the companies that provide SIGINT and COMINT capabilities are run by former senior NSA officers.

– International communications from the United Kingdom and the United States and those directed to these same countries have been intercepted since the early 1920s. In the United Kingdom, a law passed in 1920 on official secrets provides access to all types of communication. Other laws followed, such as the Interception of Communications Act 1984 (also in the United Kingdom). The other countries taking part in the Echelon project have adopted laws creating obligations for telecommunication operators.

– Pre-1970 was the era of analog technologies. Post-1990 is essentially digital.

– The access to data/messages is done either "with the complicity of the network operators", or "without their knowledge" [CAM 00].

– International communications are systematically intercepted, including messages sent by or to American citizens.

– Internet interception: "Since the early 1990s, fast and sophisticated COMINT systems have been developed to collect, filter and analyze the types of fast digital communication used by the Internet" [CAM 00]. "Access to communications systems is likely to be remain clandestine, whereas access to Internet exchanges might be more detectable but provides easier access to more data and simpler sorting methods" [CAM 00].

– In the 2000s, the task of interception became more complicated by the shift from telecoms to fiber optic networks. "Physical access to the cable is necessary for interception" [CAM 00].

---

15 Duncan Campbell is a British investigative journalist, who in 1988 revealed the existence of the Echelon network to the general public, in an article entitled "Somebody's Listening". The article is available at: www.new.duncan.gn.apc.org/menu/journalism/newstatesman/ Somebody's_Listening.pdf.

During the Cold War, the NSA, whose primary function was the analysis of signals (SIGINT), focused on the passive interception of (over-the-air) wireless transmissions, such as satellite communications. enshrining the analog–digital transition, the Internet changed the game. Conventional interception became ineffective on optical cables, and the expansion of computer networks required an in-depth review of interception methods. They had to be practiced as close as possible to the source, with physical access to the transmission equipment. The considerable increase in the volume of communications has induced a change in scale which has jointly called for the development of surveillance capabilities. As the United States are at the heart of global Internet networks, the NSA has a considerable advantage from this point of view [CLE 14]:

> On August 14, 1962 [REU 62], the Australian newspaper *The Age* published a news brief relating to the interception of communications between Moscow and a soviet space station: "The Japanese Government radio station N.H.K. in Chiba, east of Tokyo, reported that it had intercepted Soviet radio instructions to Vostok IV, ordering it to prepare to return to Earth".

1.2.4. *Bulk cyber surveillance*

The September 11, 2001 attacks seem to have been a breaking point in the NSA culture:

> Ex-NSA analyst J. Kirk Wiebe recalls: "everything changed at the NSA after the attacks on September 11. The prior approach focused on complying with the Foreign Intelligence Surveillance Act ("FISA"). The post-September 11 approach was that NSA could circumvent federal statutes and the Constitution as long as there was some visceral connection to looking for terrorists". While another ex-NSA analyst also remembers: "The individual liberties preserved in the US Constitution were no longer a consideration [at the NSA]"[16].

This analysis can be called into question. The NSA had already extended surveillance to American citizens before the September 11 attacks, as evidenced by the great United States public intelligence crisis throughout 1975 which had resulted in an unprecedented conflict between the Congress, the White House and the agencies, following the revelations about the CIA and the FBI activities by the press [LAU 14].

---

16 Quoted in "Timeline of NSA Domestic Spying" [Online]. Available at: www.eff.org/fr/nsa-spying/timeline.

In 2001, William Binney and J. Kirk Wiebe resigned from the NSA and denounced the excesses of the activities carried out there, especially via the *Thin Thread* program, which they had contributed to develop within the agency. *Afterward, Binney and Wiebe denounced the existence of the Stellar Wind program, which intercepted communications within the country (telephone, email messages)*[17].

The disclosure of classified documents by E. Snowden brought to light the existence of NSA cyber surveillance practices and capabilities on a massive scale. At present, practices are part of the long term and affect all citizens, unlike the programs for the interception of satellite communications denounced in the 1990s, which mostly concerned states and businesses.

At that moment, the issues mainly concerned economic espionage, unfair competition, political espionage, etc. Echelon reflected the state's quest for power. The practices denounced by Snowden mark America's power strategy, but they are part of a security policy in the war against terrorism. At the same time, according to Snowden, they create risks for citizens.

Internet and the various applications having developed since the early 1990s worldwide have offered intelligence agencies new opportunities for collecting and accessing data.

The "Interception Capabilities 2014" report[18] highlights the difference between old and new interception methods. Old methods are characterized by the legal and targeted interception model, the proportionality of the means and the European security exception. New methods, on the other hand, are characterized by scale, depth level, the multiplicity of methods, secret partnerships, illicit attacks and compromised hardware.

1.2.5. *Foreign companies in national telecommunication infrastructures*

Recently, international relations have brought to the fore the question of technological sovereignty, due to the risks posed to states by the level of control/penetration of foreign companies into sensitive and critical infrastructures, including communication systems. International tensions have particularly crystallized around 5G technology.

---

17 "The National Security Agency (NSA) Controversy: Timeline" [Online]. Available at: www.discoverthenetworks.org/viewSubCategory.asp?id=1933. [Accessed March 1, 2017].
18 See: www.duncancampbell.org/PDF/CoECultureCommittee1Oct2013.pdf.

Chinese telecommunication companies are under the sight of Western countries, because they provide telephone operators with the means to deploy their vast networks (formerly 3G, then 4G and finally 5G). However, these companies are accused of acting as Trojan horses, of opening backdoors in national networks, of authorizing foreign powers (in this case, China), to capture feeds for espionage purposes. They allegedly even have the capacity to take control of the networks, something which, in a conflict scenario, could represent a major vulnerability for the countries dependent on such technologies. The Chinese operator Huawei has thus been accused, among others by the Netherlands, of having accessed the data of millions of customers from the KPN operator and to have had the possibility of listening to all their communications for years [BAY 21].

1.2.6. *Actions over undersea Internet cables*

In the 1960s, the United States secretly operated in international undersea spaces. As part of the Holystone program, the US Navy carried out espionage tasks using submarines. The practice was debated in the United States in the 1970s [HER 75] due to the confrontation risks posed by intrusions into the Soviet maritime space, on the one hand, and the interception of submarines themselves by the Soviet Defense Forces, on the other. More generally, the debates focused on intelligence-gathering and the control of government initiatives in this area. While the whole challenge for the Americans was to remain undetectable, it seems that the USSR was informed about the program's existence. The submarines were able to tap into Soviet undersea communication cables and to intercept high-level military messages which were not transmitted via other channels such as the radio, due to the vulnerability of other modes of communication. The submarines used for these operations were Sturgeon or 637 Class attack submarines to which specific electronic equipment was added.

When, in the early 1970s, the Americans became aware of the existence of undersea cables near the Kuril Islands, they launched Ivy Bell Operation, which lasted until 1981, placing sensors on these cables, regularly collecting data which were then processed by NSA services [KHA 13].

According to the Corpwatch website, the Californian company Glimmerglass offered government agencies the CyberSweep software that can intercept undersea cable signals [CHA 13] and analyze Gmail, Yahoo! and social media feeds such as Facebook or Twitter:

> With the introduction of fibre-optic cables and the ensuing dependence
> of businesses and governments on trans-ocean communications, the
> world's oceans have become a target-rich environment that provides

adversaries with incentives to develop undersea operational competence and strike these difficult-to-defend systems [ZIO 13].

The disclosures by E. Snowden reported the existence of multiple communication interception programs installed in undersea infrastructures. To accomplish this, the states benefited from the contribution of private companies (the British agency GCHQ is said to have used technologies from the Vodafone company[19]).

Internet undersea cables, fiber optic cables, are no less vulnerable to interception attacks than other communication technologies:

> There is a prevailing, misguided belief that fibre networks are more secure than other media, such as copper and wireless technologies. Fiber networks are vulnerable to tapping through the use of well-known techniques such as man-in-the-middle, re-routing and exploiting protocol vulnerabilities and software vulnerabilities in network devices. There is also a perception that fibre networks are much better protected against physical interference and the installation of tapping equipment. This is a misunderstanding: fiber networks are at least as vulnerable to physical tapping as traditional copper [DEL 17].

1.2.7. Interceptions in planes and airports

Aircraft on board GSM services were introduced on March 20, 2008. The number of its users rapidly grew. NSA SIGINT systems, as well as GCHQ British services, were mobilized to intercept these communications [FOL 16].

Intelligence-gathering agencies or the police monitor and intercept communications at the airports. In 2017, a Canadian journalist detected the presence of IMSI-catchers in Trudeau airport (Montreal)[20].

1.2.8. International interceptions as a product of secret alliances

Companies in charge of securing communications can act as intelligence providers for the states, according to the findings of an investigation published by the *Washington Post* in February 2020, which affirms that the German company

19 See: www.securityaffairs.co/wordpress/30438/intelligence/gchq-wiretapping-undersea-cables.html.
20 See: www.cbc.ca/news/canada/montreal/trudeau-airport-spying-1.4055803.

Crypto AG (providing encryption solutions to a hundred countries) was allegedly bought by the CIA in 1970, thus enabling the American agency to intercept encrypted communications. The systems are said to have been rigged with backdoors so that intelligence services could access the contents. The operation was supposedly called "Thesaurus", then "Rubicon", and according to a former German intelligence official, it made it possible to make the world a bit safer [AGE 20].

1.3. Interception of diplomatic correspondence

Intelligence gathered from the interception of communications in all their forms plays a central role in the political and diplomatic life. Interceptions are organized methodically:

> All the dispatches from the Prince of Kaunitz, all those from imperial ministers in foreign courts, all those from foreign courts and ministers which are intercepted, pass through what we here call the cabinet. This is where the decipherers' offices are established. The Baron de Pichler is its director; he discusses directly with the Empress and reports only to her. This director always gives the princess five copies of each dispatch, either imperial or intercepted. From these five copies, the Empress gives one to the Emperor, sends one to Florence, to the Grand Duke of Tuscany, as the eventual successor of the Austrian monarchy, if the Emperor has no children; one to Brussels to the Prince of Starhemberg, as appointed to replace the Prince of Kaunitz; and one to the Count of Rosemberg, as confidant, whose advice is believed to be useful [...] Another singular and very true anecdote is that the Empress sometimes adds or removes information from the intercepted dispatches.

The author of these lines continues the description, referring to the extensive interception of the private correspondence from the King of Prussia to his minister in Vienna:

> Through this channel, we have real and very interesting notions about the politics of the two currently befriended courts, their hidden designs, the nuances of their liaisons with the court of Petersburg, and the monarch's language and maneuvers [...] We have been able to know the full weight of this interception by the successive sending of the sequence of these Prussian dispatches, which already form a voluminous series [...] I would like to finish this presentation of my discoveries by announcing an infallible key that I myself carry to the king to get to know the most secret details of the correspondence of

the king of Prussia with his minister in Paris. It is the decryption of their cipher [...] Vienna, July 4, 1774 [FAV 93].

This document sheds light on the various facets of the profession of diplomat and spy, the place occupied by postal interception, and the various tactics and subterfuges deployed by the actors to take full advantage of it.

The encryption and decryption of couriers are two integrated functions within the French Ministry of Foreign Affairs, as depicted by Jean-Baptiste-René Robinet in his Universal dictionary of moral, economic and political and diplomatic sciences (*Dictionnaire universel des sciences morale, économique, politique et diplomatique*) at the end of the 18th century [ROB 77]:

> The Department also maintains two sorts of decipherers: the first are responsible for ciphering the dispatches the Court sends to its Ministers residing in foreign Courts, and for deciphering the reports they receive from them. This is a laborious and confidence-requiring work, which deserves to be rewarded with a good salary [...] The other decipherers have applied themselves to deciphering without a key the ciphered dispatches the foreign Courts address to their Ministers residing with us, or that the latter send to their Masters. This art is not as infallible as many people claim, and we will show instead that a well-sealed letter, properly ciphered with a solid key, is absolutely indecipherable. However, as not all the Courts have ciphers so difficult to guess, and not all Chancelleries are so accurate in ciphering well, nor in closing their letters with sufficient precaution, the Department sometimes avails itself of their negligence, and, by employing the know-how of these kinds of decipherers, manages to discover very dangerous projects, or matters of the greatest importance.

Powers operate outside their territories: "We have certainly not forgotten the declarations of Mr. Clemenceau, who promised to put an end to the zeal of the Russian secret police, which, in the heart of Paris, openly 'stole' the correspondence received by the political escapees from the Tsar's Empire" [MAH 13].

The construction of the electric telegraph vast cable networks in the 19th century quickly raised questions about the risk of exposure to indiscreet ears, of the messages conveyed by these infrastructures extending over thousands of kilometers:

> We are sure of the approval of every intelligent man when we say that the most perfect and most exclusive control is absolutely necessary to ensure the regular reception of our political and commercial

dispatches from India without any interception or indiscretion. It is not enough to have our employees or our stations, when the wires belong to another government and are maintained by foreigners [DES 58].

1.4. Political surveillance: targeted and bulk interceptions

1.4.1. *Interception of correspondence*

King Louis XI of France (1423–1483) was, it is said, one of the first to organize a royal courier service, which afterwards enabled the transport of private correspondence. But in return for the transport of private correspondence, the royal services had to be aware of the messages' contents:

> The ancient legislation teaches us that the postal administration has always made it its business to unseal letters. It was forbidden for all post offices, post clerks and postmen, to open any letters or packages entrusted to them, under penalty of death, so odious was considered such a crime. A sovereign judgment issued by the Police Lieutenant-General of Paris on May 3, 1741, condemned Louis Leprince, an office clerk from the Paris post office, to death by hanging for prevaricate in his functions, having intercepted, unsealed and opened two letters coming from Caen. The following year, positive law stated that any postal employee convicted of having fraudulently unsealed letters and diverted its contents to make profit, would be condemned to death; this proves that the practice was quite common. For the case of suppression or simple interception, and depending on the gravity of the facts, the penalty was the galleys in perpetuity or for a period of time, banishment or a reprimand [ATH 28].

But this right of scrutiny would continue to arouse reservations and criticism. The inviolability of the secrecy of letters was well enshrined in law, and its violations severely punished: "Nothing is more fatal and more prejudicial to society's order than the power to violate, under any pretext whatsoever, the inviolability of postal secrecy" [ATH 28].

But the practice of interceptions made the 19th century the object of a dispute opposing citizens and those who supported this form of espionage.

Let us recall the order given by the English Minister of the Interior, Graham in 1844, to intercept the letters from Mazzini, who at this moment was a refugee in London (he would later become a statesman in Italy). Mazzini protested, the British people were indignant, Graham resigned. In the popular slang of the time, *to grahamise* meant to intercept communications. The surveillance Graham wished to bring against Mazzini did not limit the information exploited to the benefit of his own government. He communicated the contents to partner governments on the continent. This sharing of information between powers echoes more contemporary practices.

For a long time, politicians and statesmen have succumbed to the temptation to intercept mail, messages, communications, intrigued by the contents passing within their reach. But the victims of these practices are not easily fooled. Interceptions are more or less discreet, leaving more or less traces. One of the major challenges of those in charge of interception is to ensure that their intervention is invisible. The other challenge concerns the decryption of messages the most cautious senders have thus tried to protect. It is also remarkable that since the 19th century the civil society, the population, turned out to be an actor of resistance, of opposition. This practice was denounced by the press in several European countries in particular (Spain, England, for example). This meant that state actors were forced to be even more discreet, on the one hand, and to enshrine in law the principles consecrating the inviolability of secrecy: "Following too flagrant abuses in 1826, a paragraph was inserted in the Constitutional Act in Portugal instituting the absolute inviolability of the secrecy of correspondence" [MAH 13].

Notwithstanding these resistances, denunciations and principles enshrined in law, 19th-century states intensively practiced interceptions. The situation was so critical that the number of letters never arriving at their destination have reached considerable proportions [MAH 13].

1.4.1.1. *The cabinet noir*

The term "cabinet noir" (black room or dark chamber) refers to secret premises, placed under the control of states during the *Ancien Régime*, which existed in most European countries. These services were in charge of intercepting postal mail and cryptography in order to "identify and censor political opponents, and to inquire about diplomatic or military couriers"[21]:

> In the month of December 1880, during the somewhat resounding fall of the Ristics ministry in Belgrade, one could read in numerous Serbian newspapers that in the ex-Premier's bureau over two thousand letters had been suppressed and opened by the "cabinet noir", and among them many insured letters. This was a revelation, and its repetition should be carefully avoided. Nevertheless, the practice

---

21 See: www.fr.wikipedia.org/wiki/Cabinet_noir.

persisted. For the adversaries of successive governments, in all the Balkan states without exception, the secrecy of letters was violated without the least scruple. Since hostilities broke out in the Balkans, many facts (and foreigners' testimonies) have proven that the interception of correspondence is practiced on a vast scale, both on the side of the Allies and in Turkish circles [MAH 13].

In France, these cabinets have existed since the appearance of the postal service. The edict signed by Louis XI on June 19, 1464 specifies in its Articles 13 and 14: "Couriers and messengers will be reviewed by the clerks of the Grand Master, to whom letters will have to be shown in order to find out whether there is anything detrimental to the service of the King, or which many contravene his edicts and ordinances"[22].

These "cabinets noirs" were particularly developed under Louis XV. There even existed a secret cabinet for the postal service, where the superintendent instructed opening certain packages. These services unsealed the letters, recomposed the stamps and sent the copies to the Police Lieutenant-General and the Minister of Foreign Affairs.

In 1789, many registers of grievances demanded the abolition of dark chambers [LAU 15]. The Constituent Assembly and the Convention proclaimed the inviolability of correspondence. Despite this, the dark chamber was restored by the French Directory, limiting surveillance to foreign letters. It was maintained under the Empire, the Restoration and would last until the Second Empire [LAU 09].

Aware of the fact that they were being observed, listened to, spied on, that their official and private correspondence could be intercepted, statesmen, politicians and diplomats ended up writing mere trivialities on their letters, a sign of self-censorship on the part of those concerned, as well as a clever way to deceive actors who were too indiscreet. Furthermore, the banalities could sometimes conceal hidden messages. Ordinary language became a code, a mask. The awareness that correspondence – regardless of its form or method – could be opened, read, seen or intercepted by third parties modified the behavior of correspondents. Humans never stopped imagining countermeasures, circumvention methods, aimed at protecting the messages from undesirable eyes. The history of interceptions, the history of interception methods, techniques and technologies is closely related to that of countermeasures, of all the ways invented to prevent interceptions. "Unencrypted", unprotected communication can sometimes be part of a broader tactical or strategic choice.

---

22 See: www.cosmovisions.com/Cabinet-Noir.htm.

1.4.1.2. *The Nazi state and the interception of telegrams and telephony*

In 1933, the activity of the National Socialists in the Saar was a major concern. The pressure exerted by the Nazi party against the population and the political leaders resorted to the interception of communications among other instruments, thus contributing to the construction of an authoritarian government:

> Rivaling the government of Society, a secret Nazi government seeks to exercise authority [...] Police officers, even the highest and senior ones, are secretly at its orders [...] The public services: the posts and telegraphs, taxation offices, municipal authorities, mayors, many bishops and prelates, even the judges and magistrates, obey, to a large extent, to this Nazi state within the state. Strictly speaking there is a reign of terror – including intimidation and espionage, anonymous denunciations, abductions of individuals, transported across Germany's frontiers, internments in concentration camps in Germany, threats of dismissal and withdrawal of pensions addressed to civil servants who do not obey the orders of the unofficial government, the interception of letters, telegrams, and telephone conversations... [SLO 33].

1.4.2. *Bulk domestic surveillance in East Germany*

The surveillance operated by the security services in the German Democratic Republic was part of bulk surveillance practices.

The practices of the Stasi in the former East Germany undoubtedly made the greatest impact. It is hard to think about a "political police" without bearing in mind the Stasi's name. On the eve of the fall of the Berlin Wall, the Stasi had over 100,000 employees. This potential was based on systematic recourse to informants, ruling the East-German society with an iron fist. The organization was completed by recourse to systematic tapping and interception of correspondence, tasks performed by approximately 2,000–3,000 members of the Stasi. The statistics seem to show a very strong correlation between the number of individual arrests and the density level of surveillance [CHE 16].

1.4.3. *Cyber surveillance in Russia: the SORM system*

The Russian SORM (*System of Operative Search Methods*) makes it possible to monitor the traffic of radio, telegraph, telephone and electronic networks (Internet) [GAÜ 16]. This system was implemented by the Soviet KGB to wiretap telephone communications. The next generation, also known by the acronym SORM-2, enables the interception of telecommunications in Russia, capabilities which now include Internet flows. The latest generation SORM-3 incorporates all telecommunications. The law authorizes intelligence-gathering services (FSB) to collect and analyze metadata and contents, to store the data for three years and compels access providers to install surveillance equipment on their networks, with a direct access to traffic [LAW 14].

1.4.4. *Fixed and mobile telephone tapping*

1.4.4.1. *Wiretapping in American politics*

From October 1963 to June 1966, the FBI wiretapped activist Martin Luther King under the COINTELPRO program (*COunter INTelligence PROgram*), operated by the agency between 1956 and 1971. The targets of this program were the political organizations or movements representing a destabilization risk in the eyes of the government. It was not limited to the electronic surveillance of leaders and members of radical groups, but also implemented denigration or influence operations. The agency was also suspected of assassinations [WOL 01]. An investigation on assassinations, carried out by the Congress in 1979[23], concluded that the FBI had exceeded its surveillance prerogatives. The purpose of wiretaps was to identify contacts between Martin Luther King and the Communists, but targeted all private communications as well as exchanges government members without any discernment[24].

Lyndon Baines Johnson, a Democrat who unwillingly became President of the United States in November 1963 following the assassination of J.F. Kennedy, and who was later elected in 1964, was in office until January 1969. In 1964, he had to address the issue of racial riots in several cities across the country.

At the time of the 1964 Democratic Convention, L.B. Johnson wished to make sure that the protesters would not disrupt debates, which is why he required being kept informed about the opposition's negotiations. For this, he summoned the FBI services, who tapped the telephones of his opponents [MAY 01].

Between 1969 and 1971, Henry Kissinger was involved in telephone tapping ordered by the White House due to national security reasons, targeting several members of the *National Security Council* (NSC) as well as journalists. Wiretapping

---

23 *Select Committee on Assassinations, US House of Representatives, 95th Congress, 2 session*, 1979.

24 See: www.archives.gov/research/jfk/select-committee-report/part-2e.html.

was intended to find out who was behind media leaks of secret bombings in Cambodia[25]:

> Former President Richard M. Nixon said his efforts to undermine the presidency of the late Salvador Allende in Chile were prompted by the 'same national security interests' which led Presidents Kennedy and Johnson to intervene secretly in that country [...] The former President's responses covered a range of questions touching on the Chile intervention as well as his authorization of domestic operations by the CIA and FBI such as break-ins, wiretapping and interception of cable traffic. In dealing with the Chilean intervention as well as the controversial surveillance programs targeted against American citizens, Nixon repeatedly argued that he has followed the lead of his predecessors in the White House [...] In the arena of surveillance activities within the United States, Nixon said: "I remember learning on various occasions that during administrations prior to mine, agencies or employees of the United States Government, acting presumably without a warrant, conducted wiretaps, surreptitious or unauthorized entries, and intercepts of voice and non-voice communications". In a sharp response to the former President's answers, chairman Franck Church of the Senate Intelligence committee criticized Nixon's advocacy of a doctrine of "the sovereign presidency" as a "pernicious and dangerous doctrine" [STE 76].

In a testimony released on March 10, 1976 by his attorneys, Nixon confirmed that he had ordered a wiretap program in 1969. But he tried to disavow himself by placing the responsibility on the shoulders of his national security adviser, H. Kissinger, for choosing the targets [HOR 76].

1.4.4.2. The Élysée wiretapping affair

This scandalous affair took place during the first term of President François Mitterrand, between 1983 and 1986. The Élysée's anti-terrorist unit, headed by a GIGN (*Groupe d'intervention de la Gendarmerie nationale*) officer, wiretapped numerous personalities (media, entertainment, politics, etc.) on the orders of the President of the Republic. These wiretaps diverted the means of the state to private ends, because they only served the personal interests of Mitterrand. A judicial procedure was opened in 1993 and a trial took place in 2005. The unit used part of

---

25 "Kissinger Telephone Conversation Transcripts" [Online]. Available at: www. nixonlibrary. gov/index.php/finding-aids/kissinger-telephone-conversation-transcripts.

the GIC (*Groupement interministériel de contrôle*) means, dedicated to administrative interceptions.

1.4.4.3. *Argentina wiretapping scandal*

A scandal broke out in Argentina in 2009, relating to espionage practices not only aimed at the victims (and relatives) of the AMIA (Spanish for Argentine Israelite Mutual Association) headquarters 1994 attack in Buenos Aires (causing 85 deaths and 200 injuries), but also targeting politicians and journalists. The case took a new turn when it was discovered that President Cristina Fernández and her husband Nestor Kirchner could also have been the object of wiretaps. Personal data relating to numerous political personalities, civil servants, trade unionists and businessmen were found on the computers of the agency who performed the interceptions. In November 2009, the justice ordered the detention of the former police head of the city of Buenos Aires. This scandal motivated several interventions from the Supreme Court, who still insisted in 2019 on the need to strictly limit interceptions to investigations conducted by the judge[26]. The Court was concerned about the systematic use of interceptions, a practice erroneously considered as an ordinary means of investigation, despite the fact that it should only be used as a last resort for the most serious crimes. This warning was issued in 2019, after wiretapping records were leaked. These cases raised the question as to the limits of the actions pursued by the intelligence services and their connections with the justice, the police and politics.

1.4.4.4. *The case of Chile: "W" and Topógrafo operations*

"W" (in 2016) and Topógrafo (in 2017) operations designate surveillance actions conducted by the military intelligence. This was the first time a journalist was targeted, and the second time it happened to four soldiers, who denounced embezzlement within the institution. According to military intelligence officials, these operations involving telephone tapping were completely legal and were carried out with the judge's authorization. These practices raised the question as to the judge's role and the authorization procedure in general. The responsibilities weighing on judges are important. Are they still able to perform their role without any pressure, in total autonomy? Are authorizations always in accordance with what is provided for by the law? Do any spurious arrangements exist "among friends"? The question was posed by the media: who were the judges who had granted the authorizations [VED 19]? In any case, the fact that an interception has been authorized does not necessarily make it lawful.

---

26 See: www.mundo.sputniknews.com/america-latina/201906191087698866-corte-suprema-argentina-restringe-escuchas-telefonicas-judiciales/.

1.4.4.5. *Scandals in Peru*

In 1997, a scandal broke out after it was revealed that the government had wiretapped political opponents and journalists. Wiretaps are carried out by the military intelligence services (SIN, Spanish for *Servicio de Inteligencia Nacional*).

In 2018, legal wiretaps as part of an investigation against drug trafficking led to the revelation of a vast network of corruption at the top of the justice.

1.4.5. **The interception of electronic communications in the political sphere**

1.4.5.1. *The scandal of fierce interceptions in Colombia*

Political interceptions arouse strong reactions in the societies which experience such phenomenon, because they are considered as a severe attack on the principles of democracy.

In Colombia, many scandals related to the interception of communications in the political arena have been grabbing the headlines for years. Interceptions are often associated with corruption cases.

A case of illegal wiretapping, known as the "Chuzadas", tarnished President Uribe's second term (2006–2010). Among other scandals, let us mention: Parapolitica, Yidispolitica, Falsos Positivos [DUB 11]. The government was called into question in 2007 by revelations concerning fierce wiretapping. The Colombian President Alvaro Uribe was accused of transforming the intelligence services (the DAS, Spanish for Administrative Department of Security, who acted as frontier police, intelligence and counter-intelligence police)[27] into a force working for his sole political interest. The fight against all forms of opposition resulted in the surveillance of journalists, politicians, trade unionists, human rights defenders and magistrates, to mention only a few. These extrajudicial interceptions (telephone tapping, email and written correspondence interception, etc.) made it possible to surveil political opponents for several years. The information collected during the wiretaps made it possible to surveil individuals, their relationships and networks, their activities and ideological positions. These practices allegedly took place between 2004 and 2008.

In 2007, a dozen generals were dismissed. But the practice persisted. In February 2009, the magazine *Semana 13* published revelations regarding the extent of DAS's

---

27 During President Uribe's first term, the DAS had already suffered a scandal, accused of having bonds with the paramilitary forces.

illegal activities. In 2010, the justice took up the case and several officials were indicted, including officials from the intelligence services and the Secretary General of the Presidency of the Republic. In their defense, the defendants claimed that the activities were aimed at finding out the relationship between organized crime and the Supreme Court judges. Agents working in these intelligence services also reported using surveillance technologies provided by Washington [FOR 11].

These interceptions were only one of the bricks of the political surveillance strategy implemented within the country to ensure that the power in place could keep a grip on anti-establishment speeches. Wiretapping and the interception of electronic communications were only a supplement to stalking, threats and the violation of private homes.

The government dissolved the DAS and replaced it with the ANIC (Spanish for National Intelligence Agency). The purpose was to break with a past of corruption and criminal practices. In September 2017, the former director of the DAS was sentenced to seven years and 10 months in prison for the interception of private communications and surveillance without any orders from the judicial authority.

But new revelations at the end of 2019 seemed to bring to life those moments in Colombian history. New illegal wiretaps were carried out, this time targeting magistrates, opposition politicians and journalists. But this time wiretapping was due to the workings of the military [PAN 20] and targeted all those who had denounced corrupt practices within the army. Wiretapping had been carried out at two military garrisons, in an attempt to evade justice. The press published the disclosures of a Colombian cyber defense junior officer at the end of 2019. Armed with cyber education capabilities, the military intercepted WhatsApp and Telegram exchanges, the content of mobile phone communications and accessed computer contents.

1.4.5.2. *Espionage in Togo*

In August 2020, the Togolese authorities were accused[28] by the newspapers *Le Monde* [TIL 20] and the *Guardian* of having spied on members of the opposition, clerics (playing a role in the efforts to establish a dialogue between the power and the opposition) and civil society actors, by intercepting mobile telephone communications (geolocation, reading emails and messages, taking control of the camera and the microphone), with Pegasus[29] software provided by the Israeli

---

28 "Togo: Media reveal acts of espionage from the authorities", RFI, August 4, 2020 [Online]. Available at: www.rfi.fr/fr/afrique/20200804-togo-médias-révèlent-actes-despionnages-la-part-authorities.

29 See: https://en.wikipedia.org/wiki/Pegasus_(spyware).

company NSO[30] Group. When they were informed of being the targets of such practices, the victims were hardly surprised because "in Togo[31], it is common knowledge that everyone can be wiretapped".

1.5. Criminal interceptions

As soon as new communication technologies emerge, they can be used fraudulently. Without it technically being an interception, let us recall the misappropriation of the Chappe optical telegraph in France between 1834 and 1836 by clever crooks gambling on the stock market. Their goal was to get to know the stock values in Paris before the arrival of the information by mail, and to sell or buy depending on the trend.

Two bankers from Bordeaux, Louis and François Blanc, had the idea of exploiting the speed of the telegraph to transmit the information subliminally. This is how the issue No. 3506 of the *Gazette des tribunaux* from December 10, 1836 described the operation:

> An agent from Paris transmitted to Tours, *poste restante*, certain items, such as gloves, etc., whose color conveyed a rise or fall in stocks. Upon seeing these objects, the telegraph employee gave an agreed signal [...] The Tours employee sent out an *error* signal, which was repeated all along the line, and consequently did not figure in the official dispatches.

Informed via a third agent, our two accomplices were certain of winning and could handsomely remunerate their accomplices. The affair was revealed following numerous errors made on purpose, detected by the Telegraphs' administration.

During the 19th century, interceptions became quite common, to the point that the states felt obliged to pass law on the question: "Shortly after the telegraph came into existence and wires were strung from pole to pole, wiretappers were busy intercepting the coded communications [...] As early as 1862, California found it necessary to enact legislation prohibiting the interception of telegraph messages [DAS 59].

---

30 A Wikipedia entry indicates that this Israeli company is majority controlled by the British company Novalpina Capital: https://en.wikipedia.org/wiki/Pegasus_(spyware).

31 "Togo: Media reveal espionage actions from the authorities", RFI, August 4, 2020 [Online]. Available at: www.rfi.fr/fr/afrique/20200804-togo-médias-révèlent-actes-despionnages-la-part-autorités.

In the United States, the same skills, which had been acquired in the army during the revolution war, were recycled into the criminal field:

> After the Civil War, a number of former telegraph operators engaged in wiretapping for private gain [...] As early as 1893, "past posters" were busy at work. They employed former linemen and operators for the Western Union Company to flash race news to gang members, so that bets could be placed with bookies before official race results had arrived [DAS 59].

Companies also engaged in these practices, particularly in the media:

> Equally active wiretapping practices existed at the same time among newspaper rivals. Telephone calls by reporters of one newspaper were being intercepted by reporters of a rival newspaper for the purpose of picking up "scoops." This practice existed across the country. It was reported in Boston, New York, Chicago, and San Francisco. In 1895, Illinois enacted legislation prohibiting wiretapping for the purpose of intercepting news dispatches [DAS 59].

The 19th-century "hackers" proved that they could cleverly exploit vulnerabilities in wired communications:

> A fraudulent interception of cable telegrams from Marseilles. We borrow from *Anales de la Electricidad* the following account of a real attack against the secrecy of telegraphic correspondence, committed in Barcelona by intercepting underground cables and whose authors have not yet been discovered. For a year and a half, over the section of the Marseilles cable, (between the Company's office in Barcelona and the landing gate), current diversions had been observed, increasing on a daily basis [...] The technical observations made by the cable's offices (measurement of resistances), indicated that the fault should be found in the vicinity of the Promenade of San Juan [...] We immediately proceeded to the opening of the channel on this short route and Mr. Brown was shocked to discover four conductor branches at the corner of the Rond de San Pedro and the Promenade de San Juan, which, starting from the four cables, went towards house No. 47 [...] The thieves, who had to perfectly distinguish Marseilles' cables from those of the government [...] had preferably made a connection over those from Marseilles, since the information from the Paris Stock Exchange was the only correspondence they could intercept. These telegrams

were transmitted by Morse apparatus, whereas those from Madrid were transmitted by the Hughes system, whose signals cannot be received by sound"[32].

1.6. Police, justice: the fight against crime, lawful interceptions

The introduction of tools for the interception of electronic communications in the police sphere remarkably varied from state to state (done at different moments and paces). They sometimes even took place too late, after relatively isolated initiatives. Australia, for example, only became interested in these practices near the end of the 1960s according to the findings established in a report by the Royal Commission of Inquiry into alleged telephone interceptions, published in 1986[33]:

> In approximately 1967 Sergeant D.R. Williams was attached to the Communication Branch of the NSW Police as a senior technician. In that year, according to Williams, the Commissioner of Police, Mr. N.T.W. Allen, asked Williams to attend Police Headquarters in order to discuss new electronic means of obtaining criminal information [...] Williams' recollection of the conversation is that the Commissioner requested him to explore the possibility of utilizing both listening devices and devices for the interception of telephone conversations [...] Williams said he was joined in the task by Constable G.P. Smith early in 1968. Smith had been attached to the Radio Technical Unit of the Police Communications Branch since 1966. His recollection was that during the period 1966 to 1967 he developed, on a part time basis, several small transistorized transmitter devices. These devices were used as listening devices and were not at that stage used for the interception of telephone conversations" [...] Smith began to experiment with the notion of using the transistorized transmitter devices on telephone lines. Williams said that the first device suitable for the interception of telephone conversations was constructed by himself and Smith in 1968. [...] In 1969 Williams visited the United States to study the progress and development of radar speed detection equipment.

---

32 *Le Journal télégraphique*, July 25, 1889, p. 155–156 [Online]. Available at: www.gallica. bnf.fr/ark:/12148/bpt6k5575657j/f15.image.r=interception?rk=42918;4.

33 *Report of the Royal Commission of Inquiry into alleged telephone interceptions*, volume 1, April 30, 1986, Melbourne [Online]. Available at: www.parliament.vic.gov. at/papers/govpub/ VPARL1985-87No96.pdf.

Williams then tried to look further into the development of interception technologies in the United States, but "he obtained very little information relating to such devices".

The interceptions implemented by the police forces have nourished the images of multiple works of fiction, novels or cinema. Policemen are portrayed as stationed in vehicles, earphones on their heads, recorders on and after hours of often fruitless waiting, capturing a few snatches of conversation which provide the keys to the case in progress. However, these taps result from microphones placed inside the buildings, not from the interception of communications between a transmitter and a receiver. This practice is illustrated by the images of police placing "contact clips" on telephone cables, and then listening to communications from a distant exchange. An audible, rasping, parasitic noise would signal to correspondents the presence of these indiscreet devices.

Today, the police practice "legal interceptions", contemplated by the law (few countries do not have such legislation), technically relying on legal interception systems or platforms. However, marginal practices persist, as evidenced by the recent confessions from the Israeli police services who admitted to illegally using the Pegasus application, although at first, they had strongly denied using this software.

In prison, the use of the telephone is not forbidden, but strictly limited. On the contrary, the introduction of mobile phones and any form of electronic communication tool is prohibited. This ban should allow the institution to monitor the prisoners' activities and to prevent criminal pursuits outside the prison. This prohibition does not always prevent the introduction of mobile phones, which surprisingly manage to enter the prison through various means. To counter this risk, prisons can equip themselves with detection tools which locate phones as soon as they are activated. Prisoners' telephone communications may be monitored, their exchanges intercepted and recorded[34]. These taps are not secret, the prisoners are informed.

1.7. On the usefulness and effectiveness of interceptions

During a cybersecurity conference held in France in 2018, the technical director of the DGSE spoke about the difficulties of the intelligence-gathering profession, and more particularly its technological challenges:

---

34 See: www.le.alcoda.org/publications/point_of_view/files/IPC.pdf.

> [...] The first challenges for an intelligence service like mine, a technical service, is to keep up with technological developments. It may sound trivial, but in fact we completely suffer from technological developments, we can anticipate absolutely nothing [...] We suffer from crypto labs attacks who are trying to crack crypto. We have people who make the interceptions [...] Historically [...] we developed these different capacities: crypto, interception [...] As a technique, it no longer works. Crypto on its own, in broad terms, we no longer break. Interceptions, if you just intercept, as it is encrypted, it is useless since the crypto won't be able to break it. Despite all, computing is still required, there are vulnerabilities, there are pieces of keys in circulation [...] So very often when, we have a problem to solve, we articulate our capacities"[35].

Interceptions alone would be of limited use if the contents could not be accessed. And to achieve this, intelligence actors have to mobilize techniques, methods, different capacities, expertise called upon to work together.

It is difficult to dispute the usefulness of interceptions because they are at the heart of intelligence practices, whether in times of peace, crisis or armed conflict. Intelligence based on interceptions enriches the knowledge acquired by other techniques (HUMINT or OSINT, for example). However, they do not provide an absolute mastery of reality. While interceptions provide information of unequal quality, their real usefulness is assessed by the use we make of them. Quality interceptions could not prevent strategic-surprise attacks (such as the Pearl Harbor attack) or tactical ones (the attack on British law enforcement agents on Easter Monday 1916 by Irish revolutionaries, although the authorities had been informed of imminent activity on the basis of intercepted secret Irish messages) [BER 16].

In 1973, in their report made on behalf of the Control Committee of the administrative services involved in telephone tapping [MAR 73], Pierre Marcilhacy and René Monory critically scrutinized past interception practices and called into question their usefulness in terms of security:

> If we try to make an assessment of two centuries of systematic espionage, we can see that its contribution to the internal and external security of the state was rather negligible, even when the interception of private messengers supplemented the opening of postal "packets": the spies' arrests at the end of the 16th century, the discovery, at the same time, of the transport routes for forbidden books from Holland, a

---

35 Conference by DT Patrick Pailloux, SSTIC 2018 [Online]. Available at: www. youtube.com/ watch?v=eGi1vuwHQFQ [Accessed October 25, 2021].

few "conspiracies" under the Restoration, diplomatic intrigues, the interception of political pamphlets under the Second Empire, none of this justifies a general and permanent inquisition, nor can it make us forget the excesses and intrigues bolstered by the "cabinet noir" system [MAR 73].

Although of limited utility, interceptions have long been an instrument of political power. "All regimes have resorted to the violation of private correspondence", carefully arrogating to themselves the monopoly on practices strictly prohibited to ordinary citizens ("a Royal Declaration of 1742 equated [*interception*] to the embezzlement of public funds and this could be even punished by the death penalty") [MAR 73]. Political powers have been able to use and abuse their prerogatives, disregarding the rights of individuals: "[...] It is striking, on the other hand, to note that in this matter the most vibrant affirmations of principles, the most formal assurances of respect for the rights of nations have only ever served to conceal the worst abuses [...]" [MAR 73].

And when the Republic practices fewer interceptions – by continuing the two rapporteurs – it is not so much the result of political will than a technical incapacity. This might have been the case during the French Third Republic, a period during which the significant increase in the volume of communications made it more complex to carry out interceptions.

A few years before the publication of this French report, American judges had also deemed the interception of electronic communications to have only relative utility in terms of national security. Most importantly, they considered that the element justice needs can be obtained by means other than electronic surveillance [CON 67]:

> The Task Force believes that the Congress must act – and act quickly – to preserve the privacy of all Americans. New and sophisticated electronic bugging devices are used today with few restrictions and little restraint. The Federal statutory law is silent on electronic bugging. All who have examined the existing law on wiretapping agree that it is inadequate, confused and often self-defeating. The Federal wiretapping statute – enacted in 1934 – neither protects privacy nor promotes effective law enforcement. Privacy, appropriately described by Justice Brandeis as "the most comprehensive of the rights and the right most valued by civilized men", is nothing less than the foundation of freedom. [...] The Attorney General [...] on March 16, 1967 [...] declared [...] that "the legitimate needs of law enforcement can be met without the use of such abhorrent devices (i.e. electronic surveillance devices)" and concluded:

All of my experience indicated that (electronic surveillance) is not necessary for the public safety, it is not a desirable or effective police investigative technique, and that it should only be used in the national security field, where there is a direct threat to the welfare of the country.

However, the actors in the field of security have a different opinion on the matter: "The great majority of law enforcement officials believe that the evidence necessary to bring criminal sanctions to bear consistently on the higher echelons of organized crime will not be obtained without the aid of electronic surveillance techniques. They maintain these techniques are indispensable [...]" [COR 67].

Today, the usefulness of interceptions is hardly questioned by those who practice them. For security stakeholders, interceptions are not only useful, but essential, in order to fight against crime on equal terms This pursuit elicits an ever-increasing intensive use of telecommunication means:

Electronic intercepts are essential in helping law enforcement battle against criminal elements. Criminal entities, including drug trafficking organizations (DTO's), criminal street gangs, and dangerous individuals, frequently rely on telecommunications to advance their criminal enterprises (California Department of Justice)[36].

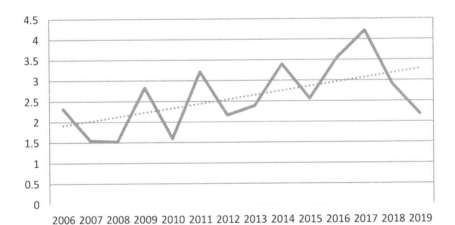

Figure 1.2. *Average number of people arrested due to interception practices in Hong Kong, between 2006 and 2019*

---

36 California Department of Justice, Office of the Attorney General, California Electronic Interceptions Report, Annual Report to the Legislature 2018, California [Online]. Available at: www.oag.ca.gov/sites/all/files/agweb/pdfs/publications/annual-rept-legislature-2018.pdf.

The effectiveness or usefulness of interceptions can be appreciated by means of a few figures.

For mass interceptions practiced by intelligence agencies, the side effects are important: "90 percent of messages intercepted by the NSA were not foreign targets but ordinary users, like you and me, from the United States and abroad" [KHA 14].

Let us recall that these amounts of data are not systematically subject to anonymization or secure storage and access, nor methodical erasure [GEL 14].

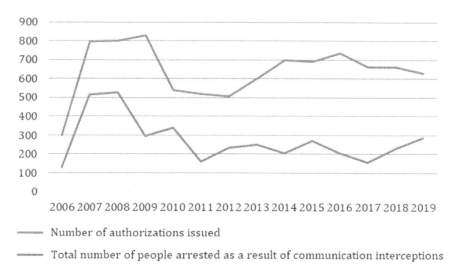

Figure 1.3. *Number of interception authorizations issued, and total number of people arrested as a result of interceptions (annual data) in Hong Kong, between 2006 and 2019. For a color version of this figure, see www.iste.co.uk/ventre/electronic.zip*

In the battle against crime, the effectiveness or usefulness of interceptions is generally assessed in terms of the number of arrests directly or indirectly resulting from them:

> Interception has not always proved an effective means of detection or deterrence. The interception of letters did not greatly reduce the traffic in lottery tickets, and this was one reason for the abandonment of this use of interception in 1953. But, with regard to the present day uses of interception, we received conclusive evidence of their effectiveness.

We were told of many major wrong-doers who had been brought to justice, and of the frustration of espionage. We give here only a few examples of results directly achieved by methods of interception [...] Between 1953 and 1956 the number of arrests made by the Metropolitan Police of important and dangerous criminals as the result of direct interception was 57 per cent of the number of telephone lines tapped. The effectiveness of interception by the Police has been getting steadily greater, especially in the last few years. So far in 1957 every interception but one has led to an arrest[37].

The annual reports from the supervising authorities in matters of intelligence have published quantified data on this.

In Hong Kong, the average number of arrests resulting from interception practices fluctuated between 1.5 and 4, over the period of 2006–2019[38].

The number of people arrested was proportional to the number of interceptions made. In the case of Hong Kong, the curves move at the same rate. Although these figures may seem low, in no way do they diminish the importance given by the law enforcement authorities to interception practices:

It is and continues to be the common view of the LEAs that interception is a very effective and valuable investigation tool in the prevention and detection of serious crime and the protection of public security [...] The intelligence gathered from interception very often leads to a fruitful and successful conclusion of an investigation. During the report period, a total of 120 persons, who were subjects of prescribed authorizations, were arrested as a result of or further to interception operations. In addition, 169 non-subjects were also arrested consequent upon the interception operations[39].

---

37 Report of the Committee of Privy Councilors appointed to inquire into the interception of communications, presented to Parliament by the Prime Minister by Command of Her Majesty, October 1957, London [Online]. Available at: https://www.fipr.org/rip/Birkett.htm.

38 Annual Reports to the Chief Executive by the Commissioner on Interception of Communications and Surveillance [Online]. Available at: https://www.sciocs.gov.hk/en/reports.htm.

39 Office of the Commissioner on Interception of Communications and Surveillance, Annual Report for 2019, June 29, 2020, Hong Kong [Online]. Available at: www.sciocs.gov.hk/en/pdf/Annual_Report_2019.pdf.

In the United States, the statistics from the *Wiretap Report* also show that the number of arrests is globally increasing at the same rate as interceptions[40].

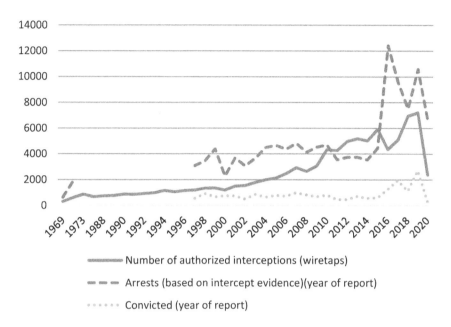

Figure 1.4. *Statistics produced from the American Wiretap Report[41] annual data. For a color version of this figure, see www.iste.co.uk/ventre/electronic.zip*

Here again, the average number of arrests made on the basis of interception fluctuates between one and three.

American reports also provide information on the barrier encryption represents in the context of interceptions: the number of interceptions involving encrypted communications and the number of communications which were successfully decrypted (or not).

---

40 This data set only takes into account national interception requests. The FISA (Foreign Intelligence Surveillance Act) requests from 1978 are not included in these data.

41 Wiretap Report, Administrative Office of the United States Courts [Online]. Available at: www.uscourts.gov/statistics-reports/analysis-reports/wiretap-reports.

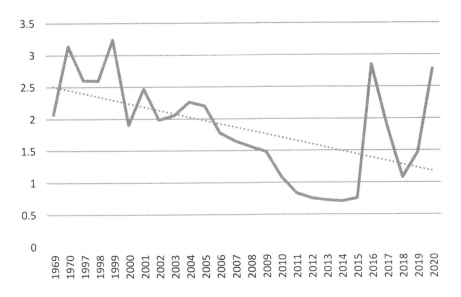

Figure 1.5. *Average number of arrests made based
on interceptions, in the United States (Wiretap Report)*

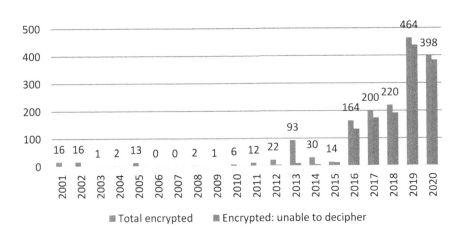

Figure 1.6. *Number of interceptions where the communications requiring processing
were encrypted, and number of communications which could not be decrypted
(United States, Wiretap Report). For a color version of this figure, see www.iste.co.uk/
ventre/electronic.zip*

According to a study published on the Mercatus Center website (George Mason University), over the period of 2001–2014, only 147 interception operations (*wiretap*) were hindered by encryption techniques (i.e. 0.45% over a total of 32,392)[42]: 132 could be decrypted and only 15 remained inaccessible (0.046% of a total of 32,392, about 10% of 147). Those data are based on figures published in the *Wiretap annual report – United States Courts*. For the said period, we can deduce that: "The charts show that, contrary to popular assumption, encryption technologies have only complicated a minuscule percentage of reported wiretap investigations in recent years" [OSU 16].

But by reconsidering these statistics and extending them to 2020, we observe a significant change in the trend.

In 2001, 16 interceptions out of 1,491 concerned encrypted communications. In 2019, this represented 464 out of 7,210 interceptions. The proportion is quite low: 1% in 2001 and 6% in 2019. On the other hand, encryption has been increasingly resistant since in 2019, in 94% of cases, the authorities were unable to decipher communications.

> The 2012 annual report was the first to mention decryption impossibilities (even if this still represented only about four impossibility situations out of 22). The share of interceptions hindered by encryption continued growing, reaching almost 100%. Despite this trend, the number of interceptions hindered by encryption was still limited compared to the total number of interceptions carried out (398 encrypted, out of a total of 2,377 in 2020; or 464 encrypted out of a total of 7,210 in 2019). In the 2020 report on "wiretaps" the American justice system mentions a few hundred encrypted[43] messages: "The number of state wiretaps reported in which encryption was encountered decreased from 343 in 2019 to 184 in 2020. In 183 of these wiretaps, officials were unable to decipher the plain text of the messages. A total of 214 federal wiretaps were reported as being encrypted in 2020, of which 200 could not be decrypted".

---

42 Data compiled from the annual reports, published on the site https://www.mercatus. org/publications/technology-and-innovation/going-dark-federal-wiretap-data-show-scant-encryption.

43 Drawn from: "Public Law 106-197 amended 18 U.S.C. section 2519(2) (b) in 2001 to require that reporting should reflect the number of wiretap applications granted in which encryption was encountered and whether such encryption prevented law enforcement officials from obtaining the plain text of the communications intercepted pursuant to the court orders". Wiretap Report (2010), United States.

Encryption was encountered more frequently, but its proportion remained relatively low compared to all the interceptions made. This first observation seems to contradict the main argument of the "Going Dark" debate. In relation to these figures, it does not appear that the actions of investigators are globally paralyzed due to a generalization of encryption. Furthermore, in a significant number of cases, it is clearly indicated that investigators were able to access the desired information despite encryption. The use of encrypted communications is therefore not as frequent as it has been generally asserted.

2

The Central Issue of Encryption

Based on the catalogs of companies marketing interception "solutions", it is now allegedly possible to intercept pretty much anything. However, in order to prevent this, ensure the confidentiality of communications and guarantee their inviolability, encryption has become widespread.

Naturally, this barrier is exposed to attacks. The efforts to circumvent it or weaken it are multiplying, especially because cryptography is not infallible.

2.1. The capabilities required for interceptions

Intercepting communications does not require the same resources, and depends on whether it is a question of targeting a spouse's cell phone communications, following a suspect in an anonymous crowd, intercepting the communications of a moving individual, investigating a wider or narrower network of suspects on national territory or, on the contrary, internationally. Resources will also differ depending on whether communications are by wire or wireless, traveling by undersea or terrestrial cables, by satellite, civil or military communications, established in times of peace or war, for the purpose of investigating crime or spying on foreign territories or actors, and of course, whether the communications are encrypted or not, and whether the interceptor has the means to read them in clear text.

Therefore, the range of intercept categories is ample. The technical means to be implemented are just as important. Here, two types of capabilities are differentiated: material and human.

2.1.1. *Material, technological capabilities*

The NSA's capabilities are difficult to estimate with accuracy, because their secrecy is closely guarded. An article published in 1986 by a magazine in the United Emirates Republic, whose excerpts are included in the NSA's Internet journal *Cryptolog* [CRY 86], estimated that, at the moment, the American agency has very advanced computers for the analysis of ordinary and encrypted phone calls, capable of receiving and reading 300,000 normal calls and 200,000 coded calls daily, and analyzing coded messages at up to 600 lines per minute, in all languages. The agency's "brain" is equipped with four linked IBM 3033 computers attached to impressive printers, with the ability to print 22,000 lines per minute, as well as supercomputers weighing 5 tons each, with the ability to perform 200 million operations per second, and write 320 million words per second. The agency mainly relies on satellites that are specialized in espionage, 200 km from Earth, photographing any object that is two feet (61 cm) long, anywhere on the planet. The article concludes that the reason some of the NSA's secrets were revealed was to preserve part of America's image of technological superiority, which needed to be restored after the Challenger tragedy.

Interceptions can be applied according to different techniques. For "source" interceptions, the principle is to place microphones in the premises where the conversations to be monitored will take place. This was the case for the "*Plombiers du Canard enchaîné*", where two "plumbers", who were actually agents from the French Directorate of Territorial Surveillance (DST, *Direction de la Surveillance du Territoire*), were caught placing bugs in the new offices of the weekly satirical magazine on December 3, 1973.

On the other hand, communications may be intercepted during transmission. We may think of postal mail interception, for instance. As for telephone interception, the method involves placing crocodile clips on the copper cables of the telephone network, and is carried out either by the police or by private[1] agencies. This practice is rather inconvenient though, due to its difficulty of implementation, its visibility and its illegality[2]. Legal wiretapping requires the technical cooperation of the operator. Data interception in the age of fixed telephony was a relatively simple task, as summarized by FBI Director James Comey [COM 14]: "In the past, conducting electronic surveillance was more straightforward. We identified a target phone being used by a bad guy, with a single carrier. We obtained a court order for a wiretap, and, under the supervision of a judge, we collected the evidence we needed for prosecution."

---

1 See: www.lexinter.net/JF/interception_de_telecommunications.htm.

2 Huyghe, F.B. (2009). *Les Écoutes téléphoniques*. PUF, Paris.

In the age of Internet, several variables have been modified. Flows have accelerated and are increasingly numerous, individuals and objects provide a space where everyone is increasingly interconnected and dependent on technologies and on a broad system to place their trust in. This socio-technical system (not only the technologies themselves, but also the people interacting with them, or building them) is fragile and vulnerable, despite all the efforts to secure or protect it. The interception of communications strives to exploit any vulnerabilities or open up possibilities within this system.

The privacyinternational.org website identifies four categories of technologies which can be implemented for the surveillance of communications:

– Internet monitoring;

– mobile telephony monitoring;

– fixed telephony interception;

– intrusion technologies.

Here, the concept of interception is reserved for operations relating to fixed telephony. For Internet and mobile telephony, the site gives preference to the notion of "monitoring". Intrusion refers to a set of aggressive surveillance practices.

While the notion of "cyber surveillance is not used, the authors prefer to speak of "surveillance of communications":

– Here, Internet monitoring refers to data capture. Technologies can be deployed at any point of the Internet's physical and electronic systems: cables, servers, routers, providers, etc. Technical tools make it possible to physically connect to networks. Software can monitor and analyze network activity without this necessarily being interception.

– Mobile telephony monitoring comprises capturing information (namely, data). One of the leading technologies of this surveillance is the IMSI (International Mobile Subscriber Identity) Catcher. Not only does this tool make it possible to intercept data – in the sense of "capturing" – but it also makes it possible to send messages to telephones. This does not merely involve passive interception, but active interference with the network and exchanges.

– Fixed line interception concerns the capture of information circulating on fixed telephony networks (Public Switched Telephony Networks – PSTN). Nowadays, the technological solutions sold by companies make it possible to monitor networks of this type at the level of an entire country.

Intrusion enables the clandestine deployment of malware on mobile phones and computers, whereby operators can take control of the targeted devices. The Privacy International website declares that intrusion is undoubtedly one of the most invasive forms of surveillance.

To illustrate our point, let us describe (in a non-exhaustive way), some of the technologies or techniques for intercepting communications.

2.1.1.1. *The man-in-the-middle type of attack*

The security of communications not only depends on cryptographic functions, but also on the protocol for using such functions. As soon as the Diffie–Hellman key exchange was introduced, the man-in-the-middle attack showed that during a key exchange between two correspondents A and B, an intruder located between them could pretend to be B in relation to A, A to B, and exchange secrets with one another. The intruder was therefore able to intercept, decrypt and re-encrypt communications, which became totally accessible to them. Counterbalancing this attack requires signing exchanges, with the signatures being generated using the sender's private key, and verified with the public key.

This approach immediately raises the question of the public key's validity. Does it match the legitimate correspondent? Or does it belong to the intruder? Here we enter a signature and verification loop, something which has led to the deployment of the public key infrastructure (PKI). Trust in a public key ultimately lies with a recognized certification authority in charge of signing user public keys.

If an organization can access user private keys – and the following section will show that this assumption is not unreasonable – the man-in-the-middle attack is still operational.

However, it is not impossible for blockchain technology, which is currently in a great boom, to replace this infrastructure in the long term.

This example shows that cryptology is no longer the business of individual actors wishing to communicate discreetly as in the times of the telegraph, but rather an integral part of the communication system. However, this system is increasingly complex and involves multiple actors: machine operating systems, application software, access providers, network routers, cable and satellite equipment managers, etc. The level of complexity has reached a point where no actor can claim to control all the parameters governing the security of communications.

2.1.1.2. *From traffic analysis to the exploitation of metadata*

Traffic analysis was introduced by Gordon Welchman during World War II. It denotes the interception and examination of messages not based on the contents – which can be encrypted without disrupting the process – but on the data accompanying such messages: date, time, origin, recipient, etc.

These few data can provide information as to the intentions and actions of the stakeholders related to the message. Traffic analysis requires proceeding by deduction, cross-checking, cross-referencing, network analysis, etc. In particular, traffic analysis is based on social network analysis tools and methods:

– Traffic analysis and intelligence-gathering based on the exploitation of metadata do not process the contents of messages.

– Cryptography is applied to the contents, so it does not constitute an obstacle to the analysis of traffic and metadata.

– The higher the number of intercepted messages, the more information the traffic reveals, and the greater the amount of deductions, cross-references and quantity and quality of the information revealed. Traffic analysis gave birth to the analysis of metadata. Both procedures require massive data interception and storage. During World War II, code breakers at Bletchley Park conceived traffic analysis so as to partially circumvent the limits of decryption. The messages encrypted by Enigma contained information or data in the header, a preamble including certain discriminators. From the analysis of those data (and without delving into the message's contents), the Bletchley Park teams managed to classify the messages into different categories, depending on their origin (country, type of force, etc.). These data, once refined, provided information on the transfer of troops, for example [HIN 01].

2.1.1.3. *DPI (deep packet inspection)*

Let us bear in mind that on the Internet network, information circulates in the form of data packets or datagrams, made up of a header and a data block. The header contains information not only about the recipient, but also regarding the treatment undergone by the data, so that the latter reaches the recipient in its entirety.

Certain network layers can re-encapsulate packets into other packets, for example, to fragment them (dividing a packet into two smaller packets), encrypt them (adding data regarding the key encryption, as well as additional data due to encryption), sign them (adding sender authentication data), compress them, add automatic error correction data, etc.

Deep packet inspection (DPI) is the activity which analyzes the packet beyond the header and processes the related data block in order to extract the successive encapsulations and attempt to arrive at the final informational contents.

The header contains abundant information relating to the packet's body. For example, for an email, it will contain data: regarding the sender and the recipient, the message's subject, its timestamp, some information concerning the final electronic messaging server. Each protocol has its own header format: the IP[3] protocol (source and destination IP address, communication protocol, etc.), DNS[4] (Domain Name System), ARP[5] (Address Resolution Protocol), etc. Headers are adapted to the types of communications (wired, wireless) and to the types of files (images, videos, etc.) As DPI equipment does not settle for these header data, packets will be analyzed in depth until their contents are reached, in the search for supplementary pieces of information. This processing necessarily has consequences on flow quality, which may be slowed down. It also requires the implementation of substantial resources, because large data volumes need to be processed in real time. Despite their setbacks, these techniques can be used to improve the quality of the service and optimize the allocation of resources, and are actually implemented by Internet service providers (ISPs).

Intelligence authorities are said to have been using "probes" or "black boxes" for several years, fit into the equipment of telecommunications operators. The whole issue revolves around the depth level of data analysis: is it limited to headers (the metadata) or does it reach the contents? The analyses performed by intelligence-gathering actors focus on identifiers, which are considered metadata, and not on the contents. From a legal viewpoint, the identifiers embedded into packets are considered as metadata [TRE 17].

The goal of this processing is to monitor the nature of Internet traffic, access contents or block access. Its purpose can be openly declared (as in the management of transmission priorities for real-time applications, such as voice or image), or unconfessed, as in the surveillance of opponents and censorship.

DPI can also detect and counter certain attacks by analyzing and detecting the malicious (viruses, worms) or illegal (child pornography) nature of certain communications.

---

3 For further consultation, the reader may refer to the following sites, which accurately explain the structure of IP headers (IPv4 and IPv6). See, for example: www.frameip.com/entete-ip/#1-8211-definition-du-protocole-ip.

4 See: www.frameip.com/dns/#32-8211-lrsquoentete-dns.

5 See: www.frameip.com/entete-arp/.

A DPI tool produced by Blue Coat is used by the authorities in Bahrain to analyze and monitor Internet traffic, and block access to certain content. Other states such as Iran or Libya used DPI equipment for surveillance or censorship purposes (Nokia-Siemens Network in Iran, Amesys in Libya).

Although DPI can be a very powerful and effective tool, it comes up against the following obstacles:

– Deep packet processing is time-consuming and can significantly slow down traffic.

– Data encryption can block access to data themselves and to in-depth analysis.

DPI is the technology on which the Eagle system was based, produced by the French company, Amesys. This system monitors and intercepts Internet communications (emails, VoIP, http, queries in search engines, etc.), at the country level. Specific applications can be associated with the system: automatically translating the content of exchanges, transcribing voice into text, geolocating calls, performing semantic analysis, identifying individuals via voice recognition. Several countries have acquired the system, such as Saudi Arabia, Dubai, Gabon, Kazakhstan, Libya, Morocco and Qatar, to mention a few.

In 2017, the Dutch police supposedly used DPI techniques to monitor Russian hackers defrauding on the Internet[6]. The technique was allegedly deployed on the infrastructure of a Dutch host which had been used to perpetrate the offences. These means were used by the police force (LEA) and not by the intelligence services, who also have the means for intercepting Internet communications. Created in 2005, the premises for the legal interception of Internet communications and telephone tapping were installed in Driebergen. In the context of an investigation searching for the hackers who authored the malware "Zeus" in 2008, the Dutch police cooperated with several countries, and benefited from the fact that the offenders communicated via ICQ, an unencrypted application. To intercept the communications associated with the identified ICQ accounts, the police implemented the DPI technique on the servers of the Dutch company Leaseweb (used by the criminals), analyzed all the ICQ flows from Russia and filtered them. Around 50 gigabytes of data per second went through the DPI machines. The method raised some questions, because the police seemed to incur into bulk interceptions, instead of targeted interceptions, which is what the law generally constrains the police to do in Europe. Stricto sensu,

---

6 "Dutch–Russian cybercrime case reveals how the police taps the Internet", June 8, 2017 [Online]. Available at: www.electrospaces.net/2017/06/dutch-russian-cyber-crime-case-reveals. html.

was the concept of targeting still respected on the grounds that only 436 ICQ numbers were sought within the bulk of processed data?

2.1.1.4. *Integrating source interception equipment into telecommunications infrastructure*

In many countries, telecommunications providers have been forced to adapt their infrastructure to enable direct surveillance, dispensing with the authorization of judges. This was the case in Colombia in 2012 and in Uganda in 2010 (where the law regulation of communications[7] interception provides for the creation of a monitoring center and compels telecommunications providers to transmit intercepted communications to this center) [LAR 13]. Indian authorities have proposed that a centralized monitoring system redirects all communications to the government, thus enabling security agencies to dispense with any request to providers, or for that case, any judge authorizations. In many countries, the trend is to separate police from justice, central power from any form of control or judicial restriction, and to shorten procedures, as well as processing times. The states want to have a real-time and all-encompassing vision of communications. The option envisaged by India even aims to remove the intervention of providers. The risks are significant in terms of transparency and justice, because they leave the door open to all kinds of abuse of power, consecrating a state of surveillance without any responsibilities.

Is the cooperation of telecom operators really necessary? The scenarios will depend on the goals pursued and the conditions for carrying out the interceptions, as well as the type of data actors want to intercept, and the technology capabilities:

> Any operator of telecommunications services is required to put in place the necessary means to intercept communications exchanged on a public network [AUD 10].

> Interception does not give rise to any recording on the part of the operator, which is legally prohibited, except for the "switching" of the communication towards the appropriate state service (flows traveling via the mediation platform). Only duly authorized staff from the Ministry of Justice or the Prime Minister's services may proceed with the tapping, the framework of this type of action being strictly controlled by the law [AUD 10].

---

7 Regulation of Interception of Communications Act 2010.

Telecommunications companies allowed the NSA to install surveillance equipment (such as the powerful DPI instrument Narus Semantic Traffic Analyzer)[8] directly connected to the networks, set up in protected areas at the premises of the telecommunications[9] companies themselves. These practices took place outside any legal framework (no authorization from the judge, no discrimination between American and foreign citizens' data, etc.). The collected data were then analyzed and processed (data mining). This equipment was installed following the September 2001 attacks. Interception and processing capabilities rapidly increased. A dozen pieces – or perhaps twice as many – of this equipment may have been deployed among American operators during the 2000s. Afterwards, the volumes of communication data continued to grow, which in parallel led to an increase in collection capabilities, in the computing and processing power of the data collected, as well as in storage requirements. In response to the expansion of the masses of data produced by Internet users, security and defense actors deploy an "always more" strategy, apparently with no other option than to expand their own means and capabilities, focusing on three key points: collection (how to collect more, better, faster), processing and analysis (of new computers, new algorithms), and storage (retaining as many data as possible, likely to be used later, by being crossed-referenced with new data).

The immensity of the capabilities required could hardly remain a secret. The ambition to ensure a total vision, as broad as possible, by means of the exploitation of electronic data pushes the limits of possibilities one step further every day, because it is now necessary to be able to collect data from emails, websites, social networks, all types of Internet applications (deep and dark web, encrypted content, etc.) and from a diversity of sensors (the Internet of Things, car parks, vehicles, terminals, electronic organizers, etc.). It is with a view to massive storage that the Utah[10] data center was conceived.

---

8 According to claims (2006) from the Electronic Frontier Foundation, invoking the role of the operator AT&T regarding the surveillance of their customers' communications by the NSA.

9 "How the NSA's domestic spying program works" [Online]. Available at: www.eff.org/nsa-spying/how-it-works [Accessed 1 February 2017].

10 See: www.nsa.gov1.info/utah-data-center/. The Utah Data Center was the first data center belonging to the "Intelligence Community Comprehensive National Cyber-security Initiative" (IC CNCI), which aims to meet the ever-increasing needs for storing and processing the amounts of data processed by American intelligence agencies. The project is codenamed Bumblehive. The center has been operational since 2014. This is one of the largest, if not the largest communications data storage centers in the world.

On the other hand, with the support of ETSI[11], Europe wants cloud computing providers to deploy lawful interception capabilities directly into cloud technology, so as to grant the state authorities straightforward access to the contents stored by providers (including email, text and voice messages)[12].

2.1.1.5. Downstream and upstream collections

These two forms or categories for the interception of Internet communications distinguish the two main methods used by the NSA in order to collect network information.

Downstream collection constitutes 91% [FIS 11] of the interception of foreign communications carried out by the NSA on the Internet. It is done at the level of Internet service providers (ISPs) and with their involvement. PRISM is a program of agreements initiated in 2007 between the NSA and American Internet operators (Microsoft, Yahoo, Google, Facebook, PalTalk, YouTube, Skype, AOL, Apple, which successively entered the PRISM program between 2007 and 2012).

Upstream collection designates the tapping and the Internet traffic/telephone analysis of communications passing through the Internet's backbone, with the participation of telecommunications operators such as AT&T. The backbone is made of land and undersea cables, and switches. The intention is to grasp the information which circulates between two undefined points.

The main upstream programs are called Fairview, Blarney, Stormbrew and Oakstar (data collection outside the United States):

– Telecommunications companies filter the data (data whose origin or recipient is abroad).

– The NSA applies "strong selectors" or "tasked selectors" to these data provided by the operators (data concerning these targeted actors, such as telephone numbers, email addresses). The data of US citizens may be referenced and communications intercepted, for the sole reason that their data have been mentioned in emails or

11 ETSI (European Telecommunications Standards Institute) is an international organization created in 1988, which currently totals 800 members (among industrialists, universities, operators, administrations, etc.) from 67 countries (see: http://www.etsi.org/about/who-we-are [Accessed October 21, 2022]). It works on the production of norms/standards in the field of information and communication technologies. At the beginning, the project was part of a European logic, but since its creation, it has expanded its actions further. The institute's headquarters are located in France, in Sophia Antipolis.

12 ETSI DTR 101 567 VO.0.5 (2012-14), Draft Technical Report: Lawful Interception (LI); Cloud/Virtual Services (CLI).

other electronic communications. This is known as intelligence-gathering or data collection "about" a certain actor. Despite the person being neither the message's sender nor recipient, they have been mentioned in the communication. The minimization procedures implemented by the NSA have not sufficed to remove the risks of collecting data on people who should not be subject to it. Those preceding the 2011 FISC (Foreign Intelligence Surveillance Court) report were not strict enough and did not guarantee the respect for the rights of individuals (especially the 4th amendment). New minimization rules were established following this report. FISC requests included not only reducing the data retention period to two years instead of five, but also preventing analysts from using the identification data of American citizens to carry out research in the upstream collection results.

These operations are performed using specific technological systems, both physical and software infrastructures, such as:

– Room 641A, a communications interception facility at the AT&T premises (in San Francisco), operational since 2003. The facility intercepts and analyzes the data passing through one of the most important communication channels on the American Internet. The data are analyzed by Narus Insight.

– Internet traffic data filtering tools, such as Narus Insight, a Narus STA (Semantic Traffic Analyzer), subsidiary of Boeing. The Big Data application analyzes content on networks in real time and can be used for individualized monitoring.

– Secret agreements with ISPs in several countries worldwide, enabling the NSA to intercept Internet communications outside of American territory.

These surveillance programs are supplemented with several other levels and action tools such as the Bullrun program[13], Stellar Wind[14] or even Xkeyscore, which were publicized after Edward Snowden's revelations. Communications surveillance

---

13 Program focusing on decryption and which is of interest for all UKUSA partners. The goals of the program are multiple: to ensure that the United States (and its UKUSA partners) control international standards for encryption, to cooperate with companies in order to introduce backdoors into systems from the very beginning, to recover encryption certificates from ISPs, to acquire supercomputers that are able to break the codes (brute force) and to develop decryption solutions (e.g. Turmoil).

14 Program which collects communications information from American citizens (emails, telephone communications, banking transactions, activities on the Internet, etc.). Based on the information collected, large databases are compiled, including the Mainway database, which groups telephone communication data (a priori metadata, not the contents). The base is maintained by the NSA.

programs have been established in several countries around the world, such as Tempora (in the United Kingdom)[15] and Levitation (in Canada).

2.1.1.6. *IMSI-catchers*

IMSI-catchers are surveillance equipment for intercepting the communications of mobile telephones within a limited perimeter. Originally, they were used for IMSI (International Mobile Subscriber Identity) detection, a number which uniquely identifies a user in order to determine their presence within the detector's wave propagation perimeter. Nowadays, the term refers to the equipment simulating a relay antenna and which can intercept telephone traffic. IMSI-catchers are called CSS (Cell Site Simulator) devices or "WITT gear" [FBI 12], Stingrays or Triggerfish [FBI 12]:

> Law enforcement possesses electronic devices that allow agents to determine the location of certain cellular phones by the electronic signals that they broadcast. This equipment includes an antenna, an electronic device that processes the signals transmitted on cell phone frequencies, and a laptop computer that analyses the signals and allows the agent to configure the collection of information. Working together, these devices allow the agent to identify the direction (on a 360 degree display) and signal strength of a particular cellular phone while the user is making a call [FBI 12].

The investigator must know the telephone number (Mobile Identification Number – MIN), which they enter into the machine. Then, they scan for the phone in the area. When a communication is established by this target phone, it emits a signal to the operator's relay antenna. As long as communication is maintained, the tracker can record the target phone's direction and signal strength. These operations do not collect communications contents. In this regard, since 1994, the American law has considered that the use of these instruments for tracking and locating mobile phones does not call into question the 4th amendment nor the law on wiretapping.

---

15 This is a project managed by the GCHQ, which makes it possible to intercept the data which travel through the undersea fiber optics cables between the United States and Europe (in place since 2011). The principle is to collect as much data as possible, over 200 cables, keep these data in a buffer zone for a few weeks, and peruse them when necessary, for useful intelligence information. The data relate to e-mails, Internet user search histories, etc. Despite the computer processing power deployed, the amount of data requires the mobilization of several hundred individuals solely for the work of data analysis, both for the British (GCHQ) and American (NSA) agencies.

The IMSI-catcher interferes between the user's mobile phone and the operator's relay antenna by means of a man-in-the-middle attack. When used by the intelligence services with the participation of operators, these devices can access encryption and authentication keys. Otherwise, they can exploit faults in the encryption algorithms. The simplest way is to impose the absence of encryption (A5/0) on the mobile, so that the conversation is unencrypted. Cryptographic attacks exist against standard algorithms (A5/1), but require access to a large amount of data which can be collected from a previous communication.

A questionable property of this type of equipment is that it captures all the users within a given perimeter and not merely the identified target who is being monitored under judicial control. This raises a question of a political and legal nature. Due to the operating mechanism of these technologies within a given radius of action, the interception or tapping performed using this equipment does not seem capable of differentiating between the devices which must be tapped into and those which are accidentally caught in the net (passing through the perimeter). The IMSI-catcher is not capable of accurate targeting.

IMSI-catchers can even be made by amateurs for a modest sum using generic computing platforms (raspberry-pi), associated with software-defined radio (SDR) modules. In order to limit piracy problems, the new mobile telephony standards impose the authentication of base stations by the mobile device.

Several companies have been offering IMSI-catchers since the 1990s: the German company Rohde&Schwarz (in 1993), Harris Corporation (which offers the StingRay used by the American authorities), Digital Receiver Technology, Inc. (marketing the Dirtbox), Amesys (a French company), PKI Electronic and Gamma Group.

The implementation of these means of interception is regulated by the law, and sometimes requires multiple permissions, depending on various use cases.

However, in addition to these well-identified problems, other issues have been singled out. Complaints from the American Civil Liberties Union, relayed by US senators and research websites (City Lab), claim that the use of these technologies reveals discriminatory uses. Surveillance could mainly affect the poorest social strata in the United States, especially neighborhoods where Black populations reside [MIC 17]. According to the observers, these populations are victims of violation of their digital rights. The digital sphere prolongs and increases inequalities, with access being forbidden or restricted due to insufficient resource levels. Digital technology does not reduce inequalities, on the contrary it increases them.

In addition to this phenomenon, we should mention that police surveillance tends to focus on poor neighborhoods. An investigation from City Lab estimates that between 2007 and 2014, 78% of Stingray uses took place in these disadvantaged neighborhoods. Added to the surveillance exercised via the digital space, is the degradation of communications caused by IMSI-Catchers, which disrupt communications or even interfere with communications with the emergency services. IMSI-catchers are not neutral and have an impact on signal quality. The use of IMSI-catchers is not unbiased, with certain populations being specifically targeted. Is surveillance discriminatory due to the particularities of the technologies used, the authorizations granted, simply in virtue of the location of criminal actors, or where the efforts to fight against crime are concentrated?

2.1.1.7. Interception of satellite communications

Neither the end of the Cold War nor the revelations concerning the existence of the Echelon network (and its big ears spread worldwide) are the vestiges of a bygone era. These satellite technologies are still fully operational at present.

The number of satellites continues to grow, organized in constellations of a few tens to several thousand devices.

The infrastructures are of unequal size, depending on the means made available to the intelligence agencies, the types of communications states wish to listen to, and the state-of-the-art of science and technology. Ground infrastructure is often visible along the roads, from a great distance, its size making concealment difficult.

Satellites pursue their route around the Earth and their interest is constantly reaffirmed, due to their multiple uses, for Earth observation, for the operation of modern geolocation systems, for military transmissions or within the framework of an extended deployment of the Internet, to provide network access worldwide in wireless areas (the Starlink project and its constellation of more than 40,000 satellites, the constellation project of 648 satellites by the Anglo-Indian company OneWeb, the projects by the Canadian operator Telesat satellites, etc.).

In terms of communication, the efficiency of cables is unparalleled by satellites, because these lack the capacity to process large data volumes (the new cables are allegedly able to process some 160 terabits per second).

According to the Telegeography site, only 0.37% of the Internet traffic at a planetary scale passes through satellites. Yet, this figure is difficult to verify. Bear in mind that almost every flow of modern communications relies on land and undersea cables, including the ones used for mobile telephony or the Internet.

This being the case, is the interception of satellite communications still relevant? Yes, and probably more than ever as we are at a time when the great powers are relaunching themselves in a race to conquer space. Undoubtedly yes, because in the military field satellites are one of the central links in the communication architecture. C4ISR systems, all military communication systems deployed in the theaters of operations, are dependent on satellites, either for communication or for observation purposes. The possibilities in terms of interception are numerous:

– The number of "observation" satellites, which are actually interceptor satellites[16], can collect the telephone communications of a whole territory. The first of these spy satellites, GRAB, was launched by the US military in 1960. Its function was to capture radar signals emitted by the Soviets and relay them to ground stations. Since then, the number of spy satellites has continued to grow.

– Ground antennas are deployed to intercept messages and data which are routed via commercial satellites. While today most communications travel through cables (land and undersea), satellites are extremely useful in the case of maritime or air communications, for example.

– Satellite Internet is extremely vulnerable to interceptions. The experiments carried out and conclusions drawn up by James Pavur (Oxford University) have emphasized the weak security of satellite Internet communications.

The satellite communications (SATCOM[17]) interception consists of intercepting the flows passing through satellites (in low[18], medium[19] or geostationary[20] orbits), Internet or telephone data flows, for example, and the geographical areas served by satellites. On the ground, antennas receive the flows transmitted by satellites. Intercepting these flows comes down to pointing antennas towards the satellites and connecting to the transmission frequencies in order to recover the flows. This is the role of ground listening stations, such as the British GCHQ stations (Bude, Cyprus, Oman) or the American NSA. The geographical location of the stations is crucial, because it makes it possible to cover the communications of a given region.

Private companies produce satellite surveillance "solutions" or "products", for example:

---

16 See: www.aerosociety.com/news/eavesdropping-from-space/.

17 SATCOM: Satellite Communications.

18 LEO: Low Earth Orbit.

19 MEO: Medium Earth Orbit.

20 GEO: Geostationary.

– The German company Rohde&Schwarz[21], which markets a "portfolio of surveillance solutions by satellite [...] for the passive signal interception of satellite communications" and sells "its satellite surveillance systems only to government-authorized organizations". The notion of portfolio is important because it reflects the diversity of technologies and configurations that can be mobilized for the surveillance of satellite communications. This company was the one that first produced an IMSI-catcher in 1993.

– The Indian company Shoghi[22] Communications Ltd, which offers satellite communications surveillance solutions capable of intercepting Broadband IP traffic, voice, fax, SMS, satellite phone communications (GMPCS – Global Mobile Personal Communications by Satellite), and collecting call data, geolocation, etc. Satellite phones offer alternative communication solutions in areas that are not covered by conventional telecommunication networks or without Internet access, or can be used by actors (terrorism, criminality, etc.) that do not want to use conventional means of communication, likely to be more closely monitored.

– Stratign, a company[23] whose main customers are state actors in defense, intelligence, national security agencies and the police forces (Law Enforcement Agencies). It provides technology for the interception of satellite communications[24], for ISAT, VSAT, as well as GSM, Wi-Fi, CDMA and IMSI-catchers detection tools to help users identify attempts to illegally intercept their mobile[25] communications.

Last but not least, let us mention the Israeli company Ability Computers & Software Industries Ltd[26]; Horizon Technologies, a company who markets FlyingFish, designed as an autonomous or human-operated ISR platform, enabling governments to passively monitor satellite communications, Thuraya, IsatPhone Pro; and many others.

2.1.1.8. *Interception and storage of collected data*

While interception requires the completion of several technical and legal phases upstream, the process does not end once the data have been collected, on the one hand because collection can be a continuous process, extending over time, and on

---

21 See: www.rohde-schwarz.com/fr/produits/securite-de-l-aerospatiale-et-de-la-defense-a-d/surveillance-satellitaire/apercu-pg_64135.html.

22 See: www.shoghicom.com/about-shoghi.php.

23 See: www.stratign.com/about-us/.

24 See: www.stratign.com/product/satellite-interception-system/.

25 See: www.stratign.com/product/bts-hunter/.

26 See: www.interceptors.com/satellite-interception/.

the other hand because the collected data must then be stored and processed. Several processing techniques can be applied to the data collected during interceptions:

– analytical work (the data collected from interceptions by SIGINT, for example, are transmitted to the departments specifically in charge of the analysis);

– the data can be used as proof;

– communication data may be transcribed and translated;

– the collected data are also stored. Afterwards, they are rendered safe, and access rights are granted to legitimate users. Encrypted data are sometimes stored pending further decryption opportunities [HER 02].

> As quickly as Soviet espionage in the United States expanded during the war years, almost as quickly it began to shrink, starting in 1945 with the defection to the FBI of Elizabeth Bentley [...] Her revelations were followed by the defection of Igor Sergeievitch Gouzenko, a cipher clerk in the Soviet Embassy in Ottawa. He defected to the Canadians in September 1945 with Soviet cipher codes that, when shared with Washington, allowed the NSA to make real progress deciphering their large collection of intercepted Soviet cables accumulated during the war years. NSA decoded and deciphered part of the Venona intercepts from 1946 through the 1970s [...] Evidence on these intercepts led to the arrest of Fuchs in Britain and, from there, to the apprehension of the Rosenbergs and their accomplices [HER 02].

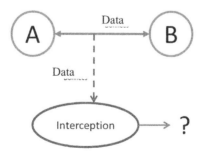

Figure 2.1. *What happens to the data resulting from interception? For a color version of this figure, see www.iste.co.uk/ventre/electronic.zip*

Although interceptions are not necessarily exploitable straight away, their use a posteriori – sometimes several years later – can retain all their interest.

2.1.1.9. *The interception of emails*

When they were created in 1981, emails did not fully integrate security. Even today we may note that a large part of emails circulates "unencrypted", without the slightest protection. Not only has this particularity been widely exploited by certain intelligence agencies, but it has also been used by many other actors and for a variety of purposes: fraud, economic espionage, etc. While the biggest providers such as Gmail, Yahoo and Outlook encrypt messages, it may appear that out of around 700,000 SMTP servers, only 35% configure encryption correctly (situation observed in 2015 [DUR 15]).

Every day, emails are used by many people to exchange both personal and professional information, and contain many "useful" data revealing the privacy of individuals (contact details, banking data, access passwords to various websites), business secrets, research projects, social activities (political, economic, etc.), etc. However, the SMTP (Simple Mail Transfer Protocol) alone neither encrypts messages in transit nor identifies senders. Additional protocols have been designed to overcome this lack of security: STARTTLS, DKIM, DMARC or SPF protect messages in transit and authenticate them. But despite the protection offered by these protocols, their poor implementation or ignoring them leaves a considerable volume of electronic communications vulnerable to man-in-the-middle attacks, for example [DUR 15].

In recent years, the use of encryption has become widespread. Nevertheless, several attacks are still possible:

– DNS MX record hijacking attacks: the "mail exchange" (MX) record directs the email to an SMTP[27] server. This attack diverts emails to a server corrupted by the attacker (see, for example, the scheme proposed by [BUR 16]).

– SMTP TLS downgrade attacks: the TLS protocol enables the encryption (public key) of a client–server connection. These attacks seek to prevent encryption.

Attacks aimed at intercepting emails seek to exploit implementation errors, protocol weaknesses or cryptographic weaknesses [PRO 18].

The susceptibility of emails to interception attacks imposes relatively strict security practices on anyone who wants to guarantee message confidentiality and transfer security.

Exploiting emails is one of the key practices of cybercrime. For example, in the United Kingdom in May 2019, several individuals were sentenced to 2–10 years in prison for organized fraud after hacking into email accounts and embezzling large

---

27 See: www.cloudflare.com/fr-fr/learning/dns/dns-records/dns-mx-record/.

sums of money. Sixty-nine victims filed complaints for these actions, which took place between 2014 and 2018. The gang resorted to malware in order to intercept the login credentials to email accounts, whereby looking for high-value financial transactions. Later, they intercepted emails relating to those transactions, interfered with them and finally deceived users so that the sums were paid into fraudulent[28] accounts.

2.1.1.10. *The interest of having control over infrastructures*

The episode of the Zimmermann telegram during World War I is significant. On the one hand, it reveals the advantage of communication cables passing through our own territory, and on the other hand, the inconvenience of having to reveal our own intercepting abilities. Admitting to knowing how to decipher the enemy's messages leads to the enemy changing the encryption, thus reducing the intelligence work, leading to this discovery of nothing. After resolving this explosive telegram, the British made a considerable effort not to reveal any hints of their intercepting capability.

At the beginning of the 20th century, British cryptology work was carried out by "Room 40", the name given to the encryption service after it moved to that room in the Admiralty. It was led by Admiral Sir William Reginald Hall (1870–1943). Reverend William Montgomery (1871–?), a Presbyterian pastor and translator of theological texts, worked within that chamber, as well as Nigel de Gray (1886–1951), who was fluent in French and German. The British were well prepared for the war in terms of communications control. On August 5, 1914, the day after the United Kingdom declared war on Germany, the British Navy cut the German undersea cables near the border with Holland, forcing the Germans to either use enemy-controlled cables or communicate by radio. A couple of German codebooks were recovered early on by the British during maritime operations, which resulted in the German light cruiser SMS Madgebourg running aground on August 26, 1914 in the Gulf of Finland. The crew urgently evacuated and abandoned ship. The Russians recovered a copy of the codebook forgotten in the captain's cabin and provided it to the British. Another codebook was recovered during the Battle of Heligoland Bay on August 28, 1914 from a trunk thrown overboard.

Contrary to the forecasts of maneuver warfare, by the end of 1916, a war of position finally set in. The blockade had a strong impact. On May 7, 1915, a German submarine torpedoed the British ocean liner Lusitania off the coast of Ireland, which was carrying a secret cargo of ammunition, killing 128 American citizens who were

---

28 "Gang of fraudsters jailed for 43 years by the Metropolitan Police after reports to Action Fraud", May 9, 2019 [Online]. Available at: www.actionfraud.police.uk/news/gang-of-frauds ters-jailed-for-43-years-by-the-metropolitan-police-after-reports-to-action-fraud.

on board. German agents committed sabotage on American soil to prevent the delivery of material to the Entente forces. Anti-German sentiment started rising in the United States. Germany then came up with the idea of proposing a war against the United States to Mexico, so as to keep them away from the European theater. Mexico had to be informed of this proposal. On January 6, 1917, the Minister of Foreign Affairs of the German Empire Arthur Zimmermann sent a telegram to this effect to his ambassador in the United States, Johan Henrich von Bernstorffs, who would be in charge of transmitting it to Henrich von Eckardt, resident minister of the German Empire in Mexico. To ensure the routing, the telegram would travel by two routes: 1) via Sweden. The transatlantic Swedish cable traveled through England. The telegram was sent to Germans living in Buenos Aires, where it was transferred to Washington. Sweden promised to stop transmitting telegrams from Germany directly to Washington; and 2) via Mr. Edward House, adviser to President Thomas Woodrow Wilson, who authorized direct Berlin–Washington connections in December 1916, so as to facilitate the peace negotiations. This route passed through Berlin – Copenhagen – London – Washington. The telegram arrived on January 16, 1914 at 6 pm at the German Embassy in Washington, but was intercepted by the British on the two routes. This enabled them to remove transmission errors. It was handed over to Room 40, where it was given the name "Zimmermann Telegram".

This telegram contained a thousand numbers, recognized as a super-enciphered code. The super-encipherment did not conceal the fact that it was an assembly of trigrams, tetragrams and pentagrams, characteristic of a code called "Code 13040", on which Room 40 had been working for six months. A partial decryption was obtained, whose translation is as follows:

> Top secret: For Your Excellency's personal information, to be transmitted to the Imperial Minister of (Mexico) with Telegram No. 1 [...] by means of a secure channel. We intend to begin on the first of February unrestricted submarine warfare. We shall endeavor in spite of this to keep the United States of America neutral. In the event of (this) not succeeding, we make (Mexico) a proposal of alliance on the following basis: make war (together), make peace (together) [...] You will inform the President of the above most secretly as soon as the outbreak of war with the United States of America is (certain) [...] (Japan) [...] and at the same time mediate between Japan and ourselves. (Please call the President's attention to the fact) that [...] our submarines [...] will compel England to make peace in a few months. Acknowledge reception. (Signed) Zimmerman.

The ellipses "[...]" denote unencrypted sections. Words in parentheses were written in pencil and their transcription was considered uncertain. The rest was written in ink and the transcription was considered perfectly safe. This reconstruction was sufficiently revealing of the German intentions to react. On February 3, in reaction to the German attacks against American interests, President Wilson announced to Congress that he would break diplomatic relations with Germany if the latter persisted with submarine warfare.

The revelation of the telegram would undoubtedly lead the United States to enter the war alongside the Entente. But the telegram's direct revelation posed serious problems:

– The United Kingdom would have to admit to having spied on the telegraph lines from Sweden, a neutral country despite its proximity to Germany. At the same time, this would lead to the suspicion that the United Kingdom had also spied on other neutral countries, such as the United States. The support taken for granted would thus become compromised.

– The telegram's solution was not complete. The telegram's missing portions cast further doubt about its contents. Was there a negation missing which could fully reverse the message's meaning?

– Revealing the contents would convey the idea that the United Kingdom was able to break the German code, which would in turn encourage the Germans to change it, thereby thwarting access to the contents of future cryptograms. It was therefore crucial to preserve this highly sensitive know-how.

On February 1, 1917, Ambassador Benstorffs transferred this telegram to Minister Henrich von Eckardt, living in Mexico. However, as the latter lacked "Code 13040", the text was translated into "Code 0075", which was older and the British knew far better. "Agent T", a British agent, succeeded in obtaining a copy of this new telegram on February 5 from Western Union services. It was immediately sent to Room 40 for its integral translation. The inconveniences of disclosure disappeared. Still waiting for the tension to rise between the United States and Germany, the British claimed to have stolen the unencrypted telegram from Mexico. They published it in the press on February 22. On March 3, Zimmermann confirmed its authenticity and attempted a justification by explaining that the proposal in Mexico was only to be considered provided that the United States declared war, and considered his proposal as a matter of loyalty in relation to this country. Despite this, on April 2, 1917, President Wilson asked Congress to declare war on Germany, which was accepted on April 6. On June 28, the first American infantry division landed in Saint-Nazaire, considerably modifying the balance of power.

The mastery of information routes is a key issue for anyone desiring to ensure their domination over an information space and acquire the means of action over information or data, whether at the national, regional or international level. At present, the undersea Internet cable network totals around 447 international cables[29], for a total length of over a million kilometers. The difficulty of the count is due to the permanent evolution of this enormous planetary network: new cables are being deployed, while others are being removed. The length of each cable is sharply variable: from a hundred kilometers to over 20,000 km.

The maps, which can generally be found on the Internet[30], show the paths taken by the cables. However, these are not always the actual routes taken. What the maps attempts to show is 1) the existence of a cable and 2) the starting and ending points. Countries with maritime coasts are practically all connected, and several cables sometimes reach their landing stations, which can also contribute to ensuring the continuity of service and countering the possibility of an incident on the one of the cables.

Despite all the precautions taken, these networks are sometimes still fragile due to the naturally hostile marine environment. A fiber is, itself, extremely fragile, having the diameter of a human hair. Fibers are therefore protected, wrapped in layers of protective materials. In spite of the precautions taken during cable installation, the choice of deployment zones and the physical strength of the cables designed to withstand extreme weather conditions, there are around a hundred cable cuts each year.

The need to increase network bandwidth justifies the incessant investments made in cable. However, they must also be renewed, their life span being limited to around 20 years. Cable networks are fragile, vulnerable and exposed to obsolescence, their condition increasingly worsening. Sizing must also evolve to accompany growing needs in terms of bandwidth. Cable architecture, on the other hand, also evolves hand in hand with geopolitical imperatives, and not strictly economic ones.

The presence of international cables in a territory exposes the communications passing through it to their interception by this territory's authorities. This is the reason why, for example, the United States try to deter new undersea cable projects in the Pacific region from passing through Hong Kong.

---

29 Information from the Telegeography site.

30 For example, see: www.submarinecablemap.com/.

The United States Department of Justice strongly advised Google and Facebook (partners of the Pacific Light Cable Network (PLCN) project, designed to link the United States, Taiwan and the Philippines) against using Hong Kong as a landing point, because the "Hong Kong landing station would expose US communications traffic to collection by Beijing"[31].

The following general principles can be inferred from this:

– When a company uses a foreign territory, no matter which, as a landing place for its cables, it implicitly accepts the capture of all the data passing through the said territory by its authorities, be it an "allied" country or not. The Interception Capabilities 2000 Report [CAM 99] makes reference to these systematic international interceptions by the United States and recalls the declarations of the NSA director, who in 1975 stated before the Pike Committee of the US House of Representatives that the "NSA systematically intercepts international communications, both voice and cable[32]". In the early 1970s, the United States intercepted communications passing through undersea cables by sending submarines to foreign waters (e.g. the American submarine Halibut, one of whose missions was to record communications transmitted via Soviet military undersea cables in the Sea of Okhotsk). This operation ended in 1982, but subsequently, new interceptions were organized following the same modus operandi in other maritime areas. Based on the information known at the time, the report estimated that only the United States seemed to have the specific capabilities to carry out such undersea tapping operations at significant depths. The arrival of fiber optic cables temporarily posed a new technical challenge in terms of interceptions, and flaws quickly seemed to be identified in these new technologies, in particular at the level of fiber repeaters.

– Global Internet cable projects are political projects, as well as economic ones.

– Any construction project or participation in the implementation of an international cable involving a foreign company, and a fortiori state funding, can (or should) be considered a spy project, or with a potential risk of spying. This approach runs up against the industrial economic logic and the globalization of the economy. When Google and Facebook want to partner up with a Chinese company to deploy an international cable, they are aware of the security dimension and potential state[33] reluctance, but all the same pursue their industrial, commercial logic and do not

31 "US wants undersea data cable to skip HK", *The Straits Times*, June 19, 2020 [Online]. Available at: www.straitstimes.com/world/united-states/us-wants-undersea-data-cable-to-skip-hk.

32 Interception Capabilities 2000 Report [CAM 99].

33 "US Justice Dept opposes Google's undersea cable from China, citing security concerns", August 29, 2019 [Online]. Available at: https://www.straitstimes.com/asia/east-asia/us-justice-dept-opposes-googles-undersea-cable-from-china-citing-security-concerns.

bring the project to an end, as long as the governmental authorities do not force them to do so.

– The threat of foreign espionage forces actors to either abandon projects and prioritize new undersea networks, reconfigure them (changes of partners in the consortium, or modification of the network's route) or have them managed by the authorities of a country replacing private investors. For example, in 2018, the Australian government decided to finance the undersea cable connecting its territory to the Solomon Islands, in order to exclude the Chinese company Huawei from this project[34]. Let us also mention the United States' decision (in 2021) to take charge of the financing of a cable linking the States of Micronesia with one another, the stated goal being to dismiss the Chinese company Huawei Marine, who was initially approached for this project[35].

– Internet undersea networks are not like other international industrial projects, in that they are constrained by the decisions of states, especially due to national security reasons and the risk of espionage, in other words, the interception of communications. But it is evident that when the networks are financed by the governments, the communications are controlled and intercepted by them.

– Global Internet cable projects are closely dependent on developments in the international context, the tensions or rapprochements between states when projects are implemented.

– The denser the network of undersea cables, the more numerous the possibilities of intercepting communications: "An expanding network of undersea fiber optic cables from the Mediterranean to the Gulf has made surveillance of regional communications easier than ever" [COC 21].

– The densification of the undersea network in a world region pursues two simultaneous intentions: expanding and improving Internet access for the populations of the region(s) concerned; refining the mesh of international interceptions. The question we should pose is: who carries out the interceptions, who benefits from them? The densification of the network in the Middle East is considered as a reinforcement of the western intelligence potential in the region [COC 21]. These two aspects are generally acknowledged by the geopolitical dimension of cables.

---

34 "Australia Spy Agencies raise concerns over Solomon Islands cable link, govt takes over project", January 26, 2018 [Online]. Available at: https://www.straitstimes.com/asia/australianz/australia-spy-agencies-raise-concerns-over-soloman-islands-cable-link-govt-takes.

35 "US funding tapped for Pacific undersea cable after China rebuffed", September 3, 2021 [Online]. Available at: www.straitstimes.com/asia/us-funding-tapped-for-pacific-undersea-cable-after-china-rebuffed.

– Undersea cables are not all the property of private companies, far from it. A recent study [SHE 21], based on data drawn from the Telegeography site, estimates the share of totally private cables at 59%, totally state-owned cables at 19%, the rest, 19%, being mixed public–private ownership. Owning the cables as well as the landing stations makes it possible to act on these infrastructures: "Cable owners can insert backdoors and also monitor incoming stations." [SHE 21].

– The cables convey a certain meaning by the mere fact of their existence: "Undersea cables are built between locations that have something "important to communicate"[36]. Thus, according to the site, the absence of direct connection cables between Australia and South America means that the two continents do not need to exchange much data.

– The cables are the property of telecommunications operators. But in recent years, content providers have been increasingly investing in cable (Google, Facebook, Microsoft, Amazon, etc.), which means that the identity of cable owners has also evolved over time.

2.1.2. Human resources

Apart from the purely technological dimension, there is the human dimension, which introduces a share of specific contingencies to interception processes. This results in the risk of errors or involuntary (or voluntary) faults while handling the technologies themselves, or compliance with bureaucratic or legal procedures. Because even though the power of technologies is the key component of vast cyber surveillance architectures, whose organization and functioning have been deconstructed by the revelations of informants such as Edward Snowden and a few others before him, human intervention is essential. Not everything can be automated.

The news continues to report on the breach of these obligations, abuse of power, practices undermining the rights of citizens, irregularities and methods contravening national laws. The denunciations of these practices (by the actors in charge of control, by "vigilant" actors, associations defending the rights of individuals) are numerous:

– In 2019, the Hong Kong police was singled out for a 50% increase in the number of wiretaps subject to irregularities [TIN 19] in 2018 (27 cases), compared to 2017 (18 cases) (and 11 cases recorded in 2016) [LEU 18] in a context of moderate growth in the number of interception authorization requests (1,416 in 2016; 1,303 in 2017; 1,343 in 2018 according to the information published in the

36 See: www2.telegeography.com/submarine-cable-faqs-frequently-asked-questions.

South China Morning Post) [LEU 19, TIN 19]. Irregularities were not necessarily the result of voluntary acts, but, as observers pointed out, due to a lack of training, knowledge of the law and how to practice interceptions within the ranks of the police. But even though mistakes are made because of a lack of skill or vigilance[37], due to the ignorance of technical or legal constraints, the ultimate responsibility lies not only with the police officers proceeding with the interceptions, but also with their insufficiently attentive hierarchies. The officers were sanctioned and a reminder of the law was notified to them. But the Commissioner in charge of surveillance and the interception of communications in Hong Kong requested reinforcing officer training.

– Errors (voluntary or not?) also seem to be made at the level of the judges in charge of granting the authorizations for interception practices. A Californian judge is said to have delegated the signature of authorizations to his subordinates, whereas the law explicitly obliged him to perform the task himself.

As a tool, the interception of communications depends as much on technology and its capacities, as on the legal architecture underlying its uses, and the quality of the organizations implementing it. The human dimension is just as essential in this case, as is the pure performance of technology. It thus becomes evident that the constructions resulting from the law, aimed at preserving the rights of citizens, result in the piling up of successive layers of controllers/controlled actors: the security forces request authorizations from judges, but their implementation may deviate from the authorized framework. In turn, it is necessary to control these surveillance actors (in order to ensure the proper compliance with the application of the law). The Commissioner in charge of controlling the interceptions in Hong Kong asked to be able to access intercepted content, in order to validate the tappings [SIU 13]. The judges who grant authorizations are themselves subject to a control of their interventions.

This section could be titled "those who hear, read or gain access to the secrets" of communications. Technologies can be considered as tools which facilitate human tasks, but it is the humans who are the ultimate recipients of the data or information collected. Humans are the ones who install the interception systems; they are the ones who listen or decipher, read, translate, transcribe, then analyze, interpret and give meaning to the data collected.

Who are the individuals involved in the implementation of interceptions, what are the categories of actors, which intelligence-gathering professions are in charge of implementing interceptions, what is their relationship to technology?

---

37 Suffice to remember the case of the Hong Kong police officers who intercepted private conversations taking place inside a vehicle, while the judge's authorization limited tapping to public places [LEU 16].

"Communications researchers use the most sophisticated electronic tools in the world to intercept and analyze electronic transmissions and computing-related data, including foreign communications. We have the highest security clearances at a national scale"[38].

The secret surrounding the missions contributes to the attractiveness of the very function of communication interceptors. The "secret", mysterious, espionage dimension is exhilarating: "The [...] secret aspect is something attractive, because you hear something that someone says, but who doesn't see you [...] it's a bit like James Bond"[39].

In the technohuman organization surrounding interceptions, several tasks are assigned to humans. Telephone tapping with recording, for example, requires further transcription, and sometimes even translation. These two stages of the process constitute crucial moments in the processing of collected data: a bad transcription or an impossible transcription (from an inaudible recording, for example) can nullify all the efforts made during the implementation of the interception itself. A bad translation can alter the meaning of the content and have an impact on subsequent decisions. Fiction sometimes feeds on these powers available to translators. Hannelore Cayre even made it one of the central elements of her detective novel *The Godmother* (originally entitled *La Daronne* in French) [CAY 18]. The protagonist, who transcribes and translates wiretapping recordings on behalf of the police, takes advantage of the information she learns about drug trafficking networks to manipulate traffickers, become a trafficker herself and thwart police surveillance. To do this, she falsifies the translations of the exchanges in Arabic transcribed by her.

But beyond fiction, intelligence and police agencies rely on these essential capacities, because they are often the last, essential step towards accessing the information collected. In the 1970s and 1980s, when artificial intelligence was beginning to develop, and defense and intelligence services became increasingly interested in it, among the first applications expected, or on which research focused, translation held an important place [VEN 20].

The interception of communications is based on a material and human organization, and the emergencies of war make it possible to concretize and confront this with action.

---

38 From the video "*Les chercheurs en communication*", published by the TheForces Canadiennes Youtube channel, July 7, 2010 [Online]. Available at: www.youtube.com/watch?v=qTYNPwxZfKs.

39 ibid.

In "*État-major général. 2ᵉ et 3ᵉ bureaux. Instruction sur la recherche et l'étude des renseignements*" (*Impr. National (Paris)*)[40], published in 1916, the author asserts that:

> Telephone tapping (the telegraph service) produces more results, day by day. [...] Telephone tapping posts are a valuable source of a variety of information. They are used in particular to check the enemy order of battle; to inform about the enemy's movements; to identify and counter-beat enemy batteries in action; to give indications concerning the effect of our shots, on enemy morale, etc. It is the Army Telegraph Service who must determine the location of the tapping posts, in agreement with the 2ⁿᵈ Bureau. The installation and surveillance techniques for tapping posts are provided by the divisional telegraph detachment, according to the instructions of a specialist telegraph officer, in charge of this service throughout the Army. The tapping service is provided by the two offices who have hired selected interpreters for this purpose. The tapping service must be sufficiently staffed so as to frequently change shifts. This is due to the extreme mental strain provoked by the continuous and serious operation of the post. In this respect, we can outline the composition of a German tapping post. (*Composition of a German tapping post. 1 Lieutenant, chief of post; 1 assistant warrant officer; 2 telegraph operators of Morse code; 2 interpreters; 2 telegraph operators responsible for ensuring the maintenance and proper functioning of communications. There is, day and night at the device, a Morse code operator and an interpreter. Duration of on-call and rest periods: two hours. The team is relieved every four days by a similar team*). The information collected is transmitted to the Division Headquarters, to the Rear Admiral and to the Army Majors, under the conditions set out in Article 9.

While technologies are at the heart of interception, what they are able to produce and deliver is largely up to the individual. Underlying the source of technologies, there is of course the production of scientific and technical knowledge. But it is also necessary to integrate acquisition policies. The deployment of technological tools, their quality, the quality of the engineers or practitioners, and their know-how depends on the functioning of interception instruments; we can also think of the human intervention during the transcription of tappings, data interception or at the translation phase. We cannot underestimate the importance of the human component in these technological architectures, which never truly work on their own. While this

---

40 The document is available at: www.gallica.bnf.fr.

may have been obvious in the past, it still applies today, despite process automation and process delegation to machines.

A 1950 report produced within the NSA differentiates three categories of staff deemed essential for the proper functioning of COMINT systems: R&D staff, analysts and interception staff [SSG 50]. For the first category, the salaries offered by the NSA do not seem attractive, and compete with the salaries from the private sector (this argument would be recurrent and constant over the decades, in all the activities where the state is engaged, and in areas where the industry is also present).

More recently, it is the field of cybersecurity that has been the subject of the same observation. On the other hand, in terms of scientific prestige, the professions offered by the NSA do not seem able to compete with university positions. The second job category concerns analysts (cryptanalysis and traffic analysis). These functions are mainly carried out by the agency's civil staff. In 1950, the NSA was confronted with problems for covering these positions, because they were not sufficiently attractive. The third group, interception operators, almost exclusively staffed by the military, is challenged by specific problems in career development, namely mobility. Staff stabilization in these positions is crucial to become familiar with the equipment, technologies and methods, and to develop advanced skills on these specific functions.

Because of their scarcity, human capabilities can nullify the efforts deployed in the construction of technological systems, as well as in the associated strategies or tactics based on a theoretical performance of these systems. For example, at the start of the Korean War, the American Army Security Agency only had two Korean language translators. Moreover, these two linguists had not been duly granted clearance relating to national defense secrets, mandatory to hire them at once and engage them in COMINT operations [HAT 00].

Changes in the behavior of communication systems users are likely to impact the possibilities of interception. According to the American authorities, in reaction to the publication of an article in the New York Times published on December 16, 2005 ("Bush lets US spy on callers without Courts"), the "leaks" relating to the fight against terrorism and the methods for intercepting communications without judicial authorization provide valuable information to the enemies. The latter could use alternative means of communication (by ceasing to use electronic communications), use methods preventing interception, secure their communications (encryption, anonymization) and use decoy techniques to deceive the authorities. These tactical modifications forced intelligence services to change their methods and sources of information, in particular those involving a significant cost. But, as the American authorities' report has emphasized, these leaks had no impact on the practices of the individuals or networks monitored: "Have reactions to the unauthorized disclosure been noted in adversary communications? As of this date, no" [ELE 15].

The strict application of the law can be a real headache for intelligence agencies. While technology is useful, human vigilance is indispensable. The law defines the conditions an individual must meet in order to be considered a legal target who can have their communications intercepted. Nevertheless, this status may change depending on whether the individual is in national territory or abroad, and the same applies to their interlocutors. The procedures within the NSA illustrate the necessary intervention of human control on the status of interception targets, so as to avoid targeting by mistake:

> [...] an analyst discovered that selectors associated with a USP had erroneously been tasked because the analyst had overlooked information about the target's USP status. All selectors associated with the target were detasked, and all collected data were purged[41].

> [...] an analyst discovered that a selector for a foreign intelligence target that had been detasked was subsequently retasked while the target was in the United States. The analyst detasked the selector [...]

> [...] an analyst discovered that selectors associated with foreign intelligence targets that had been previously detasked [...] were retasked while the targets were in the United States. All selectors were detasked and no collection occurred [NSA 13].

The number of errors made in the procedures was not disclosed to the public in the declassified NSA reports. We should bear in mind that interceptions are part of complex processes, during which errors are possible. Some of them may be detected, but many of them will probably never be identified. For this, human intervention in control processes and target tracking remains essential. Several actions are included here: error detection, target designation, error correction, the purge of mistakenly collected data, the follow-up of errors and corrective measures which will then be mentioned in the reports, etc. The function of the analysts seems crucial for the identification of targeting errors (for their subsequent correction, and to abide by the law). However, analysts can also be the source of errors:

> [...] an analyst mistakenly requested the tasking of his own personal identifier instead of the selector associated with a foreign intelligence target [NSA 13].

---

41 In this quote, the ellipses "[...]" correspond to the blanks inserted in the document published by the NSA. Information was masked in the declassified documents, and then disclosed to the public. Information on the number of errors made in the procedures was not provided.

[…] an analyst forwarded in an e-mail to unauthorized recipients the results of a raw traffic database query that included terms associated with a USP. The e-mail was recalled the same day [NSA 13].

The reports produced by the NSA for the Oversight Committee on Intelligence is a long list of procedural errors, all of which the NSA claims to have corrected.

[…] it was discovered that raw SIGINT data were stored on a server not authorized to hold it. The data were deleted and moved to an authorized location. A listing of authorized servers has been compiled to prevent future errors [NSA 13].

The reasons for errors are numerous, and in intelligence organizations they are often caused by humans: "On […] occasions during the fourth quarter, selectors were incorrectly tasked because of typographical errors. The selectors were detasked, and the information has been purged" [NSA 13].

The NSA differentiated between two categories of SIGINT actions: those covered by EO 12333 and those covered by the Fisa authorization system. For the activities included in the EO 12333 framework, the majority of errors were caused by humans [CEN 13].

The organization is not infallible. The guarantees the laws define for citizens cannot be fully respected. The reason invoked is the procedural error, the human error. According to the NSA, the errors are corrected. But once the data have been disclosed, for example, is it really possible to completely undo the effects of the error?

The types of errors made by humans which can be spotted based on these NSA documents are:

– typographical errors resulting in wrong targeting;

– target designation errors ("selectors incorrectly tasked", "the analyst believed that they had detasked the selector at that time, but it actually had remained on task" [NSA 13]);

– data stored on unauthorized servers or machines;

– bugfix errors;

– data transmitted to unauthorized persons;

– analyst queries on data concerning individuals who are no longer targets;

– unauthorized publishing of the names of US citizens and US organizations in reports.

Some causes explaining the errors are mentioned in the reports:

– insufficiently documented procedures (resulting in errors during task performance);

– rumors in particular contexts. Here is an example of the days following the attacks on September 11, 2001:

> Collection Against U.S. Persons […] Unintentional […] There were […] incidents involving the use of improper retrieval strategies against the […] raw traffic files this quarter. Several of the incidents occurred in the immediate aftermath of the 11 September terrorist attacks when rumors were rife that the rules governing SIGINT collection were going to be suspended. The NSA General Counsel subsequently made an Agency-wide appearance on 17 September on NSA's secure television network to inform the workforce that the rumors were not true; he emphasized that the rules had not been suspended or changed [CEN 13].

In addition to errors, there are intentional, illegal practices which do not comply with the rules for the use of resources[42]. These are perpetrated by individuals who have access to data and the agency's technical means (in this case, the NSA):

> A military language analyst at the […] deliberately and without an authorized purpose tasked the collection of a U.S. person's email address. The analyst's database access was immediately suspended and access to Sensitive Compartmented Information was suspended by the Navy Commander. As a result of this violation and other unrelated computer infractions, the analyst received non-judicial punishment from the Navy Commanding Officer based on a hearing under Article 15 of the Uniform Code of Military Justice [NAT 05].

Other security agencies run up against the same problem, risking the employees' improper use of the resources they have access to. FBI agents are said to have used

---

42 The reports by the NSA Inspector General address many use cases which did not comply with the rules laid down by the NSA, involving employees, contractors and civilian staff, accused of using technical resources for personal purposes. For example, these include the consultation of personal email accounts, sites, blogs, online publications, parallel professional activities carried out during working hours and on the non-classified NSA networks. All of these reports covering the period 2004–2016 are online on the NSA website, publishing the archives of declassified documents, at the address: www.nsa.gov/news-features/declassified-documents/ig- reports/.

intelligence data on US citizens for personal purposes. Their goal was to collect information on friends and family[43] members.

2.2. Protecting yourself against the threat of interceptions: encryption

Since humans started exchanging information in writing, it became necessary to take preventive measures against the interception of the written medium, so as to ensure that the information contained would not be revealed to anyone it was not intended for. The famous but misnamed "Caesar Cipher" (the figure did not exist at that time) testifies to this need:

> Finally, we have Caesar's letters to Cicero, and his correspondence with his friends on his domestic affairs. He conveyed messages secretly, through marks, following a structured order of letters so that no word could be recognized. If one wishes to delve further and peruse the message until the end, it suffices to change the fourth letter, that is to say a D instead of an A, and to do the same with all the letters, accordingly (Suetonius Tranquillus, *The Lives of the Twelve Caesars*).

History has been punctuated with increasingly clever and ingenious processes to break them, in an endless race between the protection of messages and the attacks on protection.

For a long time, the strength of camouflage relied on the secrecy of the process used, until 1883, when a famous article was publshed, entitled "*La cryptographie militaire*" by Auguste Kerckoffs. Kerckoffs showed the vanity of entrusting all the security to a confidential process that would sooner or later be revealed and bring down the whole edifice, by stating a principle now accepted by all: "The value of a cryptographic system intended for the needs of war is inversely proportional to the secrecy required for its handling and composition. [...] a cipher is only good insofar as it remains indecipherable for the master himself who invented it: *Ars ipsi secreta magistro*" (a secret art for the master themselves). Message confidentiality was based on a key shared between the correspondents, modifiable at will insofar as communications evolve, and known only to them. The key served as a parameter for an encryption algorithm, which may be made public without inconvenience. The problem for the correspondents was to agree on the keys.

---

43 See: www.developpez.com/actu/280384/Des-agents-du-FBI-se-sont-servis-d-une-base-de-donnees-de-la-NSA-pour-chercher-des-infos-sur-des-collegues-des-amis-la-famille-en-violation-avec-le-quatrieme-amendement/.

In a military context, this problem could be solved by couriers, but the difficulty quickly became insurmountable with the advent of computer network communications.

2.2.1. *The public key revolution*

A new cryptography became necessary. This was stated in 1976 in the founding article on public key cryptography by Whitfield Diffie (born in 1944) and Martin Hellman (born in 1945), *New Directions in Cryptography*. There, the key exchange protocol currently known as the Diffie–Hellman Protocol is described. The principle for public key encryption was stated, but without proposing a solution, only avenues for research.

The encryption key is distinct from the decryption key. The encryption key can be known to everyone and disclosed without this posing any security problems. It is only the decryption key that must be kept secret by the recipient. It should be physically impossible for anyone to reconstruct this private key from public data.

Another year elapsed before the RSA cipher was released. Named after its inventors Ronald Rivest (born in 1947), Adi Shamir (born in 1952) and Leonard Adlemnan (born in 1945), it was published in the "mathematical games" section hosted by Martin Gardner (1914–2021), in the Scientific American journal (issue of August 1977). The eloquent title was "A new kind of cipher that would take millions of years to break". Its success was immediate. After some reservations in principle on the paradox of a public key, the RSA became widely distributed. Even today, most Internet traffic is protected by this algorithm.

The principle is to generate an integer of considerable size, equal to the product of two very large prime factors. Their product is the public key, and the two factors constitute the private key. The article describes the encryption algorithm which raises the message to a certain power e modulo the public key, and how, thanks to the knowledge of the prime factors, it is possible to decrypt the message by extracting the cryptogram's e-th root.

This new cryptography marked a radical change in the approach to security. Until then, security had been based on the closely kept secrecy of a key shared between correspondents. While ignoring this key, the adversary could only attempt to reconstruct it via witty reasoning, relying on hypotheses about the unencrypted cryptogram contents. They had to overcome the fact of ignoring the key by means of acquiring information, in the sense of Shannon's Information Theory.

With public keys, the problem is quite different. As the factorization of integers is unique, the knowledge of the public key entirely determines the private key. The adversary has all the Shannon information about the decryption key. It suffices to apply the chosen algorithm for integer factorization on the public key to reconstitute the factors and access the decryption key. But beware! The information available, the product of the factors, has the wrong form. The factorization algorithms which transform the public key into a private key are extremely complex, and it is useless to hope to find the factors within a reasonable time. The title of the article suggested that the best estimates would take several million years. As of the publication date of Diffie and Hellman's article, the best factorization algorithm used continued fractions and had exponential complexity in the size of the integer to be factorized.

Public key cryptography is based on an algorithmic complexity asymmetry between encryption – the transformation of the message into a cryptogram with the public key – and decryption – the reconstitution of the message using the public key. Security is no longer informational, but computational. Although the information is accessible, in practice, it cannot be used.

2.2.2. Advances in factorization

Multiplication and factorization are reverse processes of each other and have a complexity which is not symmetrical. A schoolboy can quickly calculate 19×13, but finding the factors of 247 requires more work. And what about a considerably larger integer like 2,027,651,281? It is precisely this asymmetry that the RSA is based on. The search for an effective algorithm for factoring integers is a problem which has engaged the interest of many mathematicians. In a letter to Mersenne in 1643, Fermat proposed a method for factoring the integer greater than 2 billion mentioned above. For a long time, this algorithm was the most efficient algorithm known. However, its complexity is exponential, which means that adding a few digits to the integer to be factorized multiplies the resolution time by a certain factor. Preliminary progress was made by the French mathematician of Russian origin Maurice Kraitchick (1882–1957) in 1926, who proposed a method to speed up Fermat's algorithm. Although much faster, Kraitchick's algorithm also presents exponential complexity. In 1931, Derrick Lehmer (1905–1991) and Ralf Powers (1875–1952) further improved the method by using continued fractions. But its complexity was still exponential. This algorithm programmed on a computer in 1971 by John Brillard would remain the most efficient factoring method for a long time. In 1975, it made it possible to discover the factors of the 7th Fermat number $2^{127} + 1$, which was known not to be a prime number, but whose factors remained unknown. This was the state of the art in 1977, when the RSA was published. The situation was quite satisfactory. Tackling the RSA remained exponentially complex and inaccessible in practice. But its advent revivified research, and great progress was made.

A first algorithm of sub-exponential complexity was discovered in 1982. It was called the multi-polynomial quadratic sieve (MPQS), following a series of advances between 1988 and 1996 to factorize integers of a particular form at first, then more and more general integers, before reaching the algorithm known as the general number field sieve. Although the latter has sub-exponential complexity, it is still not of polynomial complexity, which is the criterion for defining an efficient algorithm.

Since then, no algorithmic improvement has been made and the algebraic sieve is still the most efficient method for factoring integers.

However, the progress made is considerable. It takes nine million times longer to factorize a 100-digit number than a 50-digit number with the multi-polynomial quadratic sieve algorithm, whereas the algebraic sieve only takes a little more than a thousand times longer. As for Fermat's algorithm, the ratio of times is of the order of 10 to the power of 41.

To prove the robustness of their process, the three inventors of the RSA algorithm founded a company which in 1991 proposed a list of integers to be factorized with a variable size between 100 and 617 decimal digits. Figure 2.2 shows the factorization record dates obtained since that moment.

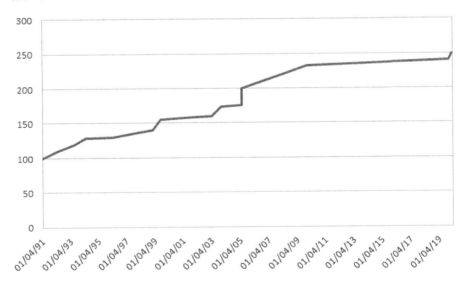

Figure 2.2. *Factorization records (reconstructed from [BOU 20]). On the abscissa: factorization date. On the ordinate: number of decimal digits of the factored integer*

2.2.3. *Shor's quantum algorithm*

The researcher Peter Shor (born in 1959) published an algorithm in 1994 to efficiently factorize integers in polynomial time and space. His algorithm is based on the quantum computer model. It is efficient, but will only work on a machine which is yet to be created.

Quantum physics offers a theoretical framework that accounts for contradictory phenomena regarding our intuitive ideas about matter and that can be observed in the microscopic world of particles. In this context, a theoretical calculation model has been developed. While in classical information theory, information is defined by the voltage level on a transistor, the binary unit of quantum information is carried by data regarding the state of a physical system, for example, the linear polarization of a photon or the spin of an electron. The quantum information unit is called a qubit (quantum bit), by analogy with the binary information unit (bit, binary digit). The value of a qubit is a piece of data that is only accessible through a measurement, making it possible to observe a quantum state. To carry out this measurement, it is necessary to choose a basis in advance, according to which the measurement will be carried out. This basis comprises two directions which are respectively associated with the binary information values 0 or 1. The state of a qubit is a normed vector expressed by this basis. The observation of the value of a qubit obeys the following laws:

1) The result of the measurement is uncertain. It is expressed by the value of a random vector, which can only be one of the basis vectors according to which the measurement is carried out. In other words, only values 0 or 1 can be observed, corresponding to the two basis vectors.

2) The components of the qubit state in the observation basis define the probabilities of observing a 0 or a 1.

3) After the measurement, if the value 0 was observed, the qubit is in the 0 state, and if the value 1 was observed, it is in the 1 state.

Principle 3) leads to the consideration that observation created the particle's state. A second subsequent observation of the same basis certainly leads to the same result. The initial particle's state is lost, making the observation process irreversible. As long as it is not observed, the particle's state is uncertain. While classical information can only take the two values 0 or 1, a qubit is in a superposition of states, covering all the combinations between 0 or 1, and whose probability depends on the state components in this basis.

Quantum computing is based on the combination of several qubits. The simplest execution is the association of independent qubits. This means that the observation of one of the values is independent from the observation of the others. But the interest of associations is the composite state of several non-independent qubits, to such a point that the observation of one of the components partly or wholly determines the observation value of the others. In this case, qubits are said to be entangled. This is a property that binds the values of two separate qubits.

Just as the logic gates enable digital electronic calculations, there are quantum analogues which perform calculations in qubits. There is a reversible logic gate that changes state 0 to state 1, and vice versa. This is the Toffoli gate, named after the Italian researcher Tommaso Toffoli (born in 1943) who invented it and which performs the AND logic function, and the controlled inverter in charge of the logical EXCLUSIVE OR (XOR) function. Thus, any calculation achievable in digital electronics is also possible in quantum computing, with equivalent doors. The peculiarity of quantum computing lies in a gate called the Hadamard[44] gate, which has no equivalent in classical logic. It achieves a symmetry of the qubit's state relatively to the diagonal of the observation basis. If a quantum register contains n of independent qubits, all with a 0 value, the application of the Hadamard gate to each of them leads to a state which is the balanced superposition of the 2^n possible states. This remarkable property amounts to considering that the register is virtually in all states, enabling the simultaneous performance of calculations with all values. Shor's algorithm takes advantage of a suitable arrangement of gates on a superposition of states to calculate which power of an integer k modulo n returns value 1, which, after calculation on a conventional computer, makes it possible to find one of the factors of the n integer.

The manufacture of quantum machines comes up against physical difficulties. Very quickly, the particles interact with the environment, which destroys the coherence of the entangled registers. Maintaining these entangled particles in a coherent state today seems to exceed our technical capabilities. Only quantum registers of a few tens of qubits have been produced. Much research is being done in the following directions:

– increasing the time when the components of an entangled register are coherent;

– reducing the time needed for observation;

– finding corrective mechanisms tolerating a certain level of inconsistencies.

In 2013, a laboratory at the University of Bristol succeeded in factoring $21 = 3 \times 7$. We are still far from being able to factorize several thousand binary digit RSA keys. It is currently very difficult to estimate the practical feasibility of factoring very large numbers on such a computer.

---

44 Named after Jacques Hadamard (1865–1963), a French mathematician known for his work on number theory.

However, research is today particularly active concerning so-called postquantum cryptography, which will come about when machines are perfected. In the quantum realm, everything is yet to be discovered. There is still no criterion of resistance to the quantum computer model. A number is labeled as postquantum only due to our ignorance of a quantum algorithm to solve it.

2.2.4. *The evolution of computing capabilities*

The 1977 article accompanied the RSA description with a security challenge for readers. It contained a message encrypted with a 129-bit public key, equal to:

m = 114 381 625 757 888 867 669 235 779 976 146 612 010 218 296 721 242 362 562 561 842 935 706 935 245 733 897 830 597 123 563 958 705 058 989 075 147 599 290 026 879 543 541

Although the article stated it would take a million years to solve the cipher, the factorization of this integer and the resolution of the cryptogram were found only 17 years later, on April 24, 1994. This result was the work of a team who ran over 600 computers in parallel. The public key factors are:

p = 3 490 529 510 847 650 949 147 849 619 903 898 133 417 764 638 493 387 843 990 820 577

q = 32 769 132 993 266 709 549 961 988 190 834 461 413 177 642 967 992 942 539 798 288 533

Such a gap between the expectation and the realization must be food for thought. While algorithmic progress is partly responsible for the result, the main reason lies in the incredible progress made by computing power during that period. On April 19, 1985, in the journal *Electronics*, an empirical law was stated by Gordon Moore (born in 1929), who was the R&D Director of the integrated circuit company Fairchild at the time:

The complexity for minimum component costs has increased at a rate of roughly a factor of two per year. Certainly over the short term this rate can be expected to continue, if not to increase. Over the longer term, the rate of increase is a bit more uncertain, although there is no reason to believe it will not remain nearly constant for at least 10 years. This means that by 1975, the number of components per integrated circuit for minimum cost will be 65,000.

To illustrate the veracity of this prediction, bear in mind that the 68,000 processor, which owes its name to the number of transistors it contains, appeared in 1979.

2.2.5. *The evolution of etching precision*

Etching precision is the thinnest band of silicon that can be etched onto an integrated circuit. The finer the etching, the larger the number of transistors that can be concentrated on a circuit, and therefore, the more numerous the calculation functions on a given silicon surface. In addition, etching precision is accompanied by an increase in the operating frequency of circuits, which has a direct impact on computing power. Moore's economic law has been corrected and turned into a technical law: the computing power of processors has followed an exponential growth for several decades, doubling every 18 months.

Since 2007, the frequency of circuit operation has no longer increased. Increasing the frequency is accompanied by higher power consumption and heat generation, which could melt silicon down.

The silicon industry admits that this period of exponential growth has reached its limit. 10-nm precision approaches the size of the silicon atom and quantum phenomena make component operation unpredictable, even though certain laboratories have managed to produce transistors operating with a single atom, with a size as small as 360 picometers [FUE 12].

Year	1971	1980	1989	1998	2007	2010	2014	2017	2023
Etching precision	10 µm	2 µm	800 nm	250 nm	90 nm	32 nm	15 nm	10 nm	7 nm

Table 2.1. *The evolution of etching precision*

2.3. Attacking encrypted communications, circumventing the hurdle of encryption

The widespread encryption of communications has been made necessary in order to guarantee "trust in the digital economy". But it immediately posed new problems to the interception services by delaying or prohibiting access to the contents of messages: "A strong cryptography interferes with intelligence collection" [BUC 16].

This situation has created new splits within the American and Western society, between the advocates of privacy protection on the one hand, and state agencies on the other, who argue the need for control in their mission to fight against the mafia and terrorist organizations.

Cryptology brings together the techniques for protecting transmitted or stored information from being tapped with or suffering malicious modifications. It is now sufficiently mature to claim it can lead to an acceptable level of trust. At present, protocols are accompanied by security proofs. But this area is permanently evolving. Processes suffer mathematical attacks, which bring weaknesses to light. Some algorithms become obsolete, such as the MD5 hash function, and very recently SHA1, used for digital signatures, or the encryption algorithmRC4, used in some Wi-Fi network protection standards.

But the main weaknesses lie in a faulty implementation, which renders protection inefficient. Flaws are regularly revealed, until they constitute a market. Moreover, the interventions of state agencies for establishing standards raise suspicions about the existence of backdoors which would make protective measures transparent.

Secured, encrypted systems are vulnerable and attackable. How do we bypass the obstacle? Because even though encrypted contents can be intercepted and collected, their interest is immediately reduced to nothing if the encryption of data renders them impossible to read.

2.3.1. *Interceptions on encrypted messaging*

End-to-end encrypted messaging solutions have often been criticized by the authorities, in particular, in the United States. The providers of these applications are accused of encouraging crime and terrorism, by building insurmountable obstacles to national security actors.

In fact, end-to-end encrypted messaging is sometimes associated with criminal use. Organized crime groups use these tools because they enable a discreet organization of their activities, at least theoretically.

Several companies have marketed and continue to sell encrypted phones. The customers of these companies can be found in the thousands. Some of these companies were created by criminals. The company MPC, for example, was controlled by "The Brothers" (James and Barric Gillespie), two members of the underworld. This company marketed encryption telephones. It notably sponsored the site "Butterfly Crime", a site specializing in underground crime (vlinderscrime.nl), created and managed by Martin Kok (the Netherlands), himself a former criminal who was murdered in December 2016, the main suspect being Christopher Hugues, who had worked for MPC. This is the universe of crime.

Although some providers specifically address their offers to a criminal clientele, this is not always the case. ProtonMail officials expressed their astonishment when the company's name was associated with terrorist activities: "we were greatly saddened last week to hear the news that ProtonMail was on ISIS's list of recommended email providers" [YEN 15], practices contrary to their values: "Our intent when creating ProtonMail was to improve online data security, and to also protect at risk groups such as democracy activists, dissidents, and journalists."

It is not possible to systematically associate encrypted messaging with crime or terrorism, as their actors do not only communicate via secure means. Encrypted messaging has other legal or legitimate uses. Failure from intelligence services or more generally, from national security agencies cannot solely be explained by the inconveniences of encrypted messaging. The co-founder of Tutanota wonders: "Would Austrian authorities have been able to stop the Vienna terrorist attack, had they had access to the encrypted chat history of the terrorist prior to the attack?" [45].

The insistence of the authorities on the dangerousness of encrypted messaging can be understood as an argument aimed at legitimizing the state's use of backdoors and permanent access to all communications. To make their point, American intelligence would profit from any security event to establish a causal link between encryption and terrorism:

> Robert S. Litt, general counsel in the Office of the Director of National Intelligence [...] argued that although "the legislative environment [for passing a law that forces decryption and backdoors] is very hostile today", it could turn in the event of a terrorist attack or criminal event where strong encryption can be shown to have hindered law enforcement [ZET 15].

Despite encryption, police forces can be credited for multiple successes in recent years, seeming to attest to capabilities or methods enabling the authorities to access encrypted messages and decrypt them.

At the beginning of 2021, the Belgian police dismantled an international network, carrying out 50 arrests, seizing weapons, drugs, GPS suitcases and one million euros. This was achieved thanks to the dismantling of an encrypted network: the criminals used encryption telephones marketed by the Canadian company Sky

---

45 "Another terrorist attack, another surveillance bill proposed. Will politicians ever learn that breaking encryption would bring more harm than good?" [Online]. Available at: www.tutanota. com/blog/posts/eu-backdoor-surveillance/ [Accessed June 23, 2021].

ECC, allowing text and images to be communicated only between network users. In this affair, about a billion encrypted messages were intercepted, almost half of which were successfully decrypted, according to the Belgian[46] public prosecutor.

During Operation Trojan Shield (IronSide, 2018–2021), which was a sting operation conceived by the Australian police forces and the FBI, the criminals were lured in. They were supplied through a fake criminal company marketing "secure" (but secretly backdoored) devices. The police had previously introduced their own communication platform within criminal organizations. The commercialized device, ANOM, was released in over 100 countries. Other sources mention 11,800 devices distributed [AMS 21]. To gain the trust of the partners in crime, the product was marketed by a pseudo crime mentor. With these telephones, the user could not make any phone calls nor send any emails. The user could only send messages within a closed network, to an interlocutor on the same platform. The tool enabled police authorities to receive more than 20 million messages exchanged over several months by criminal customers of the application who thought they were safely communicating with one another, far from any possibility of interception, hacking or espionage. The operation, triggered by the FBI, resulted in a vast police operation, simultaneously launched across several countries so as not to lose the benefits of the surprise effect. This police success resulted from engaging massive resources (number of countries involved, number of seizure operations, searches, action initiated in 2018, a long preparation time required until completion, interceptions, international procedures). ANOM devices could only exchange with other ANOM devices, but not with the outside world. It was a closed network. To acquire and use these devices, the user had to be sponsored. For the FBI, this operation was only made possible thanks to the exploitation of technologies seized from a previous criminal case. Crime technology was thus reused, reengineered and mastered for police purposes. The police operation was successful precisely because of the criminals' ignorance of the origin of the communication tools they were using. This operation is important because it illustrates how the security forces have adapted their investigation methods to penetrate and monitor criminal networks by infiltrating encrypted messaging systems.

In the same line, the EncroChat case ended with 800[47] arrests and enabled the police to break into an encrypted communications system used by criminals[48], a

46 Video published on March 10, 2021 [Online]. Available at: www.youtube.com/watch?v=nYpehd6WuH8.

47 See: www.threatpost.com/eu-authorities-crack-encryption-murder-network/157146/.

48 "Police arrest more than 800 in crackdown on EncroChat, encrypted phone system used by organized crime", July 3, 2020 [Online]. Available at: www.france24.com/en/20200703-france-united-kingdom-netherlands-police-arrests-cyber-crime-hacking-encrochat [Accessed 9 June 2021].

network dismantled by the French and Dutch police. After breaking the Encrochat encryption protocol, the police were able to intercept communications between the criminals[49] for several months.

In February 2016, the Dutch police announced that it had closed the encrypted communications network Ennetcom and arrested the platform's operator, Danny Manupassa [OSB 16]. The service used servers from the BlackBerry company. The company Ennetcom sold modified telephones, priced at €1,500, which could neither make calls nor use the Internet, but could only communicate via its own encrypted network. According to the police, the uses were mostly criminal, which supposedly elicited this reaction from the authorities. Was the real intention to prosecute the criminal users of this service, or simply to shut down a service which escaped police surveillance thanks to encryption?

Other secure networks used by criminals were infiltrated and dismantled: Phantom Secure[50], Sky Global, Ciphr[51], etc. These applications allegedly prevented any kind of interception and identification of the authors of the communications.

In 2019, a Canadian citizen was sentenced to nine years in prison in the United States for having sold several thousand BlackBerry encryption phones via his company Phantom Secure, whose communications were completely secure through the use of a network based in Panama and Hong Kong. These devices were marketed for a whole decade (2008–2018). His clients included many criminals (Mexican drug cartels, the Australian Hells Angels, etc.)[52]. The main charges retained by the prosecutor involved the criminal activities for which Phantom Secure became a facilitator and an accomplice:

> Through PHANTOM SECURE, the defendant and others facilitated
> the importation, exportation, and distribution of wholesale quantities
> of (a) cocaine; (b) heroin; and (c) methamphetamine throughout the

---

49 See: www.vice.com/en/article/3aza95/how-police-took-over-encrochat-hacked.

50 Phantom Secure, created by Vincent Ramos, summoned by the police to set up backdoors in the encrypted network. Ramos reportedly refused to comply with this request. The Anom project was supposedly born from this company. "CEO who sold encrypted phones to the Sinaloa cartel sentenced to nine years" [Online]. Available at: www.vice.com/en/article/xwn4vw/ceo-who-sold-encrypted-phones-to-the-sinaloa-cartel-sentenced-to-nine-years.

51 See: www.vice.com/en/article/bme5w3/customer-data-from-encrypted-phone-company-ciphr-has-been-dumped-online.

52 See: www.scmp.com/news/world/united-states-canada/article/3012251/prison-vancouver-man-vincent-ramos-who-sold.

world, including the United States, Australia, Mexico, Canada, Thailand, and Europe. It was reasonably foreseeable to the defendant that as part of this conspiracy PHANTOM SECURE's customers would and did use PHANTOM SECURE devices to coordinate the importation, exportation, and distribution of more than 450 kilograms of cocaine [BRA 18].

The phones provided by Phantom Secure lacked cameras and microphones, GPS, and it was possible to erase communications remotely (in case their owners were arrested, or the device was lost). The company Phantom Secure initially sold its products as privacy protection solutions. This case illustrates how the privacy argument can be misused. This case is yet another demonstration of how the interests of various stakeholders are intersected:

– During its investigation, the FBI became interested in the communications established by criminals on these networks, and instructed the CEO of Phantom Secure to introduce backdoors in his phones [ADK 19]. The CEO did not give in to the pressure.

– A former senior Royal Canadian Mounted Police official reportedly offered to sell intelligence to the company's CEO [ADK 19].

– This case provides an argument to the states hoping to ban end-to-end encryption.

Basing its entire business on the idea that it is possible to circumvent police surveillance, the company has become an important link in international organized crime. While the encryption tool was undoubtedly the cornerstone of this trade, in order to work, the system had to rely on a set of practices and techniques to gain the trust of its private customers: maintain servers outside the United States, use proxy servers to hide the servers' geographical location, use a referral system (any new customer had to be sponsored by an existing customer), use codenames to refer to customers, no identity verification of customers (exchanges only used nicknames or codenames). In the eyes of the court, which judged the person in charge of Phantom Secure, the whole architecture of this activity had been built to try to escape the surveillance of authorities and obstruct the investigations of the security forces. The international dimension of the activity also made it possible to cover tracks in the long term, because the company's pursuits spanned an entire decade.

Phantom Secure was operative on BlackBerry (Phantom Secure BlackBerry) and Samsung devices (Phantom Secure Android), offering two distinct service lines. Emails and file sharing were encrypted, remote wipes were enabled, man-in-the-middle attacks were detected, communications and chats on Samsung devices were also encrypted, as well as the Notepad app. Phantom Secure's products were not the only ones available on the market, though. Other marketed encryption mobile solutions are, for example, theZphone (from the Zezel company), Sky ECC (Sky) and Granite Phone (Sikur) developed for multiple operating systems (Secure OS, BlackBerry 7, BlackBerry 10, Android, Silent OS, Encrochat OS, etc.)[53].

In November 2018, the Dutch police announced[54] that they had accessed over 258,000 sent messages via Ironchat's end-to-end encrypted communication app during an investigation into money laundering[55]. Thanks to the exploitation of a loophole in the system, the police were able to monitor a large volume of online communications between offenders. The application ran on special telephones, and communications passed through its own servers. The company owners of Blackbox-security.com who sold the Ironchat app and IronPhone phones – two Dutch men, one from Lingewaard and the other from Boxtel – were arrested. Based on the information collected during the interceptions, a drug traffic laboratory was discovered in Enschede, as well as weapons and hard drugs. However, the mystery remains as to how the Dutch police, who remain silent on the subject, managed to take control of the systems to intercept unencrypted communications.

Europol claims to have been able to carry out major operations against organized crime in March 2021, thanks to information intercepted from users of the Sky-ECC service. This was yet another communications decryption operation the police could be credited for. The Sky-ECC company denied that its communications could have been intercepted. Sky-ECC was said to have 170,000 customers, sending three million messages each day. Europol claimed to have broken the app's encryption.

The multiplication of police operations in Europe and around the world relying on the ability to intercept encrypted communications suggests that the systems suffer from vulnerabilities. In at least one case the police forces were able to create a service acting as a honeypot, recreating all the conditions of a real encrypted system (in this case under its total control: Operation Trojan Shield). The services were offered under the cover of private companies to lure a criminal clientele. Although the communications were properly encrypted, the authorities had the keys.

---

53 See the comparative table published in the brochure [Online]. Available at: www.zezel.com/wp-content/uploads/2017/04/theZphone-SecureOS-infosheet.pdf.

54 "Police have achieved a breakthrough in the interception and decryption of crypto communication", November 6, 2018 [Online]. Available at: www.politie.nl/en/news/2018/november/02-apeldoorn-police-have-achieved-a-breakthrough-in-the-interception-and-decryption-of-crypto-communication.html.

55 Dan Gooding, "Police decrypt 258,000 messages after breaking pricey IronChat crypto app", November 7, 2018 [Online]. Available at: www.arstechnica.com/information-technology/2018/11/police-decrypt-258000-messages-after-breaking-pricey-ironchat-crypto-app/.

In other configurations, police forces may have interfered with the exchanges by posing as criminal actors. Finally, in other cases, the police were able to exploit the flaws in poorly implemented encryption systems. Encrypted phones are marketed by companies engaging in fierce competition: misinformation to discredit the competing services, the need to use phones from the same company to keep users away from other platforms[56], etc. Due to competing battles between vendors of encrypted applications and devices, signs of attempted attacks (intrusions, for example) could be attributed to operations carried out by adversaries in the business.

What are the solutions available for the police forces to circumvent the barrier end-to-end encryption poses to them?

– Taking part in exchanges using pseudonyms. Strictly speaking, this is an infiltration, not an interception method (authorized for intelligence activities and for judicial investigations in France), which makes it possible to gain knowledge about the exchanges. However, the presence in a flow of communications is likely to have an influence on interlocutors, and their actions. The difficulty comes down to not being unmasked, on the one hand, and succeeding the infiltration, on the other hand.

– Accessing data by seizing the terminal. But this involves being able to unlock the passcode and decrypt the data stored on the terminal.

– Using a Trojan horse, a technique authorized in France by the law, both for intelligence and for judicial investigations. The data entered on the terminal are captured before being encrypted. The technical difficulty lies in the ability to evade cybersecurity solutions (antiviruses, firewalls, etc.).

– Resorting to backdoors in order to decrypt the messages during their transit between terminals.

In February 2020, the French authorities publicly declared that they had entered into negotiations with software publishers to consider the possible use of backdoors (something that will nonetheless require an evolution of the legal framework) [REE 20]. But in France, as in many other countries, the use of backdoors is met with resistance, because it is synonymous with a weakening of the level of security of encryption systems. On the other hand, how do we ensure that the backdoors will only make it possible to decipher the correspondence under investigation? In other words, how do we guarantee a proper targeting? Resorting to such practices could finally have an impact on the practices of users concerned with escaping possible intrusions by the state in their private exchanges. This could tempt them to turn to other applications.

---

56 See: www.vice.com/en/article/3aza95/how-police-took-over-encrochat-hacked.

To access encrypted messages on ADSL and 3G, 4G, mobile telephony, the French Ministry of the Interior has considered requiring the decryption of encrypted information on Skype, Viber, WhatsApp, Facebook, Gmail, Twitter, Kik and WeChat [REE 16]: *"Their decryption, on the other hand, turns out to be impossible or takes too long, even with the sophisticated means used by certain specialized services."*

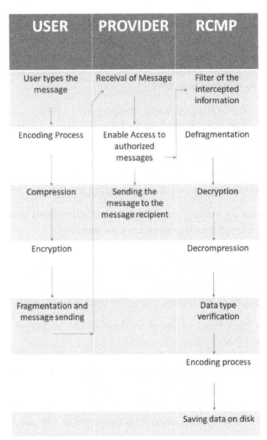

Figure 2.3. *How the Royal Canadian Mounted Police interception of BlackBerry communications works. Reproduced from the Motherboard website [PEA 16]. For a color version of this figure, see www.iste.co.uk/ventre/electronic.zip*

The French Ministry of the Interior envisaged two scenarios. A temporary one, which aimed to:

obtain electronic communications from software providers (Skype, Viber, WhatsApp, Facebook, Gmail, Twitter, Kik, Wechat, etc.), decryption keys or algorithms in order to decrypt the intercepted internet flows almost in real time, and to sanction them criminally or administratively in the event of a lack of response.

The other possibility involved changing the law (the French Post and Electronic Telecommunications Code) to compel the suppliers of electronic communications software to carry out interceptions and provide real-time and unencrypted data to the authorities (rules which are already imposed on telecommunications operators).

This diagram, published on the Motherboard website [PEA 16], shows the organization of the BlackBerry communications interception system by the RCMP (Royal Canadian Mounted Police) during Operation Clemenza. The system shows that the Canadian police were able to decipher the messages. In these situations, the fundamental question that remains, for users, is that of the degree of involvement or collaboration of the manufacturer with the state security forces. Manufacturers themselves are hardly inclined to admit to these collaborations, because of a potentially negative impact on their consumers: "it is not a good marketing thing to say we work with the police" [PEA 16].

Facts	Date
The SGDSN (*Secrétariat général de la défense et de la sécurité nationale*, the French Secretariat-General for National Defence and Security) instructed President N. Sarkozy to stop using his BlackBerry because the content of the conversations was accessible on servers based abroad.	2007
The states feel helpless in the face of encrypted messaging. Hence, they directly exercise pressure on the company: Saudi Arabia briefly interrupted BBM[57] services. There is a balance of power between the Canadian company RIM and the states that are able to block access to markets. This implies a balance of power between politics (security, counter-terrorism, counter-insurgency, etc.), trade, values, etc.	2010
RIM was reported to have reached an agreement with the government of India, enabling the country's authorities to have clear access to the content exchanged by BlackBerry users.	2010
According to the information revealed by Snowden, the NSA could have succeeded in circumventing the cryptographic protection of BlackBerrys in 2010 [ATK 13].	2010
During Operation "Project Clemenza" against the mafia, the Canadian police intercepted over a million BlackBerry messages [PEA 16].	2010–2012

Table 2.2. *Some facts regarding the questioned security of BlackBerry devices*

---

57 BBM, BlackBerry Messenger.

In addition to these message interceptions, the Canadian police used IMSI-catchers during Operation Clemenza (practices which seem to be several years old, because the article mentions former training in the use of the IMSI-catcher received by the police in 2005).

2.3.2. *The attacks against keys and PKIs*

The architecture on which Internet security is based is perhaps much more vulnerable than the user generally imagines. However, we cannot accurately estimate the extent to which the cyberspace is fragile, vulnerable and insecure.

PKI systems, on which the entire functioning of the Internet is currently based, are one of the elements embodying this vulnerability.

Persuaded about the power of his encryption methods, in 1893, Félix-Marie Delastelle (1840–1902) published a document entitled *"Cryptographie nouvelle assurant l'inviolabilité totale des correspondances chiffrées"* (Cryptography guaranteeing the total inviolability of encrypted correspondence) [DEL 93]. The ambition is the same today. But the resistance offered by encryption systems largely depends on the time factor (calculation time required to find the keys). The inviolability of communications is not always absolutely guaranteed. The weaknesses of encryption methods or systems may lie in algorithm quality, the quality of their implementation (today, weaknesses may appear both at the software and hardware levels), the reliability of the chain of actors (e.g. for PKIs), and key protection, which attackers can try to seize.

2.3.2.1. *The keys, targets of the attacks*

In encryption systems, algorithms are well known. Those currently in use are deemed secure. But the system has a vulnerable spot: the encryption keys, and no effort is too big when trying to try to recover them. Sometimes disclosures are even accidental:

– In 2010, the NSA and GCHQ allegedly hacked into Gemalto company's computer systems, one of the main producers of SIM cards. One of the attack's goals may have been to collect as many keys as possible. Gemalto acknowledged the attack, but denied the loss of keys [SCA 15].

– In 2017, Adobe accidentally published its public and private PGP[58] keys on its blog.

---

58 See: www.securityaffairs.co/wordpress/63408/hacking/adobe-pgp-key-leak.html.

– In 2018, hackers stole encryption keys from NordVPN. One of the stolen private keys was used to secure a digital certificate which enabled https encryption for nordvpn.com [GOO 19].

– In 2019, the analysis of several million "repositories" on GitHub by a team of researchers from the North Carolina State University (NCSU) revealed that more than 100,000 among them contained encryption keys [CIM 19].

– In 2020, a flaw was discovered in the VoLTE system, a security standard used on many smartphones, which could have affected the 4G LTE network. This flaw jeopardized communications' confidentiality, by enabling an attacker to recover the encryption key assigned to each user [DAC 20].

– In December 2020, US Senator Ron Wyden announced that hackers had stolen encryption keys from the Treasury Department. Because of this, the attackers were able to access emails from senior government officials.

– In 2020, the South African bank Postbank had its "master key" stolen. The company was forced to replace 12 million bank cards.

The actors (intelligence agencies, for example) with access to the keys can intercept communications without cooperation from telecommunications operators. Key acquisition can also decrypt data which may have been previously intercepted and stored, awaiting decryption. To obtain the keys, intelligence-gathering agencies are willing to use hacking methods, to hack systems. An example of this is the operation against Gemalto, revealed in 2015 [SCA 15].

2.3.2.2. Attacking PKIs

"A certification authority is a trusted third party placed at the base of the electronic certification chain. It issues and manages the digital certificates used for securing dematerialized exchanges and guaranteeing user identity." [59] It issues electronic certificates aimed at authenticating the public keys distributed across the network. When a message is encrypted with the public key of a recipient, it is crucial to ensure that it has not been tampered with maliciously, reducing the protection secured by encryption to nothing. Certificate authorities work with registration authorities, depositary authorities and escrow authorities. Together, these authorities constitute the PKI key management infrastructure.

In this architecture, where are the most vulnerable elements located? If an intelligence agency like the NSA pretends to be a certification authority, does it not

---

59 Definition published on the CertEurope website: www.certeurope.fr/blog/5-choses-a-savoir-au-sujet-des-autorites-de-certification/ [Accessed June 30, 2021].

take control of the essential element in the chain of trust? In recent years, the use of false certifications has been denounced repeatedly.

Certification authorities (service-provider certification, certificate authority) are not only targets of hacking, but are also under the pressure in certain states:

– DigiNotar, a Dutch certification authority, was the victim of an attack in 2011, which resulted in "false" certificates being issued. The hackers broke into the DigiNotar servers and were able to fraudulently generate certificates many domains recognized as valid (including Google, Skype). This attack would have been used, in particular, to intercept emails or Internet exchanges of 300,000 Internet users in Iran[60], MITM-type attack victims. Major search engines reacted by blacklisting all DigiNotar certificates.

– In 2019, TLS certificates were up for sale on the Darknet[61].

– In 2013, the press mentioned the possible use of false certificates by ANSSI (the National Cybersecurity Agency of France) to carry out MITM-type (man-in-the-middle or machine-in-the-middle) attacks on private[62] networks.

– In the first half of 2021, the Mongolian website certification authority MonPass was hacked[63] and backdoors were introduced in its installation software.

– In December 2020, ESET revealed the existence of "Operation SinSight", during which an electronic signature application issued by the VGCA (Vietnam Government Certification Authority) was hacked.

– In 2001, the Verisign authority issued two certificates to an individual claiming to represent Microsoft.

– Between 2015 and 2020, the government of Kazakhstan forced its citizens to install a certificate if they wished to access foreign Internet services. Installing this certificate enabled authorities to intercept https traffic. In December 2020, users in the capital Nur-Sultan were asked to install a certificate before they could access sites such as Google, Twitter, YouTube or Facebook. The government had done the same in December 2015 and July 2019. Nevertheless, these certificates have been blacklisted by Apple, Google and Mozilla. The Kazakh government's project intercepted https traffic (requests from around 37 domains in 2019, mainly social networks and communication tools: Google, Facebook, Instagram, YouTube,

60 ENISA, Operation Black Tulip: Certificate authorities lose authority [Online]. Available at: www.enisa.europa.eu/media/news-items/operation-black-tulip/.

61 See: www.informatique75019.com/blog/faux-certificats-de-securite.html.

62 See: www.it-connect.fr/quand-lanssi-utilisation-de-faux-certificats-google-pour-un-mitm/.

63 See: www.thehackernews.com/2021/07/mongolian-certificate-authority-hacked.html.

Twitter, etc.). However, it would seem that not all of the country's Internet service providers (ISPs) were involved in this operation. On three occasions, the government tried to implement this interception system, attempts which were apparently only temporary and came up against strong resistance: the country's ISPs did not all take part in these operations; certificates were blacklisted. The official motive argued by the Kazakh government was the reinforcement of citizen, government and business protection in the face of cyberattacks, fraud and other types of cyberthreats.

– Part of the connections to Internet sites is not secure, although it is supposed to be. It is difficult to estimate the proportion of sites using these fake certificates. In 2014, a study by a team of researchers[64] calculated this share at 0.2%.

– The dark web is like a haven for fake certificates [AHM 21]. There, we may acquire fake SSL/TLS certificates and "code signing certificates":

> Five of the Tor network markets observed – Dream Market, Wall Street Market, BlockBooth, Nightmare Market and Galaxy3 – offer a steady supply of SSL/TLS certificates, along with a range of related services and products. SSL/TLS certificates are often packaged with crimeware services and products, such as malicious websites and ransomware. Certain marketplaces, like Dream Market, appear to specialize in the sale of SSL/TLS certificates and related services [MAI 19].

Certificate prices range from a few hundred to a few thousand dollars. The authors of that report [MAI 19] nonetheless admitted they had been unable to assess the real extent of this market;

– "https" sites are not all secure: 60% of malicious sites could be headed https[65].

2.3.2.3. *Summary of the methods to weaken communications security or to exploit its vulnerabilities, in order to make interception possible*

– Exploiting security weaknesses: a few years ago, the vulnerabilities of SSL certificates could still be derived from the use of the MD5 algorithm, whose weaknesses were well known[66] (MD5[67] was cracked in 2004, and used for a long time by certification authorities; in 2020, MD5 was still in use by 25% of CMS

---

64 See: www.linshunghuang.com/papers/mitm.pdf.

65 See: www.wandera.com/hackers-leverage-https/ [Accessed August 30, 2021].

66 See: www.tbs-certificats.com/FAQ/fr/479.html.

67 MD5: Message Digest 5, cryptographic hash function, invented in 1991.

(Content Management Systems) to secure usernames and passwords[68], which made the Internet sites using these CMS all the more fragile);

– stealing certificates: one of the main purposes of stealing certificates is to intercept traffic and collect data;

– issuing fake certificates, signed with stolen keys;

– obliging operators/companies to make their technologies "exploitable" by providing concealed access (backdoors);

– reading messages before they are encrypted;

– stealing secret keys;

– launching side-channel attacks on stored secret keys, which are sometimes poorly protected. This type of attack exploits electromagnetic emissions, chips being sometimes insufficiently protected against such emissions.

2.3.3. *The use of backdoors*

A number of recent cases, such as the cellphone tapping of German Chancellor Angela Merkel by the United States intelligence services, or the controversy between Apple and the FBI regarding the revelation of mobile phone data encryption keys, show that cryptology is not always an insurmountable obstacle to accessing contents[69]. The cryptographic functions used are assumed to be strong enough to establish trust in the equipment used, ruling out the possibility of this access resulting from a mathematical attack. The solidity of the implemented cryptology should not be called into question. If the digital shield represented by encryption is not faulty, it must have been diverted, and therefore, the hypotheses on which its solidity is based are no longer satisfied. The encryption algorithm is used in communication systems which are becoming increasingly complex. Assuming that trust in the algorithm's security is unshakeable, does it suffice to communicate safely? Encryption is one of the components providing information protection. The cryptographic algorithm is embedded into a complex set, single-handedly acting among various other elements. Trust must be established for all the chain links,

---

68 See: www.zdnet.com/article/a-quarter-of-major-cmss-use-outdated-md5-as-the-default-password-hashing-scheme/.

69 Let us recall that the American firm from Cupertino refused to comply with FBI injunctions to access the encrypted contents of the telephone used by one of the perpetrators of the San Bernardino attack, which killed 14 people in December 2015 in California. Apple argued that no vulnerability enabled access to unencrypted content, supporting a company principle aimed at protecting its customers. The case was not pursued, the FBI probably having obtained the information by other means.

including: the computing device, the communication protocol, the application, the network, etc. It is not only mathematical security that must be ensured, but what Kerckhoffs called "material security", meaning security "in practical terms".

As soon as the user delegates the task of security management to the communication system itself, the latter can implement mechanisms that make it possible to circumvent protection. These mechanisms constitute intentional or unintentional security breaches. Complex systems, for example, need access to internal parameters for debugging or maintenance. These are often confidential data entry points which provide access to private content.

2.3.3.1. *Bypassing encryption*

One of the possibilities for accessing unencrypted messages is the disclosure of information through unexpected channels, such as response time, radiation or component power consumption.

Nowadays, these side-channel attacks are at the heart of security device assessment, and the problem is certainly not new. In his memoir, Spycatcher, the British counter-intelligence officer Peter Wright described how the French embassy in London was spied on at the end of the 1950s [WRI 87]. For intelligence on the French government's intentions concerning the British application for entry into the Common Market, this embassy was monitored by the British services.

In Wright's words:

> In the 1950s, the most sophisticated encryption process involved typing the unencrypted text on a kind of telegraph, connected to an encrypting device.

> At the other end, with just a click, the machine delivered an encrypted message. The security of this whole procedure depended solely on good insulation. If electromagnetic isolation between the telegraph and the encrypting machine was insufficient, the echo of the unencrypted text could have lingered throughout the cables, in parallel to the encoded text. Theoretically, with adequate amplifiers, it should be possible to recover the ghost text as it came out, and to read it.

The experiment was carried out successfully. Wright continues:

> A steady curve throbbed on my control monitor. We could very clearly see the superposition of two curves: that of the encrypting machine and the unencrypted "ghost" text accompanying it.

The GCHQ technicians changed the settings of their amplifiers so that our pirate line gave a sufficiently powerful signal to send the message by teleprinters. Portions of the unencrypted text were revealed, and within ten minutes we had a summary transcription of a telex the French ambassador was sending to General de Gaulle's office.

For almost three years, from 1960 to 1963, we were able to read all the transmissions that passed through the French Embassy.

An unintentional weakness in the communication system has been described. Preventing compromising radiation from machines handling sensitive data, such as computer screens, has been a constant concern for military circles, leading to the development of standards known as TEMPEST (Telecommunications Electronics Material Protected from Emanating Spurious Transmissions).

In 1996, the American cryptologist Paul Kocher (born in 1973) developed methods for finding secrets buried in devices such as smart cards, by exploiting the measurement of computing time or electrical consumption. For example, during a transaction and by simple measurement of the electrical current consumed by the bank card, such attacks allow a payment terminal to withdraw the private keys. Manufacturers have since taken significant steps to counter this type of weakness.

2.3.3.2. *The reduction of key entropy*

Key size often constitutes a security argument to attest to the robustness of a cryptographic algorithm. But even when keys are of a substantial size, it is technically possible to impose limited entropy onto them, facilitating an exhaustive search by the organizations aware of the malice, while displaying the appearance of robust encryption. This reduction can be performed on the hardware or on the software, but it is more discreet when the hardware is supported.

Let us recall that "key size" is the number of binary symbols required to write it out, whereas "entropy" refers to the number of questions with binary answers it is necessary to ask in order to establish it as a whole. If a key is made up of random and independent symbols, entropy is equal to the number of binary symbols in its writing, but it is possible to produce keys which are statistically indistinguishable from a true random key, depending only on a number smaller number of binary symbols. It will then suffice for organizations who are familiar with the procedure to go through this narrower number of possibilities to explore the space of all the keys produced. It is not absurd for this procedure to be used to allow intelligence services to determine the keys for cryptographic equipment exported to countries considered potentially unsafe. Recent revelations on the activities of the American National Security Agency (NSA) show that this process can also be applied to the allied countries signatories of the Wassenaar Arrangement.

A concrete example of this practice is illustrated by the results obtained by the company Cryptosence, a spinoff of INRIA, and published on the company's website. This work follows the publication of an academic paper in 2012, which showed that a considerable number of RSA keys intended to ensure Internet communications security turned out to be weak. Let us recall that RSA is an encryption procedure involving a public key signature, whose security is based on the difficulty of factorizing large numbers. By choosing two large prime numbers p and q, it is possible to publish their product $n = p \times q$ without compromising factors p and q. While the encryption function only requires the knowledge of product n, decryption requires that of factors p and q.

Researchers from UCSD and the University of Michigan noted that calculating the greatest common divisor (GCD) of the public keys available for SSL/TLS security led to an abnormally high number of RSA public key factorizations. Thanks to this process, they succeeded in factoring 12,934 keys out of 5,989,923, that is, a proportion of 0.22%. Three years later, the factored keys were 19,256 of the 13,603,691 tested, that is, about 0.14%. Obtaining these results conveys the idea that out of the 26 million prime numbers generated, nearly 20,000 collisions are observed. The birthday paradox formula shows that the real average entropy of the primes produced is about 57 bits. The prime numbers used to generate the RSA keys are finally chosen from a set restricted to 2^{57} numbers. Bear in mind Bertrand's postulate on the density of prime numbers, which asserts that the number of 512-binary-digit prime integers required for the production of RSA keys with size 1024 is 2^{503}. The average entropy of RSA keys used on the Internet network to secure exchanges corresponds approximately to the size of the DES (Data Encryption Standard) keys. Exploring 2^{57} is widely accessible to current computational means. It is possible for this weakness to result from a faulty implementation neglecting the basic security rules in force for the development of secure applications, but the suspicion on the intentional nature of this weakness should not be ruled out.

Reducing the actual entropy of keys is only one of the possibilities for introducing a backdoor into cryptographic functions. Without being exhaustive, here are a few examples:

– imposing obsolete algorithms known for their weakness when implementing networking protocols;

– leaking secret keys through hidden channels, such as error channels;

– generating particular prime numbers, enabling an easier factorization of the public RSA keys involved.

As information and communication technologies evolved, so did the means by which States sought to monitor private communications.

With increased use of telephones came the use of wiretapping, which consists of placing a tap on a telephone wire to listen to private phone conversations. With the replacement of analogue telephone networks with fibre optics and digital switches in the 1990s, States redesigned the networking technology to include interception capabilities ("backdoors") to permit State surveillance, rendering modern telephone networks remotely accessible and controllable [LAR 13].

2.3.3.3. *The control of cryptology*

As long as cryptology is controlled by states, if needed, the latter could impose features enabling them to access encrypted contents. Thus, the size of the DES keys was limited to 56 binary symbols, a value accessible to the important means available to the state's calculation, but beyond the reach of private actors. While security was granted to businesses and citizens, the state could nonetheless lift the protections. With the development of increasing computing power, the size of this key progressively weakened, until it became insufficient to provide acceptable security. The differences in computational means between the industry and government organizations were no longer acceptable. The cryptographic community estimated that a size of 80 binary symbols was the minimum acceptable to ensure security. The United States tried to impose key escrow. Thanks to this mechanism, the keys required to decrypt cryptograms are accessible to government authorities, if necessary. This escrow mechanism materialized in a component, the "Clipper Chip", an integrated circuit developed and promoted by the NSA for implementation in encryption equipment. This component required users to escrow their keys to government authorities so that law enforcement agencies (FBI, CIA) could have full access to traffic for interception, surveillance and intelligence-gathering purposes. The development of this chip was widely controversial and was finally abandoned in 1996.

At the same time, French legislation shifted to a system of trustworthy third parties. The use of cryptology was subject to prior declaration, with the obligation to deposit the keys with a freely chosen trustworthy third party. These trustworthy third parties were independent private companies responsible for providing and storing the keys used by customers for their private communications, a priori without any size limitation. These keys remained confined to the trustworthy third party until a court decision required them to be communicated for investigative purposes.

The principle was to use robust and unsolvable cryptography, while allowing state services to access communications under certain circumstances contemplated by the law.

In contrast, the business community exerted pressure to liberalize cryptology, so as to build public trust in the nascent digital communications technology and develop e-commerce.

The second position prevailed and the French "Law for Trust in the Digital Economy" from June 21, 2004, declared in Art. 30 that "the use of cryptology means is free".

However, this was far from the end of the story. Despite its use being announced as free in most western countries, states did not relinquish the control of cryptology. The Wassenaar Arrangement on dual-use (military and civil) technologies includes cryptology and obliges exporting countries to implement a certain control.

The liberty to use cryptography freely is a bone of contention for states in their surveillance mission to fight against criminal or terrorist organizations. This tension between freedom and control is reflected by many official documents. The cryptology regulations of 1991 enacted by the French SCSSI (*Services centraux pour la sécurité des systèmes d'information*, Central Service for Information System Security), ancestor of the French ANSSI (*Agence nationale de la sécurité des systèmes d'information*, National Agency for the Security of Information Systems), stated that:

> As part of the protection of people and property, interior security and national defense, the State must put in place the necessary measures to prevent these technologies (information and communication) from facilitating, with complete impunity and in total discretion, the development of illegal actions or trafficking (petty and serious crime, terrorism, mafia, pedophilia, money laundering, financial fraud, industrial spying, etc.) [70].

The question arises as to the nature of these "necessary measures" to make the contents of strongly encrypted exchanges accessible to the services requiring them. A first solution had been to limit key size, so as to make exhaustive research accessible to institutions equipped with powerful computing resources. Key size also provided information on the power of these means, following countries' regulations. While France limited the use of keys to 40 bits, the United States authorized 56 bits[71].

---

70 See: www.securinet.free.fr/crypto-regle-fr.html.

71 This contrast reveals the differences in computing power available on both sides of the Atlantic.

This solution had the prohibitive disadvantage of weakening protection for everyone, including the exchanges where this protection was fully justified, such as during contract negotiations or commercial exchanges.

A second solution was to introduce backdoors into the cryptographic system, unbeknown to users, but accessible to authorized services. Mathematical solutions are available to make these backdoors secure, such as, for example, encrypting the encryption keys with a public key. In this way, only the custodian state of the corresponding private key can access decryption and finally, the unencrypted exchanges.

This solution was widely contested by all cryptology[72] actors. During a congressional hearing on the "Clipper Chip", Whitfield Diffie, one of the creators of the Diffie-Hellman protocol for secure key exchange, declared:

– "The backdoor would put providers in an awkward position with other governments and international customers, weakening its value.

– Those who want to hide their conversations from the government for nefarious reasons can get around the backdoor easily.

– The only people who would be easy to surveil would be people who didn't care about government surveillance in the first place.

– There was no guarantee someone else might not exploit the backdoor for their own purposes."

Official backdoors, like the Clipper Chip implemented during the Clinton administration, were ultimately dismissed. This rejection of official escrow or trustworthy third-party methods did not seem to discourage states from designing an access solution, all the same. Since the circumvention of cryptology is not official, it is unthought-of and remains concealed under vulnerabilities regularly discovered in systems (zero-day vulnerability).

The issue of backdoors was revitalized by a letter sent by the French and German interior ministries to the European Commission.

In the letter dated February 20, 2017, signed by Thomas de Maizière and Bruno Le Roux, Ministers of the Interior of the two countries[73], it is written that:

---

72 See: www.arstechnica.com/information-technology/2015/12/what-the-government-shouldve-learned-about-backdoors-from-the-clipper-chip/.

73 See: www.regmedia.co.uk/2017/02/28/french_german_eu_letter.pdf and www.fr.scribd.com/document/340506340/2017-02-17-De-claration-FR-DE-II-Officielle.

The fight against terrorism requires providing the European authorities with the legal means to acknowledge the widespread use of communications having been encrypted by electronic means during judicial and administrative investigations. The European Commission must ensure that technical and legal measures are implemented to envisage the possibility of defining new obligations for the providers of electronic communication services, while guaranteeing the reliability of highly secured systems and, on this basis, to propose a legislative initiative in October 2017.

In general, the EU Cybersecurity Strategy of 2013 must be revised and include new actions, drawing up an inventory of the measures which still have to be taken.

To prevent and deter all forms of terrorist threats, we support the Commission's approach for updating the agenda on chemical, biological and radionuclear (CBRN) threats in order to improve the measures required to prevent, combat and reduce these threats. This modernization is essential to adapt the response of the Member States to constant technological changes. This agenda should be conducted in partnership with Europol's European Counter Terrorism Center – ECTC.

This letter clearly shows the idea of reintroducing backdoors into encryption solutions, so as to make the contents accessible for operations that would eventually require it. This proposal was opposed by many stakeholders.

In particular, the French Data Protection Enforcement Authorities (CNIL, *Commission Nationale Informatique & Libertés*) advocated for strong cryptography, without any backdoors and controlled by users, arguing the existence of binding legal mechanisms to provide encryption keys (Box 2.1).

Guillaume Poupard, former director general of the French National Agency for the Security of Information Systems (ANSSI), shared a similar position. He spoke out against any parallel access to contents inserted by technology providers and was in favor of intrusive investigative techniques for intercepting messages before or after encryption[74].

74 See: www.hightech.bfmtv.com/internet/l-anssi-does-not-believe-in-the-sovereign-bones-nor-in-the-backdoors-946311.html.

"Recent events have led to a debate on the relevance of national law introducing backdoors or a master key ultimately enabling access to data contained in a system protected by an encryption solution, and presented as available to the user. Such a device would raise many issues:

– it would create a collective risk tending to weaken people's level of security against the widespread cybercriminal phenomenon, whereas it would not technically prevent malicious actors from continuing to use encryption solutions on an individual basis to protect the confidentiality of their communications and stored data;

– it is likely not to be very robust over time, against attacks from states or from organized crime, especially considering it would be necessary to exchange secrecy or keys between the authorities;

– it would be very complex to implement safely because applications are globalized and internationalized.

Robust encryption solutions, under the user's full control, contribute to the digital ecosystem's balance and security. The introduction of backdoors or master keys could lead to weakening the security of the technical solutions currently deployed, which would be detrimental to the information assets of companies, to the stability of the ecosystem of the digital economy and to the protection people's liberties.

Consequently, the CNIL concluded that[75]:

– encryption contributes to the resilience of our digital societies and information assets;

– in the context of legal proceedings, there are already many ways in which the authorities can access and analyze the contents relevant to investigative purposes or convenient for truth to become manifest;

– the respondents and third parties have an obligation to cooperate with the authorities;

– the implementation of backdoors or master keys could weaken the future of the digital ecosystem."

Box 2.1. *Limits to the use of backdoors*

The American manufacturers from the CCIA (Computer and Communications Industry Association), an association bringing together the main Internet technology companies from the United States – in particular Amazon, Google, eBay, Microsoft,

---

75 See: www.cnil.fr/fr/les-challenges-de-2016-3-quelle-position-de-la-cnil-en-matiere-de-chiffrement.

Netflix and many others – also oppose any method potentially leading to the introduction of weak encryption into equipment.

> It remains unclear exactly how online service providers should provide law enforcement authorities with access to end-to-end encrypted user data. Any backdoors to encrypted data would pose serious risks to the overall security and confidentiality of Europeans' communications, which seems inconsistent with existing legal protections for personal data. Weakened security ultimately leaves online systems more vulnerable to all types of attacks from terrorists to hackers. This should be a time to increase security – not weaken it[76].

The ENISA (European Union Agency for Network and Information Security) has a similar[77] position (see Box 2.2).

ENISA sees that

– "The use of backdoors in cryptography is not a solution, as existing legitimate users are put at risk by the very existence of backdoors.

– Backdoors do not address the challenge of accessing or decrypting material, because criminals can already develop and use their own cryptographic tools. Furthermore, new technologies are now being deployed, making lawful interception in a timely manner very difficult.

– Judicial oversight may not be a perfect solution; as different interpretations of the legislation may occur.

– Law enforcement solutions need to be identified without the use of backdoors and key escrow. It is very difficult to restrict technical innovation using legislation.

– History has shown that technology beats legislation, and criminals are best placed to capitalize on this opportunity.

– The perception that backdoors and key escrow exist can potentially affect and undermine the aspirations for a fully embraced Digital Society in Europe.

– History has shown that legal controls are not always successful, and may harm and inhibit innovation, as seen with previous US experience."

Box 2.2. *ENISA's position regarding backdoors*

---

76 See: www.ccianet.org/2017/02/is-europe-about-weaken-encryption/.

77 See: www.enisa.europa.eu/news/enisa-news/the-importance-of-cryptography-for-the-digital-society.

2.3.3.4. *Backdoors and their political dimension*

The term "backdoor" is polysemous. Three definition levels can be differentiated [JEN 18]:

– The backdoor is a concealed door (primary meaning). The backdoor can then be considered as an alternative, an unofficial entry point, which can only be used by people who are authorized to do so, who can legitimately do so. This entry can be controlled.

– A way of acting which is indirect, furtive, illicit, disloyal or secret, in order to reach a goal.

– A mechanism for circumventing security:

- sometimes, the approach is purposely vague, with backdoors being described as tools whose technical properties should not be widely known;

- occasionally, backdoors are tools used by hackers or other malicious attackers; access points are known to a limited number of people, undocumented or poorly documented; access points can be used illegally by criminals or intelligence agencies. There are two backdoor categories: legal and illegal.

Backdoors are used by governments who claim the possibility of installing legitimate and reserved entry points, or administrator access rights; its opponents or detractors dispute this claim, alleging that this practice adds a threat level to a cyber environment already amply marked by insecurity.

The term "crypto-wars" designates the debates that took place in the 1990s, a period during which American security authorities tried to oppose the generalization of strong cryptography, something which weakened its means of action, in particular, those involving interception. These authorities lobbied to ban the free and widespread use of strong cryptography.

Backdoor	Effect
"A backdoor in a computer system (or cryptosystem or algorithm) is a method of bypassing normal authentication, securing unauthorized remote access to a computer, obtaining access to plaintext and so on, while attempting to remain undetected"[78].	Unauthorized access.

---

78 See: http://docshare01.docshare.tips/files/26796/267966800.pdf.

"Typically unauthorized hidden software or hardware mechanism used to circumvent security controls"[79].	Material or software access.
"[...] an intentional construct inserted into a system, known to the system's implementer, unknown to its end-user, that serves to compromise its perceived security" [VAN 18].	Access intentionally designed by the system designer.
"When a programmer intentionally creates an undocumented portal into its encrypted system, this opening is called a backdoor. [...] A backdoor is a malicious computer program that is used to provide the attacker with unauthorized remote access to a compromised PC system by exploiting security vulnerabilities [...] Most backdoors are malicious programs that must be somehow installed to a computer. Nevertheless, some parasites do not require the installation, as their files are already integrated into software that is running on a remote host. Programmers sometimes leave such backdoors in their software for diagnostics and troubleshooting purposes. However, hackers use these flaws to break into the system"[80].	Malware or access arranged during software design… Not always for attack purposes: it can be useful for technical diagnoses.
Trap-doors	**Effect**
"[...] entry points in the system that by-pass the control facilities and permit direct access to files. Trap-door entry points often are created deliberately during the design and development stage to simplify the insertion of authorized program changes by legitimate system programmers, with the intent of closing the trap-door prior to operational use. Unauthorized entry points can be created by a system programmer who wishes to provide a means for bypassing internal security controls and thus subverting the system" [WAR 79].	Entry point into a system. To bypass means of control. Deliberately created during system design: for technical purposes.
"When a system is implemented, traps or "hooks" are often included to allow special operating privileges to system programmers. The traps are intended for debugging or legitimate system maintenance. However, their usefulness depends on the secrecy of their existence, and secrecy is a very poor security protection method. Thus, the use of traps should be strictly limited or they should be removed" [LIN 76].	They are forced to remain secret.

Table 2.3. *Some definitions of backdoors and trap-doors*

This "war" opposed business actors against the American government. State security actors then requested the integration of backdoors into communication devices and the export of strong encryption solutions to be limited. It was in such a

---

79 (CNSSI-4009) (NISTIR).

80 See: https://www.2-spyware.com/backdoors-removal.

context that CALEA (Communication Assistance for Law Enforcement Act)[81] was adopted in 1994, aiming to guarantee security forces the access to electronic communications. While encryption became widespread in the years 2000–2010, the revelations by Snowden seemed to attest to the fact that authorities knew how to circumvent the obstacle of communications encryption. The debates were revivified with the revelations by Snowden and the San Bernardino attacks in 2015. During the investigation, the FBI tried to compel Apple to provide the access keys to the contents of the terrorists' iPhone. This was followed by a new period, the "Going Dark Debate", which conveyed the idea that an increasing part of communications escapes scrutiny by the police (or the intelligence services), due to the strong encryption means now available to users. In 2015, FBI Director James Comey reaffirmed the need to fight end-to-end encrypted applications, considering they are weapons in the service of terrorism. The Islamic State could take advantage of these means of communication and carry out their international operations under the radar of their enemies' intelligence. But the head of the FBI deplored the small margin for maneuver he had, with strong encryption hindering security actions:

> Those charged with protecting our people aren't always able to access the evidence we need to prosecute crime and prevent terrorism even with lawful authority. We have the legal authority to intercept and access communications and information pursuant to court order, but we often lack the technical ability to do so [COM 14].

The FBI may not have the same capabilities as intelligence agencies:

> Some believe that the FBI has these phenomenal capabilities to access any information at any time – that we can get what we want, when we want it, by flipping some sort of switch. It may be true in the movies or on TV. It is simply not the case in real life [COM 14].

From the Crypto Wars to the Going Dark debate, legal arguments seem to dominate exchanges (what state security forces can legitimately request, how they can collect data, what they can do with the data, the unquestionable conditions of the preservation of freedoms and privacy, etc.). Without a shadow of a doubt, questions of power are at stake: who in a society imposes its rules on others? How does the state assert its power? To what extent are non-state actors able to challenge the state's power? In the same vein, comparisons arise between agencies within the same state (note that the FBI does not have the same exorbitant means as the NSA,

---

81 H.R. 4922 - 103rd Congress, Communications Assistance for Law Enforcement Act, 1994 [Online]. Available at: www.govtrack.us/congress/bills/103/hr4922; www.govinfo.gov/content/pkg/BILLS-103hr4922enr/pdf/BILLS-103hr4922enr.pdf; www.baller.com/wp-content/uploads/calea.pdf.

for example). These are also economic issues. There are also clashes between technological fields: interception technologies dispute cryptanalysis techniques, backdoors are opposed to security (encryption) and "Privacy Enhancing Technologies" (PET).

To a much lesser extent than intelligence agencies, the police force is also immersed in a paradoxical situation. Due to the generalization of encryption, the sources of exploitable information by the police forces is becoming scarce, with data being too difficult to access, whereas at the same time, cyberspace continues to thrive with the multiplication of information flows.

The debate is quite dynamic. The proponents of unrestrained access to the contents of communications are numerous. A law project was recently filed (in 2020) in the United States by Senator Lindsay Graham (Lawful Access to Encrypted Data Act), proposing that the precise means of access to unencrypted data should be listed in the law. The promoters of this bill (Lindsay Graham, Tom Cotton, Marsha Blackburn, all three Republican senators) justified it by invoking the need to fight crime, terrorism or sexual predators. What they are actually proposing is CALEA II, CALEA already having enshrined the obligation for telecommunications operators to modify their systems and make communications accessible.

By imposing the implementation of backdoors, state security authorities aim to free themselves from their current dependence on technology-savvy private sector companies. With the use of backdoors, it would no longer be necessary to ask, demand, exert pressure, initiate proceedings and debate. The action could be direct and permanent.

The debates that crystallized around the backdoors issue seem to reveal a deep, and in any case lasting, divergence between the interests of various stakeholders: on the one hand, the security actors (police, justice, intelligence) and on the other – opposing the claims of the former – a heterogeneous combination of citizens, politicized groups, defenders of individual liberties, of privacy, of fundamental rights, as well as companies that have built their markets, in a certain number of countries, upon the guarantee of the preservation of confidentiality and the secrecy of correspondence. The industry has repeatedly expressed its opposition to government demands for the introduction of backdoors into their products: "The United States government has demanded that Apple take an unprecedented step which threatens the security of our customers. We oppose this order, which has implications far beyond the legal case at hand" [COO 16].

These are the main stakeholders in the confrontation, but cybersecurity and cryptology researchers should be added, not to mention crime hackers, who all have a particular set of skills for bypassing systems security and creating backdoors. The political field is also divided into two blocks: the appointed officials, those who propose and create the laws, those who debate democratically: one of the two blocs has so far prevailed over the other, at least officially. These are the politicians refractory to the idea of imposing backdoors, and who were able to repel the assaults of the pro-backdoors.

In recent years, the international commercial struggle that crystallized around the deployment of 5G around the world brought to the fore the security issue on backdoors. One of the main arguments put forward by the American government to try to block China – world leader in 5G technologies – focused on the threat of backdoors. The two main Chinese companies, Huawei and ZTE, were accused by America of tampering their technologies with backdoors, having no choice but to obey the orders from Beijing. Nevertheless, nothing and no one can truly guarantee the absence of backdoors in technologies, nor completely protect themselves against them. The design of cyberspace is by nature a worldwide construction, the fruit of globalization, of internationalization. The most sensitive systems, including weapon systems, can be designed using off-the-shelf components from potentially enemy countries.

The debate on backdoors has invaded many countries and is not an American-centric concern. In Russia, a counter-terrorism bill filed in 2016 required the implementation of backdoors in all encrypted messaging applications. The law was signed in July 2016 by Vladimir Putin. Corporate resistance to demands by the security agencies seems to be sanctioned, but if we are to believe the figures, this is done moderately: in 2017, the London-based company Telegram was reportedly fined with 800,000 rubles for failing to provide the FSB (Federal Security Service of the Russian Federation) with the access to six encrypted[82] communications. A similar request was reportedly made to the company by the FBI. Telegram's lack of response to the FSB's request could have been due to two reasons: on the one hand, it could simply be technically impossible to access the contents themselves, and on the other hand, this would amount to breaking the Russian law, which recognizes the citizens' right to privacy. The FSB's request was an attempt to expand its influence, to the detriment of the law.

2.3.3.5. *Concrete examples of the introduction of backdoors by the states and crime*

In 1993, the United States tried to impose the use of the Clipper Chip using the Skipjack encryption algorithm, as a tool for encrypting voice and data messages. It turned out that this chip, made by VLSI Technology, Inc., had been conceived and

---

82 See: www.bleepingcomputer.com/news/government/russia-fines-telegram-14-000-for-not-giving-fsb-an-encryption-backdoor/.

designed by the NSA and equipped with an official backdoor for use by local, federal and state security forces. During this operation, the algorithm used was classified, which factually excluded any scrutiny from the research community. The algorithm was declassified and published in June 1998. In the end, this experience did not last long, and was dismissed in 1996, as the system had proven to be inefficient and imperfect, with many vulnerabilities and having been barely used.

In 1999, Andrew Fernandes from Cryptonym Corp (based in Ontario) declared that Microsoft had provided the US NSA with a gateway into Microsoft Windows 95, Windows 98, Windows NT4 and Windows 2000[83]. To use cryptographic applications in Windows, the user had to use a standard architecture named CryptoAPI. However, researchers revealed that to activate this API, there were two keys: one available to Microsoft, and the other apparently assigned to the NSA ("_NSAKEY.") .

What powers could such a maneuver confer to the American authorities?

– Having such a key would enable the agency to penetrate encrypted systems on any Windows operating system.

– Since US law prohibits the unauthorized interception (eavesdropping) of American citizen communications, the means offered to the NSA were more likely to be directed against foreign actors, and even more likely against organizations, companies or institutions; these attacks may have been targeted rather than bulk[84] attacks.

Confronted with such accusations, Microsoft was forced to deny them. But it is clear that it was the company who bore the pressure resulting from these state strategies (confirmed, or not).

The NSA may have pulled the strings to influence the development of a cryptographic standard in the 2000s (Dual_EC_DRBG, Dual Elliptic Curve Deterministic Random Bit Generator). This intervention on standards has been documented since the 1970s (with the development of Data Encryption Standards, DES). The agency was able to influence standardization procedures. But the reconstruction of the various moments of the NSA intervention, and the understanding of the way in which the agency exerts its influence (exactly when, involving which actors) is a difficult exercise. Research on this topic [GAS 16] identified some stages:

---

83 See: www.edition.cnn.com/TECH/computing/9909/03/windows.nsa.02/ [Accessed November 5, 2021].
84 See: www.edition.cnn.com/TECH/computing/9909/03/windows.nsa.02/ [Accessed November 5, 2021].

– NSA presence in meetings of standardization bodies or cryptography research conferences (the NIST (National Institute of Standards and Technology) workshop in 2004, for example);

– the Dual_EC_DRBG generator presented several weaknesses seemingly overlooked by the NIST;

– the hypothesis of the presence of a backdoor in the Dual_EC_DRBG generator was suggested by researchers in 2007;

– the constants which must imperatively be used for the calculations may have been chosen after conferring with the NSA;

– the NSA reportedly paid $10 million to the company RSA Security for it to use Dual_EC_DRBG by default in its BSAFE cryptographic library.

According to Edward Snowden, the NSA systematically injected backdoors in all US ICT (Information and Communications Technology) equipment for export. The agency was also reported to have a catalog of vulnerabilities (discovered by itself or bought) and techniques making it possible to exploit these backdoors in espionage operations. For example, a permanent backdoor is said to have been installed in Huawei routers, not only enabling remote takeover, but also tampering with firewalls. The company Cisco could also have been affected by these NSA practices. The company's chief of security also denied any kind of cooperation with the American intelligence agency [FLÉ 13].

In 2016, the company Juniper Network admitted to having placed backdoors in some of its firewalls to satisfy an NSA request [VIT 20] (vulnerability spotted in 2007 by Microsoft researchers). In doing so, the agency acquired the means for intercepting communication flows. But these methods are not without risk, because they can turn against their users when adversaries (states or criminals) manage to exploit the vulnerabilities introduced into the systems. These situations are poorly documented. It seems that in the case of Juniper, a foreign state (China?) managed to take advantage of the backdoor [VIT 20].

According to a team of researchers [BEI 21], the encryption algorithm "GPRS Encryption Algorithm-1" featured a mechanism for lowering its security level[85]. The results of this university research, published in 2021 [BEI 21], showed that a mechanism for lowering the security level (length of the encryption key) of the

---

85 See: www.01net.com/actualites/le-gprs-l-ancetre-de-la-5g-comporte-une-mysterieuse-porte-derobee-2044700.html?fbclid=IwAR0KzZolw36EYPktERdb2hFa5cQNBGOytzRXU-HTY5-hwOZ_BedkdHoWuSY.

GEA-1 encryption algorithm (GPRS[86] Encryption Algorithm-1) developed in 1998 to secure GPRS communications had been voluntarily introduced. Under certain conditions, the key length could be lowered from 64 bits to 40. The researchers claimed that the fault was intentionally present, and that in no way could decreasing to 40 bits be a fortuitous event: "The attack on GEA-1 is based on an exceptional interaction of the deployed LFSRs and the key initialization, which is highly unlikely to occur by chance. This unusual pattern indicates that the weakness is intentionally hidden to limit the security level to 40 bit by design." It thus became imperative to know: who implemented these faults? Why were the algorithms weakened? How were these vulnerabilities exploited? What were the consequences?

– In 2011, Nohl and Melette analyzed the GPRS security traffic and showed that the signal could be easily intercepted [NOH 11].

– The GEA-1 algorithm was designed by the ETSI Security Algorithms Group of Experts (SAGE) in 1998; six organizations were involved in its development. So, when was the fault introduced?

– The authors postulated that if the system was weakened to 40 bits, this was done to match the threshold chosen for export-dedicated cryptosystems.

– It was expressly required in the algorithm design specification that it should be exportable, in accordance with the restrictions in force in this area, and more specifically, complying with the rules applicable in European countries. It was in compliance with those rules that the algorithm had to provide an adequate level of security against interceptions. While the GEA-1 algorithm may well have been developed under strict export rules, its successor, GEA-2 could have benefited from the relaxation of European legislation the following year.

In a report published in February 2020, the security company ClarSky claimed that Iranian (government?) hackers had hacked VPN servers to install backdoors [CLE 20], the targets being companies and organizations from Israel and around the world, through a campaign that could have lasted a few years. Once the backdoors were installed, hackers could carry out various types of operations against the targets: stealing data, surveillance, purging data, sabotaging systems, etc. The design and use of backdoors are not the exclusive domain of state actors, far from it.

The authorities' practices and capabilities in this area remain secret, even though they are sometimes exposed by way of media revelations. This is how in February 2020, the CryptoLeaks affair broke out. The media revealed that the Swiss company CryptoAG, secretly bought by the CIA and the West German BND in 1970, could

---

86 General Packet Radio Service, a standard widely deployed in the 2000s, associated with the first generation of mobile telephony. Encryption based on GEA-1 and GEA-2 algorithms had the function of protecting GPRS communications from interception.

have supplied many foreign countries, for several years, with encryption tools containing backdoors, allowing the authorities of these two countries to intercept the communications of their customer states.

In an article published in 2012, researchers from the University of Cambridge claimed to have found backdoors in the company-designed Microsemi/Actel ProASIC3 chip (of Chinese origin), which has applications in the military and industrial fields [SKO 12]. This chip was reported to have been used, among others, by the American army. The company of course publicly and immediately refuted the accusations, denying that it had intentionally introduced any backdoors [LEE 12]. The authors of the discovery of this vulnerability detailed:

> This way an attacker can disable all the security on the chip, reprogram crypto and access keys, modify low-level silicon features, access unencrypted configuration bitstream or permanently damage the device. Clearly this means the device is wide open to intellectual property theft, fraud, re-programming as well as reverse engineering of the design which allows the introduction of a new backdoor or Trojan. Most concerning, it is not possible to patch the backdoor in chips already deployed, meaning those using this family of chips have to accept the fact it can be easily compromised or it will have to be physically replaced after a redesign of the silicon itself [SKO 12].

This incident highlights the risks that the users of integrated circuits and semiconductors, produced in foreign countries, by companies whose markets cover many countries, are exposed to in a globalized economy. Interdependence (between technology producers, purchasers and end-users) is all the more pernicious as it is part of an international framework. The discovery of backdoors can be serendipitous, and requires constant, in-depth, extremely complex and costly investigations in terms of human, material and financial resources. Technology users cannot blindly trust the assertions of industrialists – who will always swear that their technologies are safe and snare-free – but have no other choice but to rely, despite everything, on the security guarantee provided by manufacturers.

2.3.3.6. *A state "alliance" in favor of cryptographic backdoors*

Several countries, including India, Japan and the Five Eyes countries (the United States, the United Kingdom, Australia, New Zealand, Canada), signed a joint document in October 2020[87] asking ICT companies to place backdoors in their

---

87 "International Statement: End-to-end encryption and public safety", October 11, 2020 [Online]. Available at: www.assets.publishing.service.gov.uk/government/uploads/system/uploads/attachment_data/file/925601/2020.10.11_International_statement_end-to-end_encryption_and_public_safety_for_publication_final.pdf.

encryption-secured systems to enable authorities to access encrypted communications. The text calls on the responsibility, awareness and action of industrialists, so that they cooperate with the state in order to solve the current dilemma. The goal would be to find the right balance between security (which must be guaranteed to the users of communication systems), and the legitimate freedom of action of authorities in the context of the fight against crime. But today, the latter is weakened, and it is the citizens themselves who suffer: "while encryption is vital and privacy and cyber security must be protected, that should not come at the expense of wholly precluding law enforcement, and the tech industry itself, from being able to act against the most serious illegal content and activity online"[88].

Although end-to-end encrypted applications are especially in the firing line of signatories, all encryption systems are more broadly targeted: "that commitment applies across the range of encrypted services available, including device encryption, custom encrypted applications and encryption across integrated platforms."

The pressure on the industry is continuous, challenged by the states to find the solution to the problem. On the one hand, they impose maintaining the protection by encryption (essential not only for the security of citizens, privacy, and trade but also for safeguarding individuals in authoritarian regimes). On the other hand, they advocate for the access to communications, without compromising the level of communications security. An unsatisfactory hybrid solution, because "there is no such thing as a message that is "sort of encrypted." It's either encrypted or it's not." [LIN 19].

The authorities may seem to ignore the technological reality, because as Bruce Schneier has pointed out: "We cannot build a backdoor that only works for a particular type of government, or only in the presence of a particular court order. Either everyone gets security or no one does. Either everyone gets access or no one does" [SCH 16].

The October 2020 initiative followed the joint declaration by the United Kingdom, the United States, Australia, New Zealand and Canada from July 2019, which specified:

> Tech companies should include mechanisms in the design of their encrypted products and services whereby governments, acting with

---

88 "International Statement: End-to-end encryption and public safety", October 11, 2020 [Online]. Available at: www.assets.publishing.service.gov.uk/government/uploads/system/ uploads/attachment_data/file/925601/2020.10.11_International_statement_end-to-end_ encryption_and_public_safety_for_publication_final.pdf.

appropriate legal authority, can gain access to data in a readable and usable format. Those companies should also embed the safety of their users in their system designs, enabling them to take action against illegal content[89].

The contracting states to this letter have different legal provisions that do not all guarantee the same levels of individual protection against the state's surveillance powers. Opening access implies the exposure of citizens to different practices, changing from state to state:

India currently does not have judicial oversight on surveillance and the Personal Data Protection Bill does not address the issue of state surveillance. This proposal is problematic because it gives excessive powers to the law enforcement agencies of these countries [MEH 09].

These announcements invited manufacturers to discuss and cooperate with state services in order to find a balanced solution. The Council of the European Union engaged in this same approach in October 2019:

The Council urges the industry to ensure lawful access for law enforcement and other competent authorities to digital evidence, including when encrypted or hosted on IT servers located abroad, without prohibiting or weakening encryption and in full respect of privacy and fair trial guarantees consistent with applicable law. Furthermore, cooperation between national law enforcement authorities, Internet providers, Europol and Interpol should be intensified in accordance with the applicable legal framework, for instance by devising mechanisms for the encrypted exchange of information[90].

The real question, on a technical level, is whether such a balance is achievable, whether the development of the possibility of access to encrypted communications by the authorities does not jeopardize the entire security architecture, and whether it is possible to guarantee that only the legitimate recipients of access will benefit from

---

89 Five Country Ministerial, Joint Meeting of FCM and Quintet of Attorneys-General, London, July 30, 2019 [Online]. Available at: www.assets.publishing.service.gov. uk/government/uploads/system/uploads/attachment_data/file/822818/Joint_Meeting_of_FCM_ and_ Quintet_of_Attorneys_FINAL.pdf.

90 Council of the European Union, Council conclusions on combating the sexual abuse of children, Brussels, October 8, 2019 [Online]. Available at: www.data. consilium.europa.eu/doc/document/ ST-12862-2019-INIT/en/pdf.

it. The states' approach strives to achieve the transition from a regime in which backdoors exist but are secretly developed (an unsatisfactory situation because the efforts to be made to achieve this seem very demanding), to an obligation regime, like a Clipper Chip remake (in which the notion of "security by design" is supplemented by an "encryption backdoor design"), whose implementation weight and economic, political and social consequences would rest on the shoulders of the private sector. The challenge is to shift the cost of the effort towards the industrial sector and to turn it, if not into a global issue, at least into an international question, within groups of historically allied countries.

3

Power Struggles

Spanning their conception, distribution, commercialization and use, a large network of individuals, groups or organizations (motivated by their own interests) assembles around interception technologies. Here, we will examine some of the forms taken by the relationships between multiple stakeholders, which sometimes oscillate between constraint and cooperation, but more often reflect power struggles. The state is a central player in this fabric, but its action comes up against obstacles and resistance, imposing limitations on the control of technologies and on control by technologies.

3.1. State pressure on the industry: cooperation or coercion logics?

In the mid-1980s, the FBI became aware of the risk of losing control over the interception of communications, due to the arrival of technologies obstructing this activity [GEN 93]:

> Collecting evidence by wiretapping is becoming difficult because of four growing technologies: (1) the integrated services digital network – an emerging communication system to integrate voice and data; (2) extended cellular telephone communications; (3) encryption; and (4) personal communication networks – advanced cellular telephone communications that will offer new communications services via very small, portable handsets.

In 1992, the FBI wanted operators and telecommunication service providers to ensure that their technologies were not an obstacle to legal interceptions. In 1993, the FBI seemed to reconsider its position. While the FBI emphasized the "national security" variable, economic interests also had to be acknowledged in the equation [GEN 93]. In 1993, the American authorities announced the implementation of an encryption policy (key escrow system, which allows the authorities to access the keys of encrypted communications in order to decrypt them in the context of legal procedures).

In 1998, the United States approved the Digital Telephony Bill, filed on the FBI's initiative. The text established that telecommunication operators were to adapt their technologies for wiretapping interceptions to be possible and facilitated. In other words, they had to be "wiretap compatible"[1], that is, just as accessible as telephone conversations once connected to the line. Not all technologies, such as VoIP, are easily adaptable to meet this requirement. This requirement was concomitantly imposed with CALEA (Communication Assistance for Law Enforcement Act), stating that all digital telephone networks should be adapted.

In India, the Technology Act[2] from 2000, in Section 69 (sub-section (1)), contemplates the possibility of interceptions by the authorities:

> in the interest of the sovereignty or integrity of India, the security of the state, friendly relations with foreign states or public order or for preventing incitement to the commission of any cognizable offense, for reasons to be recorded in writing, by order, direct any agency of the Government to intercept any information transmitted through any computer resource.

In order to remove the obstacle of encryption (or at least partly), the legislator has also incorporated the obligation for the user to cooperate with the authorities in view of decrypting the messages: "The subscriber or any person in charge of the computer resource shall, when called upon by any agency which has been directed under sub-section (1), extend all facilities and technical assistance to decrypt the information".

Refusing to provide this assistance is punishable by a prison sentence of up to seven years.

In the United States, the Jewel versus NSA case (based on revelations from 2006, and therefore preceding E. Snowden's wave of revelations), whereby the EFF sued the NSA for spying on the communications of AT&T subscribers with the latter's complicity, illustrates how state actors – in this case intelligence agencies supported by the authorities who issued the authorizations – were able to exert pressure on telecommunication operators. In this case, the company redirected

---

1 See: www.usask.ca/art/digital/2000/lepage/wiretapp.html.

2 See: www.wipo.int/edocs/lexdocs/laws/en/in/in024en.pdf.

copies of Internet traffic to NSA servers in San Francisco[3]. These practices were revealed by the whistleblower and AT&T employee, Mark Klein[4] who subsequently published a book on the subject [KLE 09].

In the United States, as well as in other countries, companies have an obligation to work with the state's services, in particular with the intelligence services, when required to do so: "Technology control involves controlling the actors in charge of implementing such technology"; "This obligation is based on the Patriot Act [...] these are concerted plans for the control of technology" [THI 13].

During the bulk interceptions which were central to E. Snowden's revelations, the role played by the companies was essential, acting as designers/providers of interception technologies, and as partners for carrying out the interceptions. This last category particularly includes telecommunication and Internet operators, whose contribution seems essential, be it free or forced. For a long time, states have desired to gain access to communications, including in periods of corporate privatization, since the era of telegraphy. This mastery could be enforced temporarily, favored by particular conditions such as war or the threat of revolutionary movements.

This mastery or control over operators can be evidenced in several ways. Monopoly, via the nationalization of enterprises; or when the state grants itself the possibility – by the law – of regaining control over infrastructures, when conditions make it necessary (in particular emergency situations, crises, wars). This is what happened, for example, with the Electric Telegraph Company (ETC), a British telegraph company founded in 1846 by William Fothergill Cooke and John Ricardo, which was the first public telegraph company in the world, and was nationalized in 1870: "In the Act of Parliament establishing the company, the government withheld the right to take over ETC resources in the event of a national emergency. It did so in 1848, in response to Chartist agitation"[5].

This control over telecommunication companies or operators is also operative when the state decides on the level of security that communications may benefit from (the state may be the one in possession of the encryption keys, the one setting key length). Finally, it becomes evident in the operators' legal obligation to make communications "accessible", that is, they can be directly intercepted by the operator or by the state's technical services; be decrypted for the state upon request or made readable by providing the decryption keys. Telecommunication companies

---

3 Jewel *versus* NSA, article published by EFF, www.eff.org/en/cases/jewel [Accessed June 30, 2021].

4 According to Mark Klein's statement, United States District Court, Northern District of California, June 8, 2006 [Online]. Available at: www.eff.org/files/filenode/att/ser_klein_decl.pdf.

5 See: www.stringfixer.com/fr/CS_Monarch_(1830).

are said to "cooperate" with security and intelligence forces, even though such cooperation bears the appearance of a constraint. Over the decades, police services and intelligence agencies have been able to intercept communications by relying on the technical support of telecommunication companies. These situations have been mentioned on many occasions on the press since the 19th century. For long the security forces have been able to intercept communications with the assistance of telephone operators:

> The beginnings of telephone wiretapping occurred in the early and middle 1890's [...] New York police were actively using wiretapping in criminal investigations in 1895. A loose arrangement existed between the New York police and the telephone company whereby the telephone company cooperated with the wiretapping practices of the police department [...] the New York police had the means of listening in on any wire in the entire system of the New York telephone company, and that wiretapping had been engaged in by the police with the cooperation of the telephone company since 1895 [DAS 59].

> By 1894, some indication that New York police officers were intercepting telegraphic communications had reached the public. This was vehemently denied by the Western Union Company [...] in 1916, the telephone company admitted that the police had been wiretapping with the company's cooperation [DAS 59].

> New York police were actively using wiretapping in criminal investigations in 1895. A loose arrangement existed between the New York police and the telephone company whereby the telephone company cooperated with the wiretapping practices of the police department [DAN 59].

The cooperation between companies and the police, with the acquiescence of political power, sometimes led to a scandal, as was the case of the New York police practices revealed in 1916:

> New York was treated to a sensational wiretapping scandal in 1916. It was revealed that the mayor of New York had authorized New York police to tap the telephone conversations of five Catholic priests to obtain evidence for a special New York commission investigating charity frauds [...] The legislative committee learned that the New York police had the means of listening in on any wire in the entire system of the New York telephone company, and that wiretapping had

been engaged in by the police with the cooperation of the telephone company since 1895 [DAS 59].

Cooperation is not always publicly acknowledged:

The police superintendent stated that police could not get cooperation from the Bell Telephone Company in New Orleans. This was contradicted by another ranking officer, and then all the commanding officers, including the superintendent, admitted that they could get any cooperation they wanted from the telephone company [DAS 59].

The Russian SORM (System for Operative Investigative Activities), operational since 1995, uses interception equipment placed directly with the operators. The company Nokia might have been involved[6] in the supply of this lawful interception equipment to Mobile TeleSystems (MTS), a Russian operator. The constraints imposed on telecommunication/Internet operators increased after July 1, 2018, when they were obliged to start storing communication contents, and no longer just the technical data (a set of measures called "Spring Package"). These obligations explain the growth of the cyber surveillance market[7], organized around Russian companies such as MFI Soft, Malvin systems, Signatek, Norsi-Trans and many others.

"Cooperation" can also take stricter forms. Anxious to preserve its market share in China, the American company Apple, ended up giving in to Beijing's demands: all the data belonging to Chinese citizens had to be stored on servers located in China (and not in the United States, as Apple originally wanted), and encryption/decryption keys also had to remain on the Chinese territory, within reach of the authorities.

Are companies in a position to refuse the "cooperation" imposed by the state? Can a company permanently block the pressing demands of intelligence agencies? Lavabit was an encrypted email service created by Ladar Levison, made famous after being used by E. Snowden and the fact that the FBI asked the company to grant access to the contents of the whistleblower's[8] communications. In order not to respond to the FBI's request, the company closed the service, preferring not to call into question the guarantee on communications confidentiality. The service was reopened a few years later, in 2017, offering new features to further strengthen this

6 See: https://techcrunch.com/2019/09/18/russia-sorm-nokia-surveillance/.

7 See: www.handofmoscow.com/2019/08/07/manufacturers-of-means-of-wiretapping-russians-abound-on-the-spring-package/.

8 See: www.theintercept.com/2017/01/20/encrypted-email-service-once-used-by-edward-snowden-to-relaunch/.

confidentiality feature. It included, for example, the erasure of certain email metadata, thereby depriving intelligence agencies of any information on the recipients of communications.

3.2. The accounts of whistleblowers and their analyses of the balance of power between the state, the citizen and companies

3.2.1. *The account of Herbert O. Yardley*

H.O. Yardley published *The American Black Chamber* in 1931 [YAR 31], a book in which he described his years of work as an encryption specialist in the military MI-8 during the war, and after that, at the first civil agency devoted to the interception and decryption of communications during peacetime. At the end of the conflict, the army dismissed this intelligence service, which was nonetheless extended to the civil field, hosted by the Department of State. Thus was created the first civil intelligence agency active during peacetime. Its main mission was to break codes in order to decrypt diplomatic telegrams from abroad. Yardley was placed at the head of this new agency, the "Cipher Bureau", whose premises were no longer set up in Washington but in New York (where several operators with international connections were located). The bureau concealed its activities under the cover of a business company which provided encryption services to banks and enterprises. The bureau was closed under the presidency of Hoover, who came to power in 1928. The reasons for this decision are not well known. The new president wished to act in a fair manner on the international scene. Although the espionage of foreign diplomatic exchanges had been necessary and justified in times of war, it was deemed immoral in times of peace: "I'm glad to see that you recognize that there are certain limits that we cannot exceed in the espionage necessary for the successful operation of your bureau" ([YAR 31], pp. 333–334).

Another reason could be the takeover of these activities by the military. By publishing his book, Yardley sought to draw attention to the power of encryption specialists, as well as the fragility of American communications, which foreign countries were also likely to intercept.

Several questions are addressed in this book, relating to the boundaries which must be (or should be) respected by SIGINT agencies. First and foremost, there is the risk of potential abuse, the absence of clear boundaries and the control to regulate practices: "The Black Chamber made preliminary analyses of many codes that it was never called on to solve" ([YAR 31], p. 334).

Then, there are the technical imperatives, as those described by Yardley, for carrying the efforts of cryptanalysis over time, an essential condition for efficiency:

Only by continuity is it possible to keep up with the changes that the codes of all governments gradually undergo [...] If we read a particular government's messages over a period of years, when the code is suddenly changed, it is less difficult to break the new one ([YAR 31], p. 334).

During the war the American Telephone and Telegraph Company invented a machine that automatically enciphered and transmitted a message over the wire by merely striking the letters of the message on a type-writer keyboard, while the machine at the other end of the wire automatically deciphered the message and at the same instant typed it. Had the enemy at any point between these two machines tapped the wire, he would have intercepted nothing but a jumble of letters. In cases where instantaneous transmission and decipherment was not practicable the operator first enciphered the message by striking the letters on the keyboard and turned the resultant cipher message over the cable company. When the cipher telegram reached the addressee, he adjusted his machine, struck the cipher letters on the keyboard and the original telegram appeared before him. This machine filled every requirement of simplicity of operation, speed and accuracy. But it was not indecipherable ([YAR 31], pp. 363–364).

3.2.2. *The account of Perry Fellwock (also known as Winslow Peck)*

In 1972, Perry Fellwock gave an interview to the magazine *Ramparts* [PEC 72], where he denounced the actions of the highly secretive NSA:

Far less widely known than the CIA, whose Director Richard Helms will occasionally grant public interviews, NSA silently provides an estimated 80 percent of all valid U.S. intelligence. So secret, so sensitive is the NSA mission and so highly indoctrinated are its personnel, that the Agency, twenty years after its creation, remains virtually unknown to those employees outside the intelligence community [PEC 72].

The activity of the NSA was exercised at the margins of international law: "its systematic Signal Intelligence intercept mission is clearly prohibited by the Geneva Code".

The scope of the NSA surveillance of electronic communications was global: "So that not a sparrow or a government falls without NSA's instantaneous knowledge, over two thousand Agency field stations dot the five continents and the seven seas".

But these capabilities obviously raised some questions, because:

> It is almost superfluous to point out that NSA monitors and records every trans-Atlantic telephone call. Somehow, it is understandable, given the size of the stakes in the Cold War, that an agency like NSA would monitor U.S. citizens' trans-Atlantic phone calls. And we are hardly surprised that the U.S. violates the Geneva Code to intercept communist radio transmissions. What is surprising is that the U.S. systematically violates a treaty of its own making, the UKUSA Agreements of 1947.

The article refers to the terms of the UKUSA agreement that provided for three levels of partnership and intelligence sharing. Obviously, the NSA was ignoring the terms of the agreement by authorizing the espionage of communications from its closest allies:

> The U.S. even intercepts the radio communications of its Second Party UKUSA "allies." From the U.S. military base at Chicksands, for example, and from the U.S. Embassy in London, NSA operatives busily intercept and transcribe British diplomatic traffic and send it off for further analysis to DIRNSA.

Many of these practices remind us of the documents disclosed by E. Snowden. They equally recall what Fellwock had already stated: "The NSA, through its sites all over the world, copies – that is, collects – intelligence from almost every conceivable source", practices which the agency obviously never abandoned. The agency is the country's main provider of intelligence (80%). It is only a provider, not a user of the information it produces. According to Fellwock, thanks to the NSA, the United States have absolute control over the entire Soviet information space. The agency was reportedly able to intercept and decrypt all communication and know where the Soviet forces were located at all times. The author called into question the official American discourse alleging the existence of a balance of terror between the Western world and the USSR throughout the Cold War. However, the political argument on the balance of terror was made obsolete by this absolute dominion.

3.2.3. *The account of Mark Klein*

This is the story of the long journey that awaits every citizen persuaded of having a truth to tell, and who will have to confront the powerful in order to do so.

Mark Klein [KLE 09] is a technician who was working at the AT&T operator when the NSA came to install equipment on its premises. Their presence seemed suspicious and Klein quickly understood that the operator had opened up its infrastructure to the intelligence agency, redirecting traffic to the agency's own servers.

The whistleblower was not alone: he found support, and his action was set against a larger framework. Other actors were committed to the same topics. In 2005 journalists James Risen and Eric Lichtblau published revelations in the New York Times.

From the outset, Mark Klein placed himself in the field of political action: the defense of the democratic principles enshrined in the American Constitution. In 2007, the Congress legislated and retroactively legalized the collaboration between telecommunication companies and the state. In the eyes of American whistleblowers, the problem was the large scale surveillance of American citizens. Do denunciations, revelations, trials, accusations affect the functioning and practices of intelligence agencies and states, or do the latter stick to their positions, possibly only modifying the legal framework? The American government reacted to protect the AT&T/NSA relationship, invoking the State Secret Privilege and the Congress ordered the withdrawal of EFF's lawsuit against AT&T.

The dismantlement of AT&T in the 1980s artificially split the company into several regional, local companies, but the telephony giant nonetheless survived, because all of those small structures were physically connected via a vast, long-distance network, switches being made at AT&T.

AT&T's premises at 611 Folsom Street housed these switches, and this was precisely the location chosen by the NSA to place its interception equipment. In the premises, few technicians were present, working in shifts, and sometimes even working remotely from home. Internet cable interconnections were done using Lucent hardware. AT&T's networks were also connected to those of other major operators and to Internet Exchange Points. A NARUS STA 6400-type communications surveillance equipment was connected inside this building.

Cross-checking technical information from reports or technical working documents and observations made in the premises, Mark Klein reconstructed the architecture of the espionage systems set up within AT&T.

Optical-fiber flows were duplicated (using a "splitter"), one being directed to the legitimate recipients and the other towards government machines inside the "secret room". The process was undetectable both from the point of view of the communication's sender and recipient. This method enabled the NSA to intercept practically everything: emails, Internet queries, VoIP, etc.

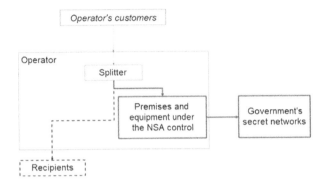

Figure 3.1. *Organization of the interception system within the operator's infrastructure. For a color version of this figure, see www.iste.co.uk/ventre/electronic.zip*

By means of this method, the NSA massively intercepted the communications of millions of individuals, foreign and national and without the slightest distinction.

At the time of Klein's revelations, the Narus company (created in 1997 by Ori Cohen, Stas Khirman and Oren Ariel) did not conceal the fact that it was selling its technologies to the United States, as well as to China, Saudi Arabia, Libya or Egypt [FOG 06]. Acquired by Boeing in 2010 and subsequently by Symantec in 2015, the company provided critical equipment: a traffic analyzer for processing contents, not only metadata. It was the context immediately after September 11, 2001 which provided the company with the opportunity to offer its technologies to American intelligence (even though, in general, the interest of intelligence actors for tools collecting web information preceded the September 11 attacks) [WAR 01]. According to Mark Klein, this tool was a secretly placed "weapon" in the hands of the executive power, without any possible control. American decision-makers pointed the finger against the powers granted to this espionage company and other foreign firms [SAN 12].

Since these revelations, the state does not seem to have modified these projects. On the contrary, it has called for increasingly significant funding for the development of colossal infrastructures hosting data from bulk collections, and to which equally massive processing is applied: infrastructures in the suburbs of Denver in Aurora, in San Antonio in Texas, in Bluffdale in Utah, etc.

Mark Klein denounced the "classic Orwellian double speak", the government's lies. Bush asserted that the tapping or interception of communications was carried out in strict compliance with the law, for which judicial authorizations had been provided, and that only a few hundred individuals were targeted. Playing on words, the government emphasized wiretapping, while omitting Internet interceptions and the scale of the collection. Furthermore, it considered that everything that passes through the Internet is "international", and therefore does not require any authorization for interception.

The amendment of FISA (Foreign Intelligence Surveillance Act) in 2008 (which Klein called the "Immunity Bill") proposed retroactive immunity for telecommunication companies carrying out bulk interceptions and legalized the warrantless interception program launched by Bush in 2002. While the amended law rested upon the principle of immunity for industrial telecom partners, it said nothing about the immunity of state services. On the contrary, state services can abide by the notion of "sovereign immunity" which emerges from the Patriot Act.

This "doctrine" can be summed up by Nixon's phrase: "When the President does it that means that it is not illegal."

From this observation, Klein reached a dark conclusion about America: nothing differentiates the American democracy from the dictatorships it intends to confront: "Wiretapping without warrants, denial of habeas corpus, torture, secret prisons, wars of aggression – all the crimes long associated with dictatorial regimes are now flaunted by the United States government" ([KLE 09], p. 107).

The Obama administration did not change the line traced by its predecessors: "the new Obama administration quickly stepped into the shoes of the former Bush regime without hesitation" ([KLE 09], p. 116).

Successive presidents maintain the same line of conduct and the projects denounced by the whistleblowers are never called into questioned. Their developments continue over many years, gaining momentum and benefiting from increasing resources:

> Congress has ensured that the extensive infrastructure for illegal NSA spying remains in place and in operation. And there have been indications that it has expanded since my retirement. In December 2004 I was told by a reliable source that more Lucent patch panels were being installed at Folsom St. so that the splitter cabinet on the 7th floor could accommodate more data circuits to be copied into the secret room on the 6th floor. Now in 2009 I have heard [...] that the 7th floor itself has become a "secret floor" ([KLE 09], pp. 117–118).

3.2.4. *The account of James Bamford*

In an interview with the academic journal *The Fletcher Forum* in 1983 [BRE 83], James Bamford (author of *The Puzzle Palace* in 1982 and of *The Shadow Factory* in 2009) discussed his vision of the role of the main intelligence agencies (NSA, CIA, NRO), their missions at the service of governments, and their evolution, conditioned by multiple political and financial, internal and external variables:

– Clandestine intelligence is a legitimate activity for the modern state, on the sole condition that it is directed externally. Strictly speaking, the NSA activities are not clandestine because the agency's existence is not hidden, and cannot be so long as the big antennae deployed in the field are visible from afar. Its action is not illegitimate from the very moment that its targets are foreign countries, it is just as legitimate for them to spy on America.

– Intelligence is centuries old, as old as civilization. Clausewitz reaffirmed its indispensability. We cannot therefore call into question this fundamental usefulness of intelligence.

– The role of modern intelligence is to provide governments with a third eye. This view now essentially relies on technological means, human intelligence being less used. The NSA is the main representative of this technical intelligence. Then comes the NRO (National Reconnaissance Office). The CIA lost ground when the profile of spies changed, now basically made up of engineers, technicians and technology specialists. It represented less than 10% of the American intelligence community in 1975. This evolution of intelligence has resulted in a shift of power in agency influence for the benefit of the NSA and the NRO, both dependent on the Department of Defense. If the importance acquired by the NSA is little known to citizens, the fault lies with the media who do not sufficiently talk about it, whereas the information exists and is readily available.

– The American intelligence community does not suffer from a duplication of effort, because each agency is specialized and provides a specific type of information: HUMINT is done by the CIA, SIGINT by the NSA, controlling satellite espionage by the NRO, military intelligence and military analysis by the DIA, State Department intelligence services, etc. These functions are clearly distinct.

– Despite the hierarchical relationship between the NSA and the Department of Defense, the Secretary of Defense has very little direct control over the NSA. The NSA is on the whole very autonomous for daily operations (choice of targets, locations of interception infrastructures) and only really goes to the Department of Defense and the Secretary of Defense for budget control.

– The NSA is not legally supposed to have analytical capabilities (which falls under the CIA) but only collection capabilities. Data from the interceptions are forwarded to the CIA for analysis. But it does not necessarily send the bulk of collected messages to the CIA. Cryptanalysis remains the responsibility of the NSA because it is not part of the human analysis. The NSA is continually increasing its collection capabilities, without a corresponding increase in analytical resources.

– During the Cold War, most of the NSA's efforts and resources were concentrated on the USSR, the number one enemy, to the detriment of other parts of the world where many conflicts and crises were nonetheless taking place. Whole areas of the planet, sometimes sensitive regions, escaped the gaze of the NSA, whose limited means did not allow it to claim to exercise global surveillance, even though it relied on its multiple alliances around the world to broaden its spectrum of vision. These weaknesses, which were the result of strategic choices – political but also financial ones – were undoubtedly one of the reasons why the Iranian crisis or the Falkland conflict came up as a surprise for the NSA.

– In theory, NSA systems are not supposed to spy on the countries hosting the agencies' facilities. But the NSA manages to spy on them indirectly, from facilities located in other countries:

> [...] the Third World is very underwatched. Two of the NSA's most sophisticated listening posts were Traksmen 1 and 2 in northern Iran, which were turned entirely towards the Soviet Union [...] Theoretically, such posts are not supposed to listen to a host country. We could have still listened to them from Turkey [...] ([BRE 13], p. 209).

– The NSA is dependent on the countries where its infrastructures are deployed, and at the same time, it is unable to set them up in sensitive and hostile countries or zones. "One of the problems is that you are really hostage to a host country if you have a valuable listening post there" ([BRE 83], p. 209).

Since then, the agency has attempted to overcome these difficulties by developing more efficient interception systems, to capture data over ever greater distances.

– International relations are permanently evolving. The NSA installed interception posts in China to monitor the neighboring USSR. Since then, the geopolitical scenario has changed a lot, as Bamford had already observed: "To try to make up for the listening post we lost in Iran, we put a new listening post in western China [...] Who knows what will happen with our relations with China – they might take over the listening post like Iran did" ([BRE 83], p. 210).

– NSA targets are not unaware of the existence of this technological espionage. The USSR has learned to counter this risk. "The Soviets allow almost no communication to slip into the NSA net". To circumvent the difficulty of directly intercepting Soviet Union communications, the NSA intercepts that of third countries, in particular in the zones where communications are practically not secured.

– Finally, James Bamford insists on the fact that no charter governs the NSA activities and that all American citizens should be aware of the vulnerability of their communications, which can be intercepted. In foreign countries, no NSA target is unaware of this, whereas American citizens are kept in the dark.

Multiple factors or variables (geopolitical choices, the risk incurred by the countries' infrastructure, the lack of infrastructure sufficiently close to the targets, dependence on third parties, lack of financial resources) constrain the actions of the intelligence agency and decide over its claims. It is therefore not as free in its movements as James Bamford asserts, he who also declines these constraints himself. The trajectory of the NSA over the last few decades can be read as the mark of a constant effort to try to free itself from these constraints, to gain intelligence power as well as freedom of action, by legitimizing the need to cover the entire planet and rule out any possibility of strategic surprises. This approach implies that no security is possible without absolute mastery over the information field, and that collecting everything is synonymous with mastering information and reality, anticipating developments on the international scene.

James Bamford's analysis of the role of the state and its intelligence-gathering agencies can be summarized as follows:

– he emphasizes the operational autonomy of certain agencies (NSA) and the existence of a hierarchy between them (the NSA would thus be placed above the CIA, because it has more resources and is more modern. According to this hierarchy, the SIGINT function would be placed above HUMINT, and signals collection would be above signals analysis);

– he insists on the existence of functional silos:

- agencies have distinct missions (SIGINT, HUMINT, satellite espionage, etc.),

- skills perimeters marking a boundary border between collection and analysis;

– the action of the NSA is legitimate as long as it is aimed at foreign countries;

– the world is divided into three zones[9], which determine the geographical allocation of intelligence resources;

– the probability of strategic risk is proportional to the width of the geographical area covered by the intelligence services;

---

9 For the NSA, the world is divided into three zones or operational groups (according to the information provided here by James Bamford): Group A, essentially gathering the Soviet Union and its communist satellites, Group B comprising communist Asia, China, North Korea and Group G made up of the remaining countries (including the Middle East, the South Atlantic countries and all other parts of the world where crises occur). The efforts in terms of NSA resources are concentrated on Group A, to the detriment of Group G.

– for the NSA, there are several categories of foreign countries: those belonging to one of the three zones, countries hosting the agency's facilities, the targets of surveillance (priorities), those which can be technically spied on, those from where it is possible to spy on third countries (those which are likely to exchange information about the target countries), allied countries, enemy countries, countries at risk, countries with weakly secure communications;

– there is a strong dependence on host countries for setting up interception facilities;

– the choice of targets for interceptions is political in nature, and interception possibilities are constrained by financial resources and capabilities;

– among the constraints influencing the choice of targets, the effectiveness of interceptions and the power of intelligence, we can mention:

- political factors: the geopolitical context, dependence on foreign countries hosting the facilities, developments on the international scene (e.g. requiring the relocation of facilities,

- capability factors (some of which depend on political choices): technical, financial, human capabilities, the ability to intercept the target's communications, and also to collect information about the target itself.

3.2.5. *The account of Babak Pasdar*

Babak Pasdar denounced the same type of interception projects, in which the state tapped into the equipment of mobile telephone operators. In the case described by Pasdar, the project had been carried out in Quantico, Virginia, one of the FBI headquarters for the surveillance of electronic operations ([KLE 09], p. 105).

In his written testimony [PAS 08], Babak Pasdar stated:

– "[…] we came to realize that the client had implemented network devices called 'Network VCR'. They were high performance, high capacity collection devices that recorded all communications traversing any single point on the network. This allowed the client to 'Record' and 'Play Back' any communication between one or more systems at any point in time";

– "[…] I know I saw a circuit that everyone called the 'Quantico Circuit'";

– "I know that it was a third party connecting to the client's network via the 'Quantico Circuit'";

– "the third party had access to one or more systems within the organization";

– "it also would be possible in real-time to tap into any conversation on any mobile phone supported by the carrier at any point".

3.2.6. *The account of Joseph Nacchio*

Qwest was reportedly the only company to have asked the NSA to produce a warrant from a judge to engage in the espionage of its customers and intimated the agency to comply with the FISA law. The fact that this was the only one – or almost – to resist against the NSA illegal requests is indicative of the nature of the cooperation that exists between the private sector and the intelligence agency. According to J. Nacchio, the NSA began to exert pressure on his company in February 2001, several months before the New York attacks. These revelations attest to the anteriority of the extension of the NSA prerogatives as to the bulk collection of communications data within the United States territory, thereby including American[10] citizens. Unauthorized wiretapping could thus have begun well before the attacks of September 11.

3.2.7. *The account of Edward Snowden*

By the time that Edward Snowden disclosed NSA documents via the press and revealed the extent of the agency's practices, several whistleblowers had already preceded him and numerous debates had made it possible to get an idea of the practices of American intelligence actors. The United States' posture is not in itself really a surprise, but is part of an approach that is several decades old.

Snowden's main arguments [SNO 19] combine technological and political dimensions. For him, as for other whistleblowers, the two aspects are closely linked, because the possibilities offered by technologies are used by governments without any restraint, as well as by their intelligence agencies, police forces and security organizations. Whenever technology offers opportunities, governments exploit them. When capabilities are lacking, technology takes one step further or limitations are circumvented by acting on other grounds (legal, economic, etc.). This is what can be deducted from Edward Snowden's speeches, who insists on:

– the failure of oversight: the lack of control opens the door to all imaginable practices, there are hardly any limits, a complete disinhibition from the actors in control of technologies, which makes them all-powerful;

---

10 "Scott Shane, Former Phone Chief Says Spy Agency Sought Surveillance Help Before 9/11", New York Times, October 14, 2007.

– the dissemination of the "American surveillance model", which induces government through fear;

– the balance of power in the domestic front is reminiscent of the relations or confrontations between the king and his princes or vassals. The attitude of companies which overinterpret what the law dictates in terms of opening up their systems to intelligence agencies, reflecting a subordination relationship to a "superior" actor.

From his work, we will retain the following points:

– "During these seven years [...] I was able to participate in the most important change in the history of American espionage – the passage from targeted surveillance to the bulk surveillance of entire populations. Snowden evokes a transition which differs from the one described by J. Fitsanakis during the 1980s–1990s from the analog to the digital, when intelligence agencies and police forces feared losing control on interception possibilities".

– The approach underlying the bulk surveillance: "Making it technically possible, for a government, to collect all the data circulating in the world, to keep them indefinitely and to refer to them whenever they wish". The interception of data is part of a broader process since it is followed by a storage procedure of indefinite duration. The consultation and use of these data involves research, analysis and processing. This approach differs from interceptions carried out within the frame of an investigation, in which retention periods are limited and collections must be as targeted as possible. Long-term storage presupposes that today's data will be useful in the future. It has been long since American politics have ceased to honor Hoover's thoughts of the years 1928–1929 for whom loyalty was essential on the international scene. At that moment, the principle was to intercept diplomatic communications only under specific circumstances and as little as possible (war).

– The reason for bulk surveillance could have its origin in the failure to anticipate the attacks of September 11, 2001. As from that moment, the protection of America imposed the need to know everything. The CIA entered the cyber world after the attacks in New York, but by the end of the same decade, it still had very few specialists: "From 2007 to 2009, I was assigned to the American Embassy in Geneva. Under diplomatic cover, I was one of the few specialists in charge of bringing the CIA into the world of tomorrow" ([ASS 12], p. 10).

– "The year I turned 26, I was officially employed at Dell while I was again working for the NSA" ([ASS 12], p. 11). Intelligence agencies maintain close relationships with their companies, with the latter serving as a cover for the agents.

3.2.8. *The account of Julian Assange*

The book *Freedom and the Future of the Internet* ([ASS 12], p. 10) reflects upon the assertion of the state's power, a project in which the exploitation of the Internet plays a considerable role. Two categories or spaces are opposed: on the one hand, those who intercept (the states), and on the other hand, those who are the object of the interceptions (companies, citizens). The authors denounce a balance of power, a relationship based on state violence. They argue that the state distills its poison into society:

> The state would leech into the veins and arteries of our new societies, gobbling up every relationship expressed or communicated, every web page read, every message sent and every thought googled, and then store this knowledge, billions of interceptions a day, undreamed of power, in vast top secret warehouses, forever.

The state seeks to maximize its power by the all-round and intensive exploitation of data and information:

> It would go on to mine and mine again this treasure, the collective private intellectual output of humanity, with ever more sophisticated search and pattern finding algorithms, enriching the treasure and maximizing the power imbalance between interceptors and the world of interceptees.

The logic underlying interceptions changed during the years 1990–2000, when it shifted from targeted or even bulk interceptions aimed at certain groups or specific actors, to a logic of permanent interception of every communication, the data collected being stored for possible ulterior use. Current interceptions are part of the long term, data being available and usable today, tomorrow or in a few years. This is how new actors have emerged in the interception landscape: not only companies participating alongside states in the deployment of large-scale interceptions, but also companies offering storage solutions commensurate with the volumes of data collected, as well as companies offering data analysis solutions. The complexity of systems has reached such a point that any control practices would be impossible: "And the technology is inherently so complex, and its use in practice so secret that there cannot be meaningful democratic oversight".

The only way to counter this company of domination in the information space would reside in cryptography, which poses a real challenge to the state because "it is easier to encrypt information than it is to decrypt it".

The generalization of encryption, its systematic use all over the world, might be the only way to escape the coercive force of states. Through encryption, the project consists of creating a new space, where massive interception is impossible, useless, free of any control state. Encryption is a weapon, a political tool, "the ultimate form of non-violent direct action".

3.3. Limits imposed on the state's power to control technology

3.3.1. *The difficult and fragile international regulation of technologies*

In its definition of the scope of dual technologies and related regulations, the European Commission incorporated cyber surveillance technologies (reformulation dated September 28, 2016 on the export rules of dual technologies, aimed at preventing technologies from having a legitimate use in the context of legal interception, from being provided to authoritarian regimes or from enabling human rights infringement)[11]. In the document[12] from September 2016, the Commission proposed modifying the definition of dual technologies and to integrate the particularities of new technologies, including cyber surveillance, which had not been the case until the Wassenaar Arrangement:

> Cyber surveillance technologies shall mean items specially designed to covert intrusion into information and telecommunication systems with a view to monitoring, extracting, collecting and analyzing data and/or incapacitating or damaging the targeted system, including items relating to the following technologies and equipment:
>
> – mobile telecommunication interception equipment;
>
> – intrusion software;
>
> – monitoring centers;
>
> – lawful interception and data retention systems;
>
> – digital forensics[13].

---

11 Proposal for a Regulation of the European Parliaments and of the Council, setting up a Union regime for the control of exports, transfer, brokering, technical assistance and transit of dual-use items (recast), Brussels, 28.9.2016, COM(2016) 616 final, 2016/0295 (COD) [Online]. Available at: https://eur-lex.europa.eu/legal-content/EN/TXT/?uri=CELEX%3A52016PC0616.

12 This document materializes the intentions made explicit since 2011, in particular following WikiLeaks revelations on the activities of Amesys in Libya.

13 Ibid note 11.

The initial proposal for the regulatory reform provided for a broader set of categories: mobile telecommunication interception equipment, intrusion software, monitoring centers, Lawful Interception (LI) systems and data retention systems, biometrics, digital forensics, location tracking devices, probes and Deep Packet Inspection (DPI) systems[14].

The international scene is organized through multiple treaties, agreements, conventions, on the most diverse themes, from the management of common goods (Global Commons) to economy, war, cooperation in terms of policing or justice, ecology, security in the oceans, telecommunications, the activities of man on the Moon, etc. Thus, the sole question of the management of the environment has been addressed by 1,000 international treaties [BIE 20].

The Wassenaar Arrangement organizes a global control system for the export of dual technologies and armament. As with all international treaties or conventions, the Arrangement makes it possible to distinguish two spaces: that of the countries which submit to it and the others, the ones that do not adhere because they consider that the rules defined therein do not go into sense of their interests [RAJ 16].

The interests and priorities of the United States have strongly influenced the rules defined in the Arrangement. Before Wassenaar, there was the COCOM (Coordinating Committee on Multilateral Export Controls) bringing together 17 Member States and headquartered in Paris, a mechanism instituted at the beginning of the Cold War to limit and regulate technology transfers from developed countries to developing countries. The COCOM disappeared at the end of the Cold War. Decades later, a successor was proposed: the Wassenaar Arrangement, which took shape in 1995, with 41 members. This agreement is one of the first, if not the first, to establish a post-Cold War international security framework [DAV 96]. The Arrangement[15] was the fruit of five phases of negotiations, conducted under the initiative of the United States and the Clinton administration from 1993, and lasting two years. The ambition was to increase transparency and the level of responsibility of states to develop these markets. The European and Pacific countries and the United States constitute the nucleus of the Arrangement. However, Russia was also a signatory, as well as the countries from Central Europe. This agreement reflects the concerns of states against new threats following those of the Cold War, and the need to avoid the anarchic proliferation of weapons of mass destruction. The first

---

14 Deep Packet Inspection (DPI) systems "used to examine the content of data as it passes through a communications network"; "DPI systems are also employed when a state bypasses standardized Lawful Interception processes through the use of a 'tap' or a 'black box' ('probes and DPI systems are also used in a range of non-surveillance technologies and systems')".

15 The exact title is "The Wassenaar Arrangement on Export Controls for Conventional Arms and Dual-Use Goods and Technologies".

goal was to prevent any export of sensitive equipment to four states: Iran, Iraq, Libya and North Korea. The Arrangement is based on the principle of checks to be carried out by each of the Member States. Today, this international mechanism coordinates export policies for conventional arms, dual technologies and sensitive technologies. Two lists, collectively defined by the members, classify all the technologies concerned: the list of ammunition, the list of dual-use goods and technologies.

State control aims to prevent the export of sensitive technology to non-member countries. This implies that the technologies whose export is authorized have been filtered by the state services. It is therefore rather difficult to imagine that governments would authorize the export of arms or technologies they were unable to control.

The legal framework for interceptions had to manage the transition from analog telecommunications (wired, wireless) to digital ones, adapting pre-existing frameworks to the new Internet context. A modification was deemed necessary – within the framework of the Wassenaar Arrangement – following WikiLeaks revelations from 2011, which detailed the commercial practices of European companies who had sold solutions to authoritarian regimes. It is from the Arab Spring and from the action of whistleblowers that the expression of this need for a regulatory change was born. In 2011 and 2012, the European embargoes concerning arms exports to Iran and Syria integrated cyber surveillance technologies. The Wassenaar Arrangement was modified in 2012 and 2013, including some surveillance technologies in the list of dual technologies[16]: jamming equipment, mobile telecommunication interception equipment, IP network monitoring systems and intrusion software.

It would appear that the circumvention of export restrictions regarding interception tools is relatively easy: for example, it is possible to acquire tactical interception equipment on the Internet [PAG 16]. The effectiveness of the Arrangement is difficult to measure. Some argue that the Arrangement is more theoretical than practical. The reasons for this weakness are multiple [WIN 01]. It could be due to the absence of a binding mechanism. In fact, there is no obligation to transpose the principles and standards of the Arrangement into the laws of the Member States having adhered to the agreement. The Wassenaar Arrangement does not have the status of a law or a treaty. It is only an agreement that aims to strengthen the sharing of information between members. Major states (e.g. China, Brazil) are also absent from this agreement, so it only partially covers the

---

16 The list of dual technologies is available on the official website wassenaar.org: www. wassenaar.org/wp-content/uploads/2016/12/WA-LIST-16-1-2016-List-of-DU-Goods-and-Techno logies-and-Munitions-List.pdf.

international system. The Arrangement does not require export control of encryption applications on the networks. In spite of these weaknesses, and despite the absence of a binding system, we observe that many Member States having adhered to the agreement play the game, transpose the rules into their national laws, carry out checks; we should also mention that states not having adhered to Wassenaar adopt principles inspired in it (e.g. Israel).

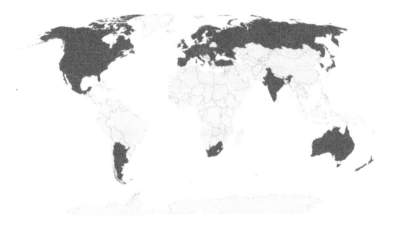

Figure 3.2. *Map of states taking part in the Wassenaar Arrangement (compiled from data published on Wassenaar.org)[17]. For a color version of this figure, see www.iste.co.uk/ventre/electronic.zip*

The debates that emerged in 2012–2013 regarding state surveillance practices sparked discussions between the members of the agreement [GOO 16]. In 2013, adhering members agreed on measures to restrict IP network surveillance systems and intrusion software. The goal was to prevent the proliferation of cyber weapons. The Arrangement was amended accordingly, by introducing the notion of "intrusion software" as well as a list of types of technologies to be placed under control.

In 2015, through the BIS (Bureau of Industry and Security), the United States attempted to transpose these elements into their national law. The conditions provided for by the Arrangement and by the American legislation were coldly received by industrialists and researchers in cybersecurity, who believed that the conditions were too drastic and would prevent the legitimate sharing of cybersecurity information at an international scale. The United States then tried to renegotiate the Wassenaar Arrangement in 2016 [KOS 17]. The European Union also wanted to implement these Wassenaar measures, but differentiating the software that should be subject to controls while preserving the possibility of

17 Online data on Wassenaar.org, February 2022.

conducting vulnerability research, thus sparing "ethical" hackers from legal proceedings. According to the European Parliament:

> Not every technology requires controls, and the exports of technologies that actually enhance human rights protection, such as encryption, should be facilitated [...] the current level of control on encryption runs counter to the fact that encryption is a key means to ensure that citizens, businesses and governments can protect their data against criminals and other malicious actors, to secure access to services and to enable secure communications, including for human rights defenders. It is therefore appropriate to further facilitate the export of encryption [SCH 17].

The European Parliament thus opposes to the checks justified by national security, a form of liberalization of encryption tools in the name of human rights, of "Human Security". The EU addition of surveillance technologies to the list of dual-use goods subject to export controls proved to be essential with regard to this human security criterion:

> Dual-use items (especially cyber-surveillance technology) are often used both to directly commit human rights violations, but they can also facilitate other serious human rights violations. Such as when illicitly obtained information of human rights defenders or journalists is used to subsequently detain and/or torture them [SCH 17].

However, the European posture does not explain how it manages to combine the defense of human security (which legitimizes the free circulation of encryption) and national security (for which encryption is an obstacle).

Germany added interception technologies to its lists from 2015 without waiting for the EU, which was accused of slowness [BOH 17].

These measures were taken to limit the possibilities of access from certain countries to technologies likely to be instruments of human rights abuses. But these states will nonetheless be able to acquire the technologies, despite international texts, whether they are EU or Wassenaar measures. Several circuits remain accessible to them: offers from companies located in non-member states of the EU or of the Arrangement – a parallel illegal market.

The offer is plethoric, customers are spoiled for choice. We also refer to the notion of "proliferation" to designate the dynamics of this surveillance technology market, which is also globalized [BOH 17].

In the industrial sector, there are always companies that pay little heed to the nature or identity of their customers, whether or not they are authoritarian political regimes. The Israeli company Verint Systems Ltd was accused by Amnesty International of having sold systems used for illegal surveillance operations to the authorities of South Sudan, resulting in pressure on journalists, creating a climate of terror and limiting press[18] rights.

3.3.2. *Illicit markets and the circumvention of laws*

A major international market for interception and Internet surveillance technologies has taken shape over the past two or three decades. The international regulation of technology exports (and the Wassenaar Arrangement, in particular) has only fairly recently incorporated interception/surveillance technologies.

3.3.2.1. *The multiplication of actors and of interception means*

The last three decades have been marked by the proliferation of actors capable of intercepting communications, as well as the producers of interception technologies. At the same time, the communications space vulnerable to interception has expanded.

In addition to its traditional actors (police forces and intelligence agencies), the surveillance ecosystem thrives with companies designing and distributing interception systems, among which some are relatively unconcerned about their customers' profiles and exploit the sometimes too loose meshes of the regulatory net, thus contributing to the proliferation of these technologies worldwide. Businesses have learned to play with circumventable rules. Markets are international and merchants sometimes pay little attention to the political or ethical considerations in their customers' choices. The consumer ecosystem of interception technologies extends to the criminal and the ordinary citizen who, benefiting from free tools available on the Internet, can take over just about any smartphone, intercept their targets' communications and spy on their private life. However, the dissemination phenomenon of interception techniques is not specific to the beginning of the 21st century. Interceptions seemed quite common in the 19th century ("Shortly after the telegraph came into existence and wires were strung from pole to pole, wiretappers were busy intercepting the coded communications" [DAS 59]) to the point that states were required to legislate on the matter: "As early as 1862, California found it necessary to enact legislation prohibiting the interception of telegraphic messages" [DAS 59].

---

18 See: www.israeldefense.co.il/node/48142.

3.3.2.2. *Interception technology producers from the private sector*

Lawful interception represents a fruitful market for the industry (further data on the development of these markets around the world are provided in the Appendices to this book). Businesses specializing in interception technologies market products whose capabilities are presented as practically limitless, if we are to believe their commercial discourse. The offer is rich worldwide. Companies offer multiple interception "solutions" to LEAs; "interception and surveillance solutions", Internet monitoring systems comprising software and hardware elements, capable of processing many Internet protocols:

– systems that can be installed at service providers, national platforms, making it possible to process several thousand targets at the same time and to find new targets thanks to heuristic analysis, monitoring wired and mobile telephone networks ("2G, 3G, WiMAX and other wireless and wired IP networks"[19];

– subscribers surveillance;

– contents interception;

– targeted or bulk interception;

– monitoring of cybercafé networks, SSL traffic interception;

– Wi-Fi interception capable of scanning multiple channels, handling all Internet protocols and applications (email, webmail, instant messaging/Chat, FTP, P2P, http, etc.)[20].

The technologies marketed promise to handle all Internet protocols, all formats (data, sound/voice, image/video), a variable number of targets, ranging from a few units to high volumes. Not only do these technologies capture all of this information, but also they sort it out, analyze it, etc. Some companies[21] wish to go past the notion of lawful interception and speak of "cyberintelligence", instead. The question is no longer to monitor only a telephone line, intercept the exchanges between two computers, two fixed or mobile telephones, but to adapt these interception practices to the reality of modern communication uses, where one individual can use many tools, several applications at the same time, switch from one to another, etc. Cyberintelligence aims to monitor these uses in real-time, to collect data in a broader environment and to offer a comprehensive, multidimensional and also real-time approach.

Technically, on paper at least, the authorities have practically unlimited capacities.

---

19 See: www.isolvtech.com/product/ip-intercept/.

20 See: www.edecision4u.com/WIRELESS-DETECTIVE.html.

21 See: www.aqsacom.com/technology/overview/.

3.3.2.3. *The spyware market*

Spyware or stalkerware are a:

> type of malicious software (malware) that collects information from a computing system without your consent. Spyware can capture keystrokes, screenshots, authentication credentials, personal email addresses, web form data, Internet usage habits, and other personal information [...] Spyware can monitor nearly any activity or data related to your computing environment. This is not limited to files on your hard drives but can also include temporary data such as screen shots, keystrokes, and data packets on connected networks[22].

Spyware makes it possible to collect traffic data:

> Network traffic is another valuable source of data. Data commonly extracted from network captures includes user names, passwords, email messages, and web content. In some cases, entire files can be extracted and reconstructed from the captured streams[23].

Keyloggers allow them to "target instant messaging clients, email applications and web browsers"[24].

Cases implementing such tools were revealed over the last decade and even further back: in July 2009 the "Interceptor" spyware (developed by the SS8 company) was installed on the customers' BlackBerrys of the UAE Telecommunication operator. To proceed with this installation, the operator supposedly asked its customers to perform an update. Using spyware, the NSA is able to intercept communications from iPhones, as shown in Operation Dropoutjeep, revealed in 2013[25].

3.3.2.4. *The sale of surveillance systems to authoritarian regimes*

Not only is the "legal" market of surveillance technology (of which interceptions are just a part) in itself already important and constantly growing, but also the news of recent years, mainly since 2010, has shed light on yet another facet of the business: the sale of surveillance technologies to countries with authoritarian regimes.

---

22 See: www.us-cert.cisa.gov/sites/default/files/publications/spywarehome_0905.pdf.

23 See: www.us-cert.cisa.gov/sites/default/files/publications/spywarehome_0905.pdf.

24 Ibid.

25 See: www.appadvice.com/appnn/2013/12/operation-dropoutjeep-the-nsa-can-intercept-iphone-communication-through-spyware.

In 2013, the British company Sophos Safeware sold Utimaco[26] to investors from Germany (Pinova Company) and Luxembourg (BPI Investment Partners). This sale took place after Utimaco was called into question for having sold interception[27] technologies to Iran, and a few years earlier to the Syrian regime.

In 2009, Nokia Siemens Network (NSN) was also singled out for supplying Iran with lawful[28] interception systems. Nokia and Siemens were reported to have integrated the Utimaco application into their solutions. Shortly after, it was the turn of the Italian company Area to become suspected of the same business practices, and later on, the Chinese companies Huawei[29] and ZTE (which allegedly provided DPI – Deep Packet Inspection – systems to Iran). A few reports have been compiled to list the companies involved[30].

Neither the existence of sanctions nor any consideration on the nature of the regimes to which the systems are sold seem to deter some companies from trading[31]. DPI systems sold to ISPs give them real power over users, monitoring all of their communications, a kind of "omniscient" power [COO 11]. Some revelations and lawsuits have been followed by regulatory change, including the Wassenaar Arrangement, after the Amesys case. The investigation on Amesys had been dismissed in 2011 for two reasons: on the one hand, the legislation did not expressly prohibit the export of its Eagle application, because it did not fall into the category of war materials. And, on the other hand, being considered interception equipment for export and not for use in the national[32] territory, it could not be subject to authorization. France only manifested its desire to control the export of surveillance technologies after the Amesys affair. It is in this context that the addition of these technologies to the list of dual-use goods was proposed and adopted by the Wassenaar Arrangement. This stage must all the same be followed by an incorporation of the principle into the national legislation of Member States having

---

26 See all the interception technologies marketed by the company on its website: www.lims. utimaco.com/fr/solutions/solution-lawful-interception-management/.

27 See: www.privacyinternational.org/blog/1561/giant-leap-backwards-corporations-divesting-toxic-surveillance-companies.

28 See: www.s3.us-east-2.amazonaws.com/defenddemocracy/uploads/documents/Tools_of_Oppression_Memorandum_-_7.7.20111.pdf.

29 See: www.reuters.com/article/us-huawei-iran-idUKBRE8B409820121205.

30 See: www.fidh.org/IMG/pdf/monitoring_technology_made_in_europe-1-2.pdf;   www.fuchs. uti.at/wp-content/uploads/DPI.pdf.

31 See: www.privacyinternational.org/blog/1561/giant-leap-backwards-corporations-divesting-toxic-surveillance-companies.

32 Libya, the Amesys affair, Fidh report, March 2016, no. 643f, 24 pages [Online]. Available at: www.fidh.org/IMG/pdf/l_affaires_amesys_2016_fr-web2.pdf.

adhered to the Arrangement. The basis of these regulations is the risk of infringement of the individuals' fundamental freedoms.

3.3.2.5. *Pegasus: targeted interception of mobile telephony*

The Pegasus/NSO affair is interesting in that it illustrates the modes of "cooperation" between industries and states, as well as the essential role played by interception technology companies in the security and national defense landscape, not to mention in political espionage. These are companies that do not produce cybersecurity apps or tools, but only "aggressive" applications, that is, weapons.

The business practices of the Israeli company NSO, which provides the Pegasus tool used for spying on the mobile phones of thousands of people around the world by various governments (case made public in July 2021 in the international press), reveal several important points:

– Trade ignores ethical issues. Regardless of the consequences that the use of their products may have on individuals, for companies, doing business comes first.

– Businesses, providing multiple states, no matter which, directly or indirectly cooperate with the latter.

– Could the Israeli company have been able to supply several governments in the world without the approval of the authorities in its own country?

– The skills used for developing lawful interception applications can be used for more legally questionable interception products.

– Espionage technologies make it possible to circumvent security systems. End-to-end encrypted messaging does not avoid the kind of espionage made possible by Pegasus.

– Bringing to light the *modus operandi* of Pegasus opens the door to all kinds of speculation: how many other interception and espionage tools, systems, programs exist around the world? What capabilities do intelligence agencies have? Are they potentially even more intrusive?

– The absence of strict regulation on interception, intrusion, espionage technologies gives a large margin of maneuver to companies, as well as to states themselves. However, no one, except of course the direct victims – some of which no doubt indulge in the same practices that they condemn – has any real interest in regulating strictly.

– Companies such as NSO take part in the proliferation of cyber weapons.

– The software is officially sold as a tool for lawful interceptions, to track down criminals and help fight terrorism. But these tools can be easily diverted from this use. There is even no need to adapt or transform the application. As it is presented, it can serve several purposes. The company will probably try to protect itself behind this argument, according to which it is not responsible for regarding the misuse of its application. But this defense will not hold.

– We can consider that more global espionage strategies, to fight embarrassing actors for the powers, guide these operations. We may even consider that states need information gleaned from other countries, and that data have been given in exchange.

– What can the targets, the victims do? Not much to prevent this type of attack, and only a few things on the legal level. Espionage is invisible.

– The cyber surveillance actions of individuals can turn into repressive physical actions against them.

– What is behind the term "lawful interceptions"? The systems provided for these interceptions can be diverted from their use and serve interceptions that go beyond this legal framework. Besides, the notion of "legality" probably does not convey the same meaning everywhere.

The NSO company had already been talked about before 2021. It was accused by Facebook of spying on its WhatsApp messaging app in October 2019. In relation to the Pegasus spyware, it had already been discussed in the media at the end of 2019. The main concern was that the application had been sold to spy on journalists in several countries.

Pegasus can be installed on a phone by a simple call, even though the called party does not answer the phone.

NSO's practices were again under public scrutiny in July 2021, when the French company Amesys was taken to court for its past activities. At the same time, and although it cannot be considered at the same political level or similar practices, the United States and Europe accused China of carrying out cyberattacks against their interests and threatened to launch potentially destructive counter-attacks. This accusation could of course be turned around because those states had been in a permanent confrontation for years and their speeches resembled a game of reflections, each accusing the other of what it practiced itself. China could probably have as many grounds for accusing the Western world.

It is therefore in a global context of "militarization", of "weaponization", of cyberspace proliferation that the Pegasus/NSO affair was positioned, and it should be analyzed as such, before worrying about the intrusions into privacy or into the political life of foreign states.

The case illustrates the internationalization of markets, the real absence of "frontiers" and of blocking regulations, despite international agreements such as the Wassenaar Arrangement. The market is global, no matter where the technology comes from, no matter who it will be sold to, the underlying logic is not that of a reason guided by ethics, morals or fundamental principles, but that of commerce. Political etiquette is not an obstacle, either. The Chinese authorities were reported to have invited a member delegation of the Brazilian congress belonging to the far right party PSL (*Partido Social Liberal*) in order to sell them surveillance technologies (facial recognition, drones, etc.)[33]: "NSO is not the only private company exploiting such weaknesses and offering commercial exploitation services"[34].

A report from the American DHS referred to a great international bazaar of cyber weapons[35].

Although the espionage revelations of thousands of people around the world in July 2021 caused a stir, the company had already been accused of its intrusive practices in previous years.

The Pegasus tool seeks to trick its targets by sending them misleading messages. There is a succession of practices in the process that relate either to intelligence uses or to those of crime.

The effects produced by these industrial and state practices are multiple. They give rise to disputes, legal proceedings, critical speeches and necessarily produce effects in terms of image, not only on the companies themselves, but also on the states who use, host and support these companies, all accused of supporting dictatorships[36]. These practices fuel the idea that globalization is necessarily wild, unbridled, without rules, ultimately only producing monstrosities, relationships that are merely driven by motivations such as immediate financial interest, the rule of the fittest ignoring all morals and all the principles that are supposed to characterize democracies: selling to dictators rather than letting others take market shares, while withholding the possibility of spying on them.

---

33 Fact reported in www.alsur.lat/sites/default/files/2020-04/Al%20Sur%20-%20The%20 Surveillance%20Industry%20and%20Human%20Rights_.pdf.

34 See: www.ntsc.org/assets/pdfs/cyber-security-report-2020.pdf.

35 See: www.dhs.gov/sites/default/files/publications/ia/ia_geopolitical-impact-cyber-threats-nation-state-actors.pdf.

36 See: www.bdsquebec.ca/wp-content/uploads/2018/10/Haaretz_IsraelCyberSpyIndustry-2018-10-19.pdf.

We should also note that "espionage"/"surveillance", became a social phenomenon in the 1980s. We cannot honestly be surprised at state practices that the citizens themselves have been able to adopt, thanks to technologies made available to them[37]: "infinity bug" to listen to what is happening in a nearby apartment... Espionage within everyone's reach became a possibility in the 1980s, but had been the subject of fictional stories long before (remember the series *Spy vs. Spy* in *Mad* magazine during the 1960s, a parody of the ideology of the Cold War).

The export vendors of surveillance technologies (IMSI-Catcher, IP intercept systems) know how to circumvent the bans or control systems imposed by their states, by using third countries or third-party partner companies through which the contract can be legally carried out. The resale or distribution of the product is no longer the company's responsibility a priori. When making the law, states cannot have ignored this possibility of circumvention.

While it was the Israeli company NSO who made it to the news, it cannot be the only one on a global market to have developed without any real possible control from the state. It may even have developed with the approval of the same states supposed to regulate the markets for these interception technologies. Other companies market and supply states with spyware around the world: the Italian company Hacking Team, or even the French company Amesys, accused of having sold spyware under the Gaddafi regime in the early 2010s. This market became scandalous after the fall of the regime. Previously, it had developed in a context of rapprochement or relations reconstruction between France and Libya. Was this market illegal? Was it legal, but morally or ethically reprehensible? Strictly speaking, were the tools provided by Amesys interception tools or flow analysis tools?

The authors of the report "Surveillance Technology at the fair: proliferation of cyber capabilities in international arms market" [DES 21] identified companies whose cyber technologies can be considered as belonging to the arms market. They emphasize the "problematic" nature of this offer because the capabilities they market make room for possibly hazardous practices both for individuals, organizations, allied states, internationally and on a domestic scale. This market operates mainly in a discreet way. Interception solution providers are a subset of the surveillance market. These companies are present in arms fairs all over the world, open to all business opportunities, regardless of geopolitics or the nature of government regimes who acquire such technology. It can also mean that several countries share the same type of technology.

---

37 See: www.bugsweeps.com/info/spytech.html.

Companies such as NSO, Amesys or Netsweeper have in common their location in democratic countries, which does not prevent them from trading with authoritarian regimes. Democracies bring their legislation into line with international law, the latter adapts, evolves as technology progresses, but in a certain way, law permanently lags behind technology. The states seem to grant marketing authorizations only after laws have been voted or agreements ratified. They prefer to be the leaders of these markets than to give way to other powers.

The principle seems simple: all states equip themselves with surveillance products. Then, it is imperative to maintain control of this market because the vendors mastering these technologies have power over their customers, which is strategically essential when the latter are foreign governments.

One of the challenges for the legislator who wishes to regulate the use of spyware is to penalize illegal uses, without penalizing some of its legitimate and lawful uses. In fact, the applications that are offered to parents to enable them to monitor the Internet practices of their children, hardly deviate in their functioning from spyware used for communications espionage:

> Another challenge that we face as legislators is ensuring that our responses to the growing spyware problem don't penalize legitimate uses of similar information technology designed to monitor and prevent unauthorized activity. For example, programs designed to help parents monitor the online activity of their children and legitimate online marketing techniques all use similar technology in an inoffensive and legal manner[38].

3.4. Trust

The encryption of exchanges, that is, modifying messages in such a way as to make them incomprehensible to anyone other than those for whom the message is intended, has always been the defense against interception, whether for private messages or for military communications. Today, cryptography is presented as the unstoppable weapon to ensure the confidentiality of exchanges. But to what extent is security is guaranteed? How much can we trust the mechanisms implemented to protect exchanges from prying ears?

---

38 See: www.ia802906.us.archive.org/16/items/gov.gpo.fdsys.CHRG-109hhrg99899/CHRG-109hhrg99899.pdf.

3.4.1. *How much confidence in encryption?*

Great cryptologists have always had contrasting opinions on the security provided by encryption. On the one hand, in 1585, Vigenère described the vanity of deciphering, that is, decryption without knowledge of the alphabet, a real "brain break" and ensured his great trust in the possibility of secure encryption: "There will be enough impregnable and invincible ways of ciphering against those who will not have its secret".

In contrast, in July 1841, in an article published in the *Graham Magazine*, Edgar Poe expressed his doubts about the possibility of safe encryption: "We say again deliberately that human ingenuity cannot concoct a cipher which human ingenuity cannot resolve".

These two extreme positions are perfectly defensible. The Vigenère cipher was for several centuries presented as unbreakable, ensuring throughout this time absolute trust, until finally resolved in the mid-19th century, confirming Poe's verdict. Everything would ultimately be a matter of time.

Encryption designers, often overconfident in the inviolability of their invention, present it as inviolable. However, even the most reliable encryption systems have been successfully broken, as the following examples will show.

During World War I, the German officer Fritz Nebel (1891–1977) conceived the ADFGVX cipher, named so because only those letters appeared in the cryptograms. It was used by the German army at the end of World War I. Although reputed to be solid, this cipher was manually solved in the French cipher section in 1918, by George-Jean Painvin (1886–1980). This accomplishment was kept secret until 1968. On this date, on the occasion of the inauguration of a room in the Invalides Museum devoted to the Great War, for the fiftieth anniversary of the 1918 armistice, the two men met. Painvin revealed to Nebel that he had read most of the encrypted messages unencrypted, leaving the latter in the deepest perplexity.

During the Soviet–Polish War of 1929, the Polish encryption bureau, headed by Jan Kowalewski (1892–1965), helped by mathematicians like Waclaw Sierpinski (1882–1969), regularly decrypted Soviet messages, made up essentially of super-encrypted mono and bigrammic substitutions. This achievement gave the Poles a decisive advantage for driving the Russian threat away from Warsaw. This unlikely victory was called the "miracle of the Vistula", named after the river that crosses the Polish capital.

During World War II, the Nazis had great trust in their cipher, produced by a revolutionary electromechanical machine, the Enigma. Mechanization had multiplied the possibilities of encryption. The material was simple enough to be usable on the battlefield, but exploded the number of combinations and reinforce the feeling of security. However, as from 1933, the work of Polish mathematicians (aided by documents obtained by the French intelligence and thanks to mathematical methods) made it possible to reconstitute the secret military version of the machine used by the Wehrmarch. During the conflict, the decryption factory mounted by the British at Bletchley Park managed to solve the Enigma cipher and regularly decrypt the German messages, thanks to significant human and material resources. While the Nazis did have a few alerts concerning the abnormal amount of messages that should not have been found in clear, and trusting the security of their methods, they persuaded themselves that espionage was the cause.

The RSA public key encryption method published in August 1977 in Martin Gardner's mathematical games column was publicized as "A new kind of cipher that would take millions of years to break". However, it was solved 17 years later[39].

3.4.2. The acceleration of calculations as a factor of confidence

The history of these decryptions shows a great dissymmetry between encryption and its attack. In the case of the Enigma machine, encryption was done by a machine weighing a few kilograms, operating with batteries and portable to the battle front. On the contrary, the Bletchley Park center required an industrial organization, hiring up to 10,000 people, endowed with enormous material resources. Machines occupying several rooms and consuming several kilowatts of electricity were set up to perform massive calculations, impossible to carry out manually in the urgency of the battles.

The integer factorization from Martin Gardner's article was the work of a team that ran over 600 computers in parallel, whereas RSA encryption is often performed on a simple smart card that fits in a pocket.

We may think that with the evolution of computer performances, it will be increasingly easy to lead attacks and that trust in encryption will decrease over time. But this idea is wrong! The increase in computing power mainly benefits encryption. If, for example, technical progress provides calculators twice as fast, allowing us, for example, to add 10 binary symbols to a secret key, the attack by exhaustive search will require a calculation whose complexity is multiplied by more than a thousand, far more than double of what the technique offers. Contrary to popular belief, advances in computing power contribute to greater robustness for encryption. Beyond the rudimentary example given above, as long as the attack is more complex

---

39 See section 2.2.4.

than the encryption, which is the least we can expect, the progress of the means of calculation will favor encryption to the detriment of the attack.

Should this progress accompany our growing trust in cryptography?

Unfortunately, other factors come into play.

3.4.3. *Abandoning secret methods*

Originally based on secret methods, the development of cryptographic procedures has evolved towards ever greater transparency, and this can only strengthen our trust. In the past, "cabinets noirs" instituted secrecy as the main source of confidence. Although this approach was strongly questioned by Kerckhoffs at the end of the 19th century – for whom a cipher was only good if it "did not require secrecy" and if it remained "indecipherable for the master himself who had invented it" – certain procedures have been kept secret until in recent times, leading to many setbacks.

For example, the procedures implemented for the first bank cards remained secret for a long time. However, this did not prevent Serge Humpich (born in 1963), computer and electronics specialist, from disassembling the software of a bank terminal purchased as scrap in 1998. He then discovered a secret related to the production of bank cards which is based on a 320-binary digit RSA key, a size clearly insufficient for the calculation means of the time. He factorized the key using Japanese software retrieved from the Internet and managed to produce a fake card allowing him to buy metro card and train tickets from a vending machine. He tried to negotiate his know-how with the GIE bank cards, but instead was convicted for falsification. The lesson has been understood. Today, the EMV standard – Europay Mastercard Visa – for bank cards is public and freely accessible on the Internet[40].

As for GSM telephony, the voice flow was originally encrypted by an algorithm called A5/1, introduced in 1987. The definition of this algorithm was kept secret. Its architecture was published in 1994 following leaks and in 1999, reverse engineering made it possible to reconstruct all its details. After its disclosure, many faults were discovered. In 2000, a real-time attack was published, requiring two minutes of traffic at the cost of heavy precomputation. Its improved version in 2003 only required a few seconds of encrypted stream.

---

40 See: www.emvco.com.

Pay-TV is one of the last areas in which conditional access providers to paid TV shows have protected the secrecy of their know-how. This industry experienced a huge wave of piracy from 1993 until the early 2000s. What really happened was more a faulty implementation than a real mathematical fault.

The video flow encryption algorithm, DVB common scrambling, was introduced in 1994 and kept secret until 2002. Faults were discovered and then exploited in 2004 (differential fault analysis), and were improved in 2011 (known-plaintext attack).

The above-mentioned examples show that a secretly devised cipher by a bureau having only a few designers, even though brilliant ones, is unlikely to be very robust. When the algorithm is revealed, by the analysis of a piece of equipment, by espionage or by mathematical analysis, faults inevitably appear and are exploited until the security of the whole system is called into question.

The modern approach to the design of encryption methods combines public design and assessment, like the DES and AES standards. However, this does not prevent the discovery of faults subsequent to the deployment of algorithms and protocols.

Public design and assessment make it possible to highlight any weaknesses, which are then the subject of corrective measures. After a sequence of fault finding and corrections, we can hope that over time, the process will acquire increasing security and robustness. But how much analysis is needed before we can achieve total trust? For how long will the process be considered safe?

In November 1993, version 1.5 of the public key cryptography standard PKCS#1, defining a padding scheme for RSA, was published by the company RSA Laboratories. Five years later, in 1998, Daniel Bleichenbacher (born in 1964) published a method that enabled an adversary to decrypt any message by an effective attack at selected cryptograms, taking advantage of the information on decryption failure.

In 1988, cryptologists Benny Chor (1956–2021) and Ronald Rivest (born in 1947) published a public key encryption based on the knapsack problem, which withstood several attacks until Serge Vaudenay (born in 1968) published an algebraic theory attack in 1998, marking the end of the attempts to exploit this type of problem for ciphering.

The Vigenère cipher, published by Jean-Baptiste Porta in 1563, remained indecipherable until the Prussian officer Friedrich Kasiski (1803–1881) published an attack on it exactly three centuries later, in 1863.

So do we have to wait five years? Ten years? Three centuries?

Once the algorithm has been defined by a standard, how long does this algorithm remain usable? The GIE bank cards maintained the 320-binary digit RSA keys designed in 1983 until 1998 (i.e. for a duration of 5–10 years), which made the attack by Sergei Humpich possible.

The "empirical design–attack–correction" loop can become infinite, making the quest for absolute security an illusion. Even this approach had to be called into question.

3.4.4. *Provable security*

For this reason, this approach has been called into question, bringing out the notion of proof of security. The object is to match any figure, from its conception, with an argument establishing its security.

The first formalizations date from the mid-1980s with the work of Shafi Goldwasser (born in 1958) and Silvio Micali (born in 1954), pioneers in cryptographical theory. This theory established that symmetric encryption is equivalent to an axiom of the existence of one-way functions, that is, of efficiently computable functions, except that for a random value, it is difficult to find a preimage leading to such value. This existence is today only a hypothesis based on experience and not on evidence.

It is currently not possible to efficiently find the factors of a product of two large prime numbers. Multiplication is a one-way function. If the factors are lost, it is practically impossible to find them if the number is too large. The current factorization records is that of a 250-decimal digit number, found in February 2020 by the INRIA team in Nancy, which required the use of the *Jülich Supercomputing Center* and over 2,700 years of CPU time. Given the complexity curve, the factorization of a 500-digit number seems inaccessible with the current means. The power of conventional computers seems to be reaching its limits today and little progress is to be expected in this sense. Everything points to granting great trust to current methods. But what about new quantum technologies, which are the subject of extensive research? Especially when it has not been proven that factorization is an intrinsically difficult problem. The foundations of the cryptographic edifice seem very fragile.

Let us go back to the question of the proof of security in cryptology. The provable security of encryption comes down to demonstrating that if an adversary exists, it can be used as a sub-program to solve a difficult problem, that is, a problem we do not concretely know how to solve today. The contrapositive of this implication is to logically establish that, as long as the difficult problem in question has no solution, the adversary against encryption does not exist.

But what is a difficult problem?

"A difficult problem is a problem that no one is working on", cryptologist James Massey (1934–2013) suggested as a joke. Complexity theory defines it as a problem for which there is no solution found by an efficient algorithm, that is, whose complexity is bounded by a polynomial of the size of the data processed. This does not involve a concrete impossibility for a given size key, but implies asymptotic behavior when the size of the key tends towards infinity. The proof of security is therefore the asymptotic reduction to a reputedly difficult problem.

Concluding on the security for a concrete given size key is a much more delicate problem which often has no practical answer.

For these reasons, the concept of proof of security has been strongly called into question by researchers such as Neal Koblitz (born in 1948) or Lars Kundsen (born in 1962). According to Koblitz [KOB 07], the word 'proof' refers to certainty, and is therefore not suitable for security: "to nonspecialists 'provable security' means that there's a guarantee that's every bit as ironclad as a proof of the Pythagorean Theorem. In our view this is very misleading". Indeed, the term proof or theorem used in mathematics means an absolute and indisputable truth. This is not the case in theoretical cryptography. He continues: "Unlike in mathematics, where conditional theorems usually mean something like "assuming that the Riemann Hypothesis is true" (which it almost certainly is), in cryptography the condition is of the sort "assuming that no one finds an improved algorithm for a certain math problem" – and that's anyone's guess. Koblitz prefers to speak of a security argument, and we cannot prove him wrong. Especially because sometimes the proof is false.

In 1994, Mihir Bellare and Phillip Rogaway proposed a mode of use for any type of public key encryption, called OAEP (Optimal Asymmetric Encryption Padding), to make it resistant to chosen cryptogram attacks. It applies two rounds of a Feistel scheme like those used in the DES rounds. This mode was accompanied by a proof of security. For this reason, it was adopted in the EMV standard along with the RSA, then incorporated into version 2.1 of the PKCS#1 standard in 2003.

In 2001, Victor Shoup discovered that the proof was false and launched an attack with a particular public key encryption, causing great concern in the banking community. To correct the proof, it was necessary to add an additional hypothesis about the encryption function – the function had to be "one-way separable". Did the RSA satisfy this additional hypothesis?

In 2003, Hieu and Pointcheval proposed a modification of the mode of use – with three rounds instead of two – which makes it possible to dispense with this additional hypothesis.

At last, in 2004, Fujisaki, Okamoto, Pointcheval and Stern finally proved that the RSA function satisfies the necessary additional hypothesis that would ultimately make the RSA with OAEP safe.

But the proofs assume that the functions used in this mode of use are so-called "random oracles", that is, functions that behave as if the value were the result of a random draw, which is not the case in practice since these functions are always the result of a calculation. The random oracle model is contested in the cryptologic community because it is considered to be unrealistic.

Trust provided by provable security is ultimately relative, because it is based on very hazardous hypotheses, such as the existence of one-way functions, which can be called into question by research results, leading to a collapse of cryptology. The Catacrypt[41] Congress (*Catastrophic event related to cryptography and security with their possible solutions*), held annually from 2014 to 2017 and sponsored by major organizations including public key cryptology is at the heart of the activity and testifies to this fragility.

In conclusion, these results from theoretical cryptography are neither effective nor complete proofs of security for algorithms, nor do they constitute provable security for communication systems. These are only arguments that can eventually build trust in a process or an algorithm. Lars Knudsen ironically states: "If it is provably secure, it is probably not".

3.4.5. *The worlds of Impagliazzo*

The notion of difficulty in solving a given problem is based on complexity theory, which followed the work of Turing and Church on computability. Its

---

41 See: www.catacrtypt.net.

development during the second half of the 20th century led to the distinction of several classes of problems, depending on the difficulty in solving them. As the quality of encryption is based on this difficulty, quite naturally, research in cryptology became interested in this theory. Thus, class P problems are those for which there exists an efficient algorithm of resolution, that is, running on a deterministic Turing machine whose complexity is bounded by a polynomial of the size of processed data. These problems are the ones that we know how to solve in practice, provided that the degree of the polynomial which limits the complexity is not too high. This should be the case with the encryption or decryption of a message when the key is known.

Another notable class is class NP (Non-deterministic Polynomial). It covers the problems for which there is an efficient resolution algorithm on a non-deterministic Turing machine. Such a machine may include several possible choices at each unwinding step. NP problems are also the ones that can be solved efficiently on machines with unlimited execution parallelism or problems for which there is a deterministic algorithm for verifying the efficient solution. It is clear that class P is included under class NP, but surprisingly, it is still not known whether such inclusion is strict or not. The difficulty of finding or showing the absence of a problem belonging to class NP without belonging to the class P led to the famous conjecture P = NP which is one of the still unsolved great problems of the millennium prize, proposed in 2000 by the Clay Institute of Mathematics.

Integer factorization is a problem belonging to class NP, since the solution is easy to verify by a simple multiplication. It is therefore still unknown whether or not it belongs to class P. The only algorithms known until now running on a classical computer have a complexity far superior to polynomial complexity. The difficulty of factorization is today only a hypothesis, solely based on our ignorance of an effective algorithm for solving it. We currently live in a world where – in practical terms – P is different from NP, without it being possible to say whether this situation will last. Research can either prove the intrinsic difficulty of factorization, which would prove that P is not NP or find an efficient factorization algorithm. In the first case, current cryptography would be strengthened in its security, whereas in the second case, it would collapse.

An NP problem is said to be complete if all the NP problems can be reduced to it in an efficient way. They appear among the most difficult problems of this class. In their seminal article, Diffie and Hellman invited researchers to find public key encryption procedures based on this type of problem, such as the knapsack problem. This problem involves finding, within a finite list of integers, those whose sum reaches a given value. Several proposals were brought forward, all of which were successively broken, with practical instances of this problem being on average easy to solve. This lead was eventually disregarded. Research is now thriving with the application of other NP-complete problems, such as finding a short vector in a lattice (Shortest Vector Problem), as well as so-called post-quantum cryptography, which will occur when the quantum computer becomes real.

An NP-complete problem is only hard in the worst case, but what is expected from applicable problems for encryption is an average level of difficulty, the key being randomly chosen. This theory, developed by Leonid Levin (born in 1948) [LEV 86] inspired researcher Russel Impagliazzo (born in 1963) with the possibility of five different worlds, depending on the type of problem it is possible (or not) to efficiently solve there [IMP 95]. Impagliazzo illustrated the guided tour of his five worlds through the use of cryptography, and also by a metaphorical staging of the character Grouse, an imaginary teacher of the young Gauss, who wanted a quiet and lasting peace in his class by posing a problem he considered difficult: finding the sum of the numbers from 1 to 100. According to Impagliazzo's narration, after being humbled by young Gauss's quick response, the unfortunate professor spent the rest of his days, to the point of madness, searching in vain for a problem that might end the arrogant success of his brilliant student. Here is the presentation of the five hypothetical worlds:

– Algorithmica: this world is the one that will happen if we prove that P = NP. We can produce an efficient solution to a problem from a verification algorithm to this solution. No cryptography is not possible there, since decrypting without a key has a complexity comparable to decryption with a key. Knowing how to factorize amounts to knowing how to multiply. Grouse cannot trick Gauss with any problem, since the latter can find the solution with the verification algorithm. On the contrary, information technology is revolutionized, since it can effectively solve a considerable number of practical problems.

– Heuristica: a world where NP problems are hard to solve only in the worst case. On average, the resolution remains accessible to an efficient algorithm. In practice, this world is almost in every respect comparable to Algorithmica. The difference lies in the existence of rare practically insoluble problems. But these problems are inapplicable to cryptography, being themselves difficult to find. The average time to solve a difficult problem will remain comparable to time needed to find it. The time to design an encryption proposal will last as long as this encryption remains safe. It will take longer for Grouse to find a problem that will get Gauss into trouble, than for Gauss to solve it.

– Pessiland: according to Impagliazzo, this world is the worst that can happen. There are average difficult problems, but there is no one-way function. It is possible to produce difficult instances of problems, but it is not possible to produce ones whose solution is known. In Pessiland, Grouse may present Gauss with a difficult problem, but he will be unable to offer a solution. Since symmetric encryption assumes the existence of one-way functions, Pessiland does not allow for any effective cryptography. This annoying world combines all the disadvantages.

– Minicrypt: in Minicrypt, one-way functions exist. Symmetric encryption is possible there, but not public key encryption. Two correspondents must first agree on a secret key before communicating discreetly. A one-way function can be used to pose a difficult problem, randomly pulling an item x, by calculating its image $y=f(x)$, and asking to find a preimage of y. In this world, Grouse holds his head high while proposing this challenge. He can also proudly display the solution to the amazed class and achieve a certain victory. Cryptographic Theory shows that in Minicrypt, signatures with asymmetric keys, a private one for signing and the public one for verifying, are possible.

– Cryptomania: practically our current world. Functions remain one-way, except for holders of additional information, called a hatch, which allows them to be reversed. Public key cryptology is possible. Two correspondents can agree on a shared secret, by publicly exchanging information. A public key can encrypt while decryption will be reserved for the holders of a private key. This world sees the triumph of Grouse to humiliate Gauss by posing a difficult problem to everyone and delivering an indication to the rest of the class who will be able to solve it effectively, whereas for poor Gauss, the problem will remain definitively insoluble. In Cryptomania, the possibilities of cryptology are limited only by the imagination of the designers: electronic voting, anonymous digital currency, public manipulation of encrypted data. The level of intimacy of the private sphere is not limited by technology, but only by political decisions, which dictate the knowledge of the hatches.

This guided tour of Impagliazzo ends with a cry of alarm: if an efficient factoring way were to be discovered, then not only would most cryptosystems fail, but there would be no systematic way to design a secure alternative.

Despite several centuries of research since Fermat, no effective factorization algorithm has emerged. No theoretical reason is known today for stating that factorization is an intrinsically difficult problem. Today, confidence is based on our ignorance.

3.4.6. *The contribution of quantum computing*

The security of exchanges is yet threatened by another method: the eventual advent of the quantum computer. The latter carries a different computing model from the one used by the Turing machine, that of our current computers. Remember (see section 2.3.3) that for this new quantum model, in 1994, the researcher Peter Shor (born in 1959) from AT&T published an algorithm which bears his name and which makes it possible to factorize integers with quadratic complexity in time and space.

The machine currently remains at the stage of a theoretical research model, but if it were to see the light of day, it would render obsolete the RSA and other arithmetic-based encryption systems. The numbers that we currently know how to factorize using this technology are trivial and we are still very far from being able to break the RSA, but it is very difficult to estimate the progress that can be achieved with this technology. Research remains very active in this area.

3.5. Conclusion

This book has brought to light the plurality of technologies, actors and interactions between them.

3.5.1. *Technologies*

Three categories of technologies are mainly at stake: communication technologies, interception technologies in the strict sense and technologies for securing communications, whose purpose is to prevent the access to contents by third parties uninvited to the exchanges. These technologies are distributed as follows, in the diagram of interceptions (as was posited it in the introduction to this work) (see Figure 3.3).

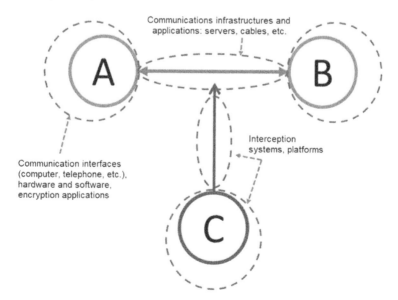

Figure 3.3. *Diagram of interceptions and technologies. For a color version of this figure, see www.iste.co.uk/ventre/electronic.zip*

3.5.2. *Actors*

The actors are also numerous: the scientist and the engineer (the one essential for his theoretical knowledge and the other for its application), technology designers, technology vendors, their customers and end-users (states, private, lawful, legitimate or, on the contrary, criminal actors, etc.), their opponents (citizen movements, politicians), their regulators, those who decide on the limits of the application and dissemination of technology (legislators, states), without forgetting the creators of standards (standardization bodies).

A, B and C are users, consumers of technologies who sometimes have power over such technologies, technological choices and their evolution, but this, to varying degrees, is never on the whole of the technological spectrum.

This whole technological environment depends on the state of knowledge, discoveries and therefore on researchers and engineers.

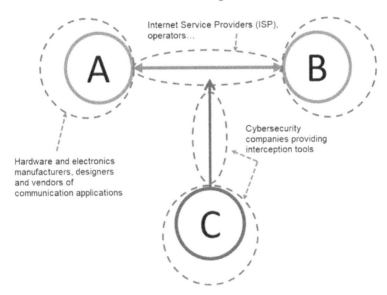

Figure 3.4. *Diagram of interceptions and technology actors. For a color version of this figure, see www.iste.co.uk/ventre/electronic.zip*

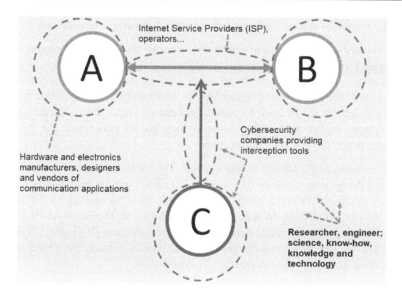

Figure 3.5. *Interception technologies are dependent on the evolution of scientific knowledge. For a color version of this figure, see www.iste.co.uk/ventre/electronic.zip*

3.5.3. *Interactions or relationships*

The interactions or relationships are multiple between all these actors. These interactions or relationships are built around practices, tactics or strategies developed by each of the actors at their level.

Among the possible interactions, there are:

– those of cooperation, for example, between the companies and states (David Lyon says they "work in tandem")[42], because the industry has at least two elements in hand that the state does not always have directly: interception technologies and communication technologies, over which the interception takes place (access providers, telecom operators)[43];

– information sharing between the states and the police or intelligence services;

---

42 David Lyon in "Surveillance after Snowden", p. 132.

43 Remember that this relationship of obligation imposed over the company is not specific to our current period. Since the privatization of postal and telecommunications services (telegraphy), this type of state–companies relationship has always taken place. The state has always been aware of the essential nature of communications and has never ceded this power to access information.

– the weight of actors, state and private, on standardization processes;

– international cooperation efforts to control the trade of interception and encryption technologies.

However, not all of these relationships or interactions are cooperative ones. A lot of room is left for the balance of power between divergent interests and conflicting relationships. Power relationships arise, which are of two types: the "power to" (capacity, potential) and the "power over".

– The "power to", defined by the systemic theory of power, as the attribute of an actor and the general capacity of a system [GOE 81] can be broken down into: the creator's power to conceive, the power to disseminate, to market, to distribute, the power to use, to decide, to authorize and prohibit, to regulate and to influence. Informational power is defined as an ability to influence [NYE 96]. Power is of course also broken down into the power to monitor or control, the power to control information, and to reduce informational asymmetries.

– The "power over" defined by the relational theory of power as a relationship between two or more actors, as a place of interplay resulting in interactions, resistance, and influence [WEB 47] is translated as a power over individuals (those who create, innovate), over citizens or politicians, over companies, over markets, etc., and also power over information, over data, or over spaces (territories, states, networks, infrastructure, etc.).

– At the forefront of these balances of power, we have insisted on the relationship between states-telecommunication companies, because while it can be characterized as "cooperative", it can also be interpreted as the constant pressure exerted by the state over private players in the sector. To keep a grip over part of the power which slipped from its hands two to three decades ago, in Western countries, the state is trying to influence the construction of technical standards on algorithms and the design of encryption tools. Despite the official rhetoric, states are probably resorting to backdoors more often than they claim.

– Technically, the state arrogates the power to intercept everything, or almost everything it wants. The only boundaries are technological and financial. They are also legal, when the law imposes restrictions, draws impassable limits, whose respect has to be guaranteed. Police or intelligence services nonetheless continue to proclaim their impotence in the face of the generalization of cryptography, which prohibits access to contents and reduces the effectiveness of their action, even though interception practices primarily targeting metadata seem to suffice. But metadata are not enough on all occasions. The state is suffering from the consequences of the policies it introduced in the 1990s and 2000s, both the privatization of telephone and Internet operators, and the liberalization of cryptology. It should be noted, however, that this situation is not universal, many states, with retaining the control over telecommunications and cryptology.

– On the international scene, the state often appears motivated by the defense of its own interests and resorts to all means, including unfair ones (when "allied" states wiretap each other's communications; when states turn a blind eye to businesses bordering with legality; when states hide behind private technology companies to better trap not only the adversary but also allied countries; the technology which, as E. Snowden described in *No Place to Hide*, is systematically tapped with before being exported). While Snowden's description features American practices, the observation is probably generalizable.

– Power lies not so much in the interception itself, as in cryptography (the power to block the access to contents) and cryptanalysis (the power to break codes and access the contents). The encryption capability is now widely shared, the real power lies more in cryptanalysis. Security rests on foundations that are perhaps more fragile than it appears. The security provided by cryptography and the trust we can grant it comes up against two obstacles. The first one is functional. The implementation of encryption protocols is ensured by the communications system and not by the actors themselves, who thereby lose control over their level of protection. It is not at all clear whether the functional hypotheses upon which the security of cryptographic solutions is based, such as the randomly unpredictable and confidential nature of encryption keys, are satisfied. The second obstacle is theoretical and mathematical. The advent of public key cryptography, which communications on the Internet network made necessary, changed the basis of protection. There was a shift from security based on the secrecy of encryption keys to security based on the computational impossibility of accessing private data enabling the reconstruction of unencrypted messages. While this computational impossibility seems effective today, it has not been demonstrated and we cannot rule out the fact that technical or algorithmic progress could lead to a security breakdown. This was evident by the existence of the Catacrypt[44] workshop, dedicated to this eventuality. Cryptographic Theory, which aims to clarify the foundations of its security, today only rests on the admitted existence of difficult problems, such as the factorization of large integers, whose solutions are difficult only because of our ignorance of an efficient solution. In terms of technology, current research on quantum computers, the existence of which would destroy the security of most current cryptographic solutions, also shows the potential weakness of current protections.

---

44 Catastrophic events related to cryptography and security with their possible solutions – www. catacrypt.net.

Appendices

A.1. Legal texts

Country	Text title	Year
America	*All Writs Act* (AWA)[1]	1789
France	On December 27, 1851, a decree following the law from August 1, 1851, was signed, regarding the repression of contraventions, misdemeanors and crimes relating to telegraph[2] lines	1851
International	Article 17 of the Convention of June 1855 (France, Belgium, Prussia) establishes the principle on the secrecy of (telegraphic) communications	1855

---

1 In 2015, the FBI proposed to refer to this text, which allows the federal courts to impose decisions in the interest of the law, so that a court ordered Apple to create ways for circumventing the encryption systems of iPhones.

2 The text provides penalties for anyone found guilty of having, recklessly or unintentionally, committed a material act that could compromise the electric telegraphy service; to have degraded or deteriorated, in any way whatsoever, the apparatus of the electric telegraph lines and the machines of the aerial telegraphs; of having (by the breaking of wires, by the degradation of apparatus or by any other means), deliberately caused the interruption of telegraphic electric or aerial correspondence; of having, in an insurrectional movement, destroyed or rendered unfit for service one or more wires of an electric telegraph line; of having broken or destroyed one or more telegraphs, or of having invaded, by means of violence or threats, one or more telegraph stations, or of having intercepted by any other means, with violence and threats, the communications or the telegraphic correspondence between the various agents of public order; or of having opposed, with violence or threats, the re-establishment of a telegraph line; attacks or resistance, with violence and assault, towards inspectors and surveillance agents of the electric or aerial telegraph lines, in the exercise of their functions. Heavy fines and prison sentences punished all these misdemeanors.

Country	Text title	Year
France	Law from June 13, 1866[3]	1866
International	Saint Petersburg Convention from July 10–22, 1875[4]	1875
India	*India Telegraph Act*[5]	1885
United States	Olmstead Judgment. 277 US 438 (1928). The Supreme Court rules that a wiretap is not a "search" under the meaning of the 4th amendment because it does not imply a physical intrusion on private property. "Private life" is not addressed by this judgment, any more than it is explicitly mentioned in the 4th Amendment[6]	1928
United States	*Congress is invited by the Court to enact statutory prohibitions on telephone wiretapping*	1928
United States	*Communications Act*[7]	1934
United States	*Communications Act of 1934*[8]	1934
France	Encryption means were governed by the decree/law of April 18, 1939 establishing the regime for war materials. Cryptography was considered a war weapon, and its use prohibited except by derogation	1939
International	UKUSA[9] Treaty	1946
International	Agreement creating the CoCOM[10]	1949

3 The general public can exchange encrypted messages on the French territory.

4 Enables encrypted communications for international telegraphic communications.

5 See: https://dot.gov.in/sites/default/files/the_indian_telegraph_act_1985_pdf.pdf.

6 The challenge of this judgment was to demonstrate whether the evidence compiled from tapping violated the 4th amendment to the US Constitution or not. The court decided that was not the case. Olmstead requested that the elements brought against him be declared null and void because they had been drawn from wiretaps targeting him. His main argument concerned the illegality of the evidence gathered through telephone tapping, constituting, according to him, a "physical search or seizure". For the courts, tapping was in no way a physical intrusion. The evidence compiled from telephone tapping was therefore admissible by the courts. It took several years before the notions of privacy and invasion of privacy were introduced, opposed wiretapping practices, and envisaged a stricter framework for the latter. See Katz vs. United States, 1967.

7 See: https://transition.fcc.gov/Reports/1934new.pdf.

8 "No person not being authorized by the sender shall intercept any communication and divulge or publish the existence, contents, substance, purport, effect, or meaning of such intercepted communication to any person".

9 This treaty laid the foundations of an International ROEM (Echelon) network.

10 Wassenaar was to succeed CoCOM in 1996.

Country	Text title	Year
United Kingdom	*Birkett Report*	1957
Australia	*Telephone Communications (Interception) Act*	1960
United States	*Katz vs. United States*[11]	1967
Germany	Law on tapping. August 13, 1968	1968
United States	*Omnibus Crime Control and Safe Streets Act*[12]	1968
United States	*Wiretap Act* (18 U.S.C.§§2510-22[13] (aka Title III))[14]	1968
United States	*Title III of the Omnibus Crime Control and Safe Street Act of 1968* (42 USC § 3789d) – The Federal Wiretap Law	1968

11 It was one of the first times, if not the first, that the Supreme Court affirmed the existence of the concept of privacy in the 4th amendment to the US Constitution. In this decision, the Supreme Court considered telephone tapping to be an intrusion into privacy ("searches", in the sense of the 4th amendment). The judge recalled that the 4th amendment protects individuals, not places.

12 See: https://www.govinfo.gov/content/pkg/COMPS-1696/pdf/COMPS-1696.pdf. This law governs telephone tapping in the context of judicial police investigations (Title III).

13 "Regulates the interception of content in real-time. It addressed interception of conversations using 'hard' telephone lines, but did not apply to interception of computer and other digital and electronic communications". Concerns interception of electronic and wire communications, which include "any aural transfer made in whole or in part through the use of facilities for the transmission of communications by the aid of wire, cable, or other like connection". "An oral communication is 'any oral communication uttered by a person exhibiting an expectation that such communication is not subject to interception under circumstances justifying such expectation'; this constitutes any oral conversation in person where there is the expectation no third party is listening".

14 "The statute regulates both government actors and private parties and it imposes strict limitations on the use of devices to intercept 'oral communications' or 'wire communications'. Prohibits the real-time interception of 'content' of any wire, oral, or electronic communications, unless an exception applies or investigators have a 'super warrant' interception order. Makes it a crime for someone who is not a party to the communication to intercept content in real-time". Envisages three communications categories: wire communications paragraph 2510 (1), (18): communications that carry the human voice and pass through wires (telephone calls, VoIP, etc.); oral communications paragraph 2510 (2): recordings of human voice, the person recorded is in a private situation; electronic communications paragraph 2510 (12): those that do not contain the human voice; includes almost all computer transmissions. The document defines several important concepts, including that of "content" – paragraph 2510 (8): "content [...] includes any information concerning the substance, purport, or meaning of that communication".

Country	Text title	Year
Australia	*Telecommunications (Interception) Amendment Act*	1973
France	Creation of the French Control Commission of Administrative Services implementing Telephone Tapping (June 1973). Its function was to "verify the missions assigned to the services ensuring the surveillance of certain private telephone communications, the human and material resources assigned to them, [to] assess in detail the quantity and quality of the tasks they perform and [to] ensure the compliance of these tasks with the laws and regulations in force" [MAR 73][15]	1973
United States	President Gerald Ford banned the CIA from using electronic and physical surveillance means to collect information about the domestic activities of US citizens; banned the NSA from intercepting communications made within, from or to the American territory, except legal electronic surveillance authorized by the judge (*Attorney General*)	1976
United States	*Fisa Act*[16]	1978
United States	*Foreign Intelligence Surveillance Act* (Fisa) of 1978. Defines the scope of SIGINT operations by the NSA: "FISA regulates the intentional acquisition of communications to or from unconsenting USPs, wherever such persons may be located, and also regulates certain collection techniques, particularly techniques used against persons located inside the United States"[17]	1978
United States	*Foreign Intelligence Surveillance Act* (Fisa). One of the key points of the law concerns the legality electronic surveillance for foreign intelligence purposes	1978
United States	*Foreign Intelligence Surveillance Act of 1978* (Fisa)	1978
Australia	*Telecommunications Interception and Access Act* (TIA Act)	1979

---

15 These lines were taken from the first report of the new Control Commission, presented to the Senate in 1973 [Online]. Available at: www.senat.fr/rap/r73-030/r73-0301.pdf.

16 See: www.govinfo.gov/content/pkg/STATUTE-92/pdf/STATUTE-92-Pg1783.pdf.

17 See: www.nsa.gov/Portals/70/documents/news-features/declassified-documents/intelligence-oversight-board/FY2013_2Q_IOB_Report.pdf.

Country	Text title	Year
Australia	*Telecommunications (Interception and Access) Act 1979* No. 114, 1979[18]	1979
United States	*Smith vs. Maryland*[19]	1979
United States	*Executive Order 12333*. Defines the scope of SIGINT operations by the NSA: "authorizes NSA to collect (including through clandestine means), process, analyze, produce and disseminate SIGINT data for foreign intelligence and counterintelligence purposes to support national and military missions"[20]	1981
United Kingdom	*Interception of Communications Act*[21]	1985
United Kingdom	*Interception of Communications Bill*[22]	1985
United Kingdom	*Interception of Communications Act*[23] (entered into force on April 10, 1986)[24]	1985
United States	ECPA (*Electronic Communications Privacy Act*)[25]	1986

18 Telecommunications (Interception and Access) Act 1979, no. 114, 1979, Australia [Online]. Available at: www.legislation.gov.au/Details/C2017C00308.

19 As part of an investigation, the police asked a telephone operator to record the numbers dialed by a suspect. In this case, the judge considered that privacy is not called into question when it comes to information freely provided to third parties (such as telephone companies).

20 NSA staff distinguish between two categories of SIGINT operations: Those covered by EO 12333 and those covered by the authorizations provided by the FISA [Online]. Available at: www.nsa.gov/Portals/70/documents/news-features/declassified-documents/intelligence-oversi ght-board/FY2013_2Q_IOB_Report.pdf.

21 The original text of the law is available at: https://www.legislation.gov.uk/ukpga/1985/56/ body/1991-02-01.

22 Debates [Online]. Available at: www.api.parliament.uk/historic-hansard/commons/1985/ mar/12/interception-of-communications-bill.

23 Original version: www.legislation.gov.uk/ukpga/1985/56/contents/enacted; and current updated version: www.legislation.gov.uk/ukpga/1985/56/contents.

24 Creates the offense of illegal interception of postal communications by means of telecommunications; introduces an authorization system for lawful interceptions. The "Interception of Communications Commissioner" function is created to ensure the application of the law. Amended by the entry into force in 2000 of the *Regulation of Investigatory Powers Act* 2000.

25 See: www.govtrack.us/congress/bills/99/hr4952/text.

Country	Text title	Year
United States	*Electronic Communications Privacy Act* (ECPA)[26]	1986
Isle of Man	*Interception of Communications Act*[27]	1988
United States	*National Security Directive No. 42* (defines NSA responsibilities)	1990
Colombia	Constitution (Article 15)[28]	1991
Colombia	*Constitution Politica de Colombia*, Article 15[29]	1991
France	The legalization of administrative wiretapping (law relating to the secrecy of correspondence)	1991
France	Creation of the French National Control Commission of Security Interceptions (CNCIS)	1991
France	Law relating to the secrecy of correspondence	1991
France	French regulations on cryptology; SCSSI	1991
France	Law relating to the secrecy of correspondence sent by electronic communications means (the rules on interception were revised in 2006 with the law for the fight against terrorism). In 2012, it was integrated into the French Internal Security Code (Title IV, Book III)	1991
United States	*United States SIGINT Directive SP0018* (July 27, 1993)	1993
Ireland	*Interception of Postal Packets and Telecommunications Messages (Regulation) Act, 1993*[30]	1993
United States	CALEA. *The Communications Assistance for Law Enforcement Act* (CALEA, P. L. 103-414, 47 USC 1001-1010)[31]	1994

26 Updates the *Wiretap Act* from 1968. It intends to expand and revise federal wiretapping and electronic eavesdropping provisions. It was enacted to promote "the privacy expectations of citizens and the legitimate needs of law enforcement". "Congress also sought to support the creation of new technologies by assuring consumers that their personal information would remain safe". The Wiretap Act was extended to "electronic communications (broadly computer communications)" [Online]. Available at: www.cs.uaf.edu/~cs393/PRES/ECPAreport.pdf http://cpsr.org/issues/privacy/ecpa86/.

27 See: www.courts.im/media/1660/interception-of-communications-act-1988.pdf.

28 See also articles from the criminal procedure code: www.eff.org/pages/mapping-laws-government-access-citizens-data-colombia.

29 Private correspondence is inviolable. Correspondence can only be intercepted or recorded following legal proceedings.

30 See: www.irishstatutebook.ie/eli/1993/act/10/enacted/en/print.

31 CALEA amends the ECPA.

Country	Text title	Year
EU	Council Resolution of January 17, 1995, relating to the lawful interception of telecommunications[32]	1995
United States	*Telecommunications Act*[33] (amendment to the *Communications Act 1934*)	1996
France	Progressive liberalization of encryption tools: limited key length or strong encryption but whose keys are managed by a trustworthy third party	1996
International	Wassenaar Arrangements	1996
France	Law 2000-230 from March 13, 2000[34]	2000
India	*Information Technology Act*	2000
United Kingdom	*Regulation of Investigatory Powers Act* (RIPA)	2000
United Kingdom	*The Telecommunications* (*Lawful Business Practice*) (*Interception of Communications*) *Regulations 2000*[35]	2000
United Kingdom	*The Telecommunications* (*Lawful Business Practice*) (*Interception of Communications*) *Regulations 2000*	2000
United Kingdom	*Regulation of Investigatory Powers Act 2000* (RIP or RIPA)	2000
United States	*USA Patriot Act*[36] (see especially Section 215)[37]	2001

32 Official Journal of the European Communities, Council Resolution of January 17, 1995 on the lawful interception of telecommunications, November 4, 1996, C329. It reaffirms the need to respect the rights of natural persons, their right to privacy and data protection; but also emphasizes the legal and technical difficulties raised by the implementation of interception measures, taking into account technological advances; and recalls that lawful interception is an important tool for the protection of national interests, national security, instruction in matters of serious crime. The text recalls the "specifications for authorized services", that is, all the duties and rights granted to the services in charge of interception in each state: must have access to "all telecommunications transmitted or caused to be transmitted to or from the number or other identifier of the target service used by the subject of the interception". "The authorized services must also be granted access to the data pertaining to the call which were used for carrying it out", etc.

33 See: www.transition.fcc.gov/Reports/tcom1996.pdf.

34 Attaches legal value to the electronic signature. "Writing on electronic media has the same probative force as writing on paper" (Article 1316-3).

35 See: www.legislation.gov.uk/uksi/2000/2699/made.

36 See: www.govinfo.gov/content/pkg/PLAW-107publ56/pdf/PLAW-107publ56.pdf.

37 Authorizes the NSA to proceed with the bulk collection of metadata from certain telephone calls.

Country	Text title	Year
United States	*Terrorist Surveillance Program* (TSP)[38] also referred to as *President Surveillance Program* (PSP). Active program from 2001 to 2007. The program targeted members from Al-Qaeda and individuals overseas having connections to the terrorist organization [JOH 06]	2001
United States	*Patriot Act*, October 26, 2001. *Uniting (and) Strengthening America (by) Providing Appropriate Tools Required (to) Intercept (and) Obstruct Terrorism Act of 2001*	2001
United States	*The Patriot Act*[39]	2001
South Africa	*Regulation of Interception of communications and provision of communication-related information act* (RICPCI)[40]	2002
South Africa	*Interception of Communications Bill*, No. 24286, January 22, 2003, Act No. 70, 2002[41]	2002
South Carolina (United States)	*Code of Laws, Criminal Procedure, Chapter 30: Interception of Wire, Electronic or Oral Communications. South Carolina Homeland Security Act*	2002
United States	*Homeland Security Act*[42]	2002
United States	In January 2002, DARPA created the IAO (*Information Awareness Office*)	2002
Jamaica	*The interception of communications act*[43]	2002
Saint Vincent	*Telecommunications (confidentiality in networks and services) act*[44]	2002

---

38 This program was granted by G. Bush. He authorized the NSA to carry out the interception of international communications towards and outside the United States for people having connections with al-Qaeda or any terrorist organizations. This decision was based on the power of decision conferred on the President of the United States by the Constitution, to carry out electronic surveillance actions without any authorization procedure, in times of war, against the enemy.

39 The Pen Register Statute was expended to the Internet. The Patriot Act clarifies and updates the ECPA to keep pace with the evolution of new communications technologies and methods.

40 See: www.internet.org.za/ricpci.html.

41 Regulation of interception of communications and provision of communication-related information act, *Government Gazette*, No. 24286, January 22, 2003, Act No. 70, 2002 [Online]. Available at: www.internet.org.za/ricpci.html#interceptionofcommunicationunderinterception direction.

42 See: www.govinfo.gov/content/pkg/STATUTE-116/pdf/STATUTE-116-Pg2135.pdf.

43 Full text in its 2015 consolidated version [Online]. Available at: https://laws.moj.gov.jm/library/statute/the-interception-of-communications-act.

44 See: www.ectel.int/wp-content/uploads/2015/12/SVG-sro-10-2002-confidentiality-in-networks-and-services.pdf.

Country	Text title	Year
United States	DARPA hosts the TIA (*Total Information Awareness*)[45] program in February 2003. In May of the same year, the program was renamed *Terrorism Information Awareness*. The project was managed by the IAO (*Information Awareness Office*)	2003
Australia	*Surveillance Devices Act* (SDA)	2004
France	Law for trust in the digital economy. June 21, 2004[46]. Liberalizes the use of cryptography	2004
New Zealand	*Telecommunications (Interception Capability) Act* 2004	2004
Chile	*Reglamento sobre interceptación y grabación de comunicaciones telefónicas y de otras formas de telecomunicación*[47] (Regulations on interception and recording of telephonic communications and other forms of telecommunications)	2005
Spain	Royal Decree 424/2005 of April 15, 2005 (transposition of the Telecom Package)	2005
St. Lucia	*Interception of Communications Act*[48]	2005
United States	*USA Patriot Act reauthorization acts*[49]	2006
Hong Kong	*Interception of Communications and Surveillance Ordinance*[50]	2006
United Kingdom	*Wireless Telegraphy Act*	2006
United States	The PAA took over from the TSP. PAA = *Protect America Act*[51]. Passed by the Congress. PAA, P. L. 110-55[52] This system's implementation was only temporary (expired in February 16, 2008) and was replaced a few months later by the amended Fisa	2007
United States	End of the TSP program	2007

---

45 The goal was to mobilize ICT to detect and identify terrorists, anticipate threats and avoid attacks. Data Mining was at the heart of this project which had to process, analyze and cross-reference huge amounts of data to try to bring out the strategic information.

46 Article 30: "The use of cryptological means is free".

47 See: www.leychile.cl/Navegar?idNorma=242261.

48 2008 Consolidated Version: www.easterncaribbeanlaw.com/wp-content/uploads/2014/07/ INTERCEPTION-OF-COMMUNICATIONS-ACT-Cap.3.12.pdf.

49 Amends the ECPA.

50 See: www.elegislation.gov.hk/hk/cap589.

51 See: www.justice.gov/archive/ll/docs/text-of-paa.pdf.

52 This program established a dual certification mechanism enabling interceptions, which emanated from the Director of National Intelligence (DNI) and the Ministry of Justice (*Attorney General*). These interceptions were part of international intelligence, and concerned individuals outside the American territory.

Country	Text title	Year
Zimbabwe	*Interception of Communications Act*[53]	2007
United States	Fisa – *Foreign Intelligence Surveillance Act, Amendment Act of 2008*[54](see in particular Section 702)[55]	2008
Guyana	*Interception of Communications Act*[56]	2008
India	*Information Technology (Procedure and Safeguards for Interception, Monitoring and Decryption of Information) Rules, 2009*[57]	2009
Namibia	*Bill on Intercepting Electronic Communications Without Court Oversight*	2009
Queensland	*Telecommunications Interception Act 2009*[58]	2009
EU	*Council Regulation* (EC) No. 428/2009[59]. New modification proposal in 2016[60] (COM (2016) 116)	2009
Zambia	*Electronic Communications and Transactions Act*	2009
Uganda	*Regulation of Interception of Communication Act*	2010
Trinidad and Tobago	*Interception of Communications Act*[61]	2010

---

53 Authorizing government agencies to intercept telephone, mobile and email communications: www.vertic.org/media/National%20Legislation/Zimbabwe/ZW_Interception_of_Communications_Act.pdf.

54 Fisa created two different procedures for the targeted wiretapping of non-US citizens outside the national territory (Fisa Title VII) [Online]. Available at: www.congress.gov/110/plaws/publ261/PLAW-110publ261.pdf; www.govinfo.gov/content/pkg/STATUTE-122/pdf/STATUTE-122-Pg2436.pdf.

55 Authorizes the targeted surveillance of foreigners outside the United States territory, under certain conditions. Amends the ECPA.

56 See: www.oas.org/Juridico/mla/en/guy/en_guy_Inter_Commun_Act_2008.pdf.

57 See: www.cis-india.org/internet-governance/resources/it-procedure-and-safeguards-for-interception-monitoring-and-decryption-of-information-rules-2009.

58 See: www.legislation.qld.gov.au/view/pdf/2017-03-30/act-2009-010.

59 See: www.eur-lex.europa.eu/legal-content/EN/ALL/?uri=CELEX:32009R0428. The amendment to regulation 428/2009, No. 1382/2014 from October 22, 2014, adds to the list of technologies whose export is controlled, IP network surveillance systems (Annex I, No. 5A001.j), in accordance with the amendments to the Wassenaar Arrangements from the December 2013 meeting.

60 See: https://eur-lex.europa.eu/.

61 See: www.oas.org/juridico/PDFs/cyb_tto_int2010.pdf.

Country	Text title	Year
Uganda	*Regulation of Interception of Communication Act*[62]	2010
Bermuda	*Electronic Communications Act*	2011
United States	United States SIGINT Directive SP0018 (new version from January 25, 2011)	2011
United States	FISC Classified Report (*Foreign Intelligence Surveillance Court*) providing encrypted data on interceptions by the NSA (FIS 11)[63] (report produced in 2011 and made public in 2013)	2011
Trinidad and Tobago	*Interception of Communications Act*[64]	2011
Australia	*Telecommunications (Interception) Act 2012. South Australia*	2012
Colombia	Decree No. 1704 from August 15, 2012 "interceptacion legal de comunicaciones"[65] (lawful interception of communications)	2012
United States	Title VII from the Fisa was extended (it is within Title VII that the important Section 702 can be found)	2012
United States	PPF-28 (*Presidential Policy Directive*) – *Signals Intelligence Activities*	2014

---

62 See: www.ulii.org/ug/legislation/act/2015/18-2.

63 The report only became known to the public a few years later, once declassified by the Obama administration in 2013. Based on the legal framework conferred by Section 702 from the Fisa, the NSA is said to have intercepted around 250 million Internet communications annually: 91% directly from Internet Service Providers (ISPs), depending on the PRISM collection mechanism ("downstream" procedure); 9% using the "upstream" method, collecting Internet transit between two unspecified locations, which therefore takes place at the level of the Internet's backbone with the help of its companies, such as AT&T, for example. The evaluation of the upstream collection made by the FISC shows an interception of international communications unrelated to the targets, as well as an amount of domestic communications. These "errors" or problems could be due to technological limitations, which do not allow for the exclusion of domestic communications. According to the report, it is these "upstream" interceptions that raise the most legal questions, due to "multiple communication transactions" (MCT) (communications that can take multiple forms – email and others) [FIS 11].

64 Version of the text amended in 2012 [Online]. Available at: www.oas.org/juridico/PDFs/cyb_tto_int2010.pdf.

65 See: www.docdroid.net/xpJJc0a/decreto-1704-de-2012-interceptacion-legal-de-comunicaciones-pdf.

Country	Text title	Year
Spain	*Ley Organica 13/2015, from October 5*[66]	2015
United States	*USA Freedom Act*[67]. Amends Section 215 from the Patriot Act, June 2, 2015	2015
United States	The NSA put an end to its bulk interception of telephone communications' metadata program on May 31, 2015 (in accordance with paragraph 215 from the *Patriot Act*) [NSA 15]	2015
United States	The NSA reactivated its bulk interception of telephone communications' metadata program on June 4, 2015 (in accordance with the *USA Freedom Act* – USAFA) [NAT 15]	2015
France	Creation of the CNCTR (French National Control Commission on Information Techniques)[68] which replaced the CNCIS. Friday, July 24, 2015	2015
Hong Kong	*Interception of Communications and Surveillance Ordinance*[69]	2016
United Kingdom	*Investigatory Powers Act 2016*	2016
United Kingdom	*Interception of communications. Code of Practice. Pursuant to Section 71 of the Regulation of Investigatory Powers Act 2000*[70]	2016
United Kingdom	*Investigatory Powers Bill. Law Project*[71]	2016
Bahamas	*Interception of Communications Bill*	2017
California	*CCIT use and deployment*	2017
USA–UK	Negotiations for a US–UK Interception[72] Treaty	2017
United States	*Military Police. Interception of Wire and Oral Communications for Law Enforcement Purposes* [DEP 18]	2018
United States	*US–UK Cloud Act Agreement*[73]	2018

66 For an analysis of the Spanish law and procedures: María Dolores Guiard Abascal, La reforma procesal, novedades en la interceptación de comunicaciones. Obtención, resolución de Ips. Identificación de titulares, terminales o dispositivos de conectividad., Artículo 588 ter LECrim, Spain.

67 See: www.congress.gov/114/plaws/publ23/PLAW-114publ23.pdf.

68 See: www.cnctr.fr/2_presentation.html.

69 See: www.elegislation.gov.hk/hk/cap589.

70 Document published by the Home Office, dated January 2016, London [Online]. Available at: www. assets.publishing.service.gov.uk/government/uploads/system/up loads/attachment_ data/file/496064/53659_CoP_Communications_Accessible.pdf.

71 One of the goals was to make interception practices more transparent and to define responsibilities (the government would be held accountable). Tags: transparency, accountability, www.gov.uk/government/collections/draft-investigatory-powers-bill.

72 See: www. epic.org/2017/05/epic-urges-transparency-in-neg.html.

73 See: www.justice.gov/dag/page/file/1152896/download.

Country	Text title	Year
Isle of Man	*Report: Interception of Communications Acts 1988 and 2001* [ALE 18]	2018
Spain	*Circular 2/2019, sobre interceptación de comunicaciones telefónicas y telemáticas*[74] (Notice on the interception of telephone and telematic communications)	2019
United States	*Intelligence Community – Legal Reference Book* [OFF 19]	2019

A.2. Timeline of technologies, standards and sciences

Country	Technology	Year
Italy	The Vigenère cipher was described by Vigenère in his *Treatise on numbers and secret ways of writing* of 1586, but had previously been published in 1553 in a small work *Cifra del Signor Belaso,* by Giovan Batista Belaso. It was subsequently reinvented several times with variations (Gronsfeld, Sestri, Beaufort)	1553
United Kingdom	Optical communication device created by Robert Hooke	1672
Germany	Johan Andreas Benignus Bergstrasser developed an optical communication device	1786
France	Optical communication test between Ménilmontant and Bagneux, by Charles-François Dupuis	1788
France	The Chappe telegraph, adopted by the French Convention in 1793	1793
United Kingdom	Installation of the first electric telegraph line between London and Birmingham	1838
United States	Invention of the Morse code (by Samuel Morse). He established a telegraphic link between Baltimore and Washington	1844
France	First electric telegraph line in France, between Paris and Rouen	1845
Germany	Friedriech-Clemens Gerke gave the Morse code its final shape	1850
France	Chappe's optical telegraph was made available to the public	1851
International	First undersea cable between England and France	1851
France	The telephone's principle was posed by Charles Bourseul (article published in *Illustration*, "Electrical transmission of speech")	1854
United States	David E. Hughes invented the teleprinter (printing telegraph)	1855
International	First transatlantic cable	1866
France	Sittler code, for compressing the amount of information to be transmitted (reducing transmission costs)	1868

---

74 See: www.fiscal.es/documents/20142/a4d45f8a-a07e-be4b-d8f6-f26c6559127c.

Country	Technology	Year
United Kingdom	Theoretical bases for wireless telegraphy. Article "Electricity and Magnetism" by James-Clerk Maxwell	1872
France	Émile Baudot improved the teleprinter (Baudot's device)	1874
Russia	Alexander Popov established the first medium-distance radio transmissions (May 7, 1875)	1875
United States	Graham Bell and Elisha Gray filed a patent for the telephone	1876
United States	First commercial uses of the telephone	1877
France	First commercial uses of the telephone	1879
Austria	Rotating grid or Fleissner grid	1881
France	"La cryptographie militaire", by Auguste Kerckhoffs, set out the principles cryptographic systems must satisfy (today known as "Kerckhoffs' principles")	1883
France	General Ferrié made a radio broadcast from the Eiffel Tower	1904
United States	Engineer Gilbert Vernam patented an encryption/decryption system which was integrated into teleprinters (patent US1310719 A from July 22, 1919)	1919
France	Article by Colonel Givierge, "Les machines à cryptographier" in the journal La science et la vie. The article described the cryptographic devices of the time and presented the new machines as "mathematically indecipherable"	1923
United States	Lester Hill introduces algebraic structures into cryptology	1929
United States	DES – Data Encryption Standard, first encryption standard for civil use (56-bit key size)	1973
France	Memory card patent by Roland Moreno	1974
United States	The idea of using the knapsack problem for encryption was published in 1976 in the seminal paper by Diffie and Hellman on public keys. There were several proposals, but were all broken. A proposal by Shor and Rivest from 1988 was solved by Vaudenay in 1998, marking the definitive end of research to use this problem for encryption purposes [DIF 76]	1976
United States	The IBM LUCIFER algorithm was standardized as FIPS (Federal Information Processing Standard) by NIST in 1977	1977
United States	Publication of the RSA algorithm in 1977 in the mathematical games section from Scientific American, then in 1978 in Communications of the ACM	1977
France	Microprocessor card patent by Michel Ugon	1978

Country	Technology	Year
United States	McEliece's cipher, published in 1978. It is a public key encryption which uses the "decoding syndrome" problem, an NP-complete problem. It was the first of a family of systems using the theory of error-correcting codes, which are realistic candidates for post-quantum cryptography	1978
United States	Adoption of the SMTP (*Simple Mail Transport Protocol*) for emails	1982
United States	A public key encryption system based on the knapsack problem was proposed by Benny Chor and Ronald Rivest (system broken 10 years later by Serge Vaudenay)	1988
United States	First publication of an attack against DES (Data Encryption Systems) by Biham and Shamir "differential cryptanalysis of des-like cryptosystems"	1991
United States	Philip Zimmermann developed the PGP (Pretty Good Privacy) software, which protects electronic mail	1991
United States	Version 1.5 of the public key cryptography standardPKCS#1 was published by the RSA Laboratories (November 1993)	1993
United States	AES was the result of a 1997 NIST request for a new standard to replace DES. After an open and public competition, the RIJNDAEL algorithm was retained and standardized as FIPS, by the NIST in 2001	1997
France	Telecommunications security; Lawful Interception (LI); Concepts of Interception in a Generic Network Architecture. Technical Report. ETSI TR 101 943 V1.1.1 (2001-07) [ETS 01]	2001
United States	NIST guideline on secure email is NIST SP 800-45, Version 2 of February 2007, Guidelines on Electronic Mail Security	2007

A.3. Chronology of political and economic events

Country	Event	Year
England	Creation of a government system of postal control [HOU 44]	1250
France	Creation of the Ministry of Posts and Telegraph	1879
France	The police headquarters from Paris intercepts the telephone communications of General Georges Boulanger, exiled in Brussels	1889
France	The Dreyfus affair started with the interception of a telegram addressed to him	1894

Country	Event	Year
France	Military postal control (1914–1918)	1914
Germany, Mexico, United Kingdom, United States	Zimmermann telegram (sent on January 16, 1917 by the German minister Zimmermann to the German ambassador in Mexico). The telegram was intercepted and decrypted by the UK	1917
United Kingdom	Interception of Zimmerman's Telegram	1917
Poland	The Enigma machine was decrypted by Polish mathematicians as early as 1933. They built the first "Bombs" in 1938. After the invasion of Poland, the information was transmitted to the French and the British, and the decryption work continued at Bletchley Park with Alan Turing, among others	1933
France	The military authority created the Technical Controls Department (TCD). The service included the control of the post, wiretaps and telegram interception	1939
France	Creation of the Technical Controls Department (TCD) by the military authorities. Function: controlling the post	1939
United States	Beginning of the Venona interception program, whose function is to intercept messages sent via the Western Union commercial telegraph from the Soviet Embassy in Washington and the Soviet Consulate in New York to Moscow. The program is implemented by the *US Army Security Agency* (ASA)	1943
International	UKUSA Agreement creating the international network international ROEM (October 1, 1942) signed between the US Navy and GC&CS within the framework of ENIGMA decryption, achieved by the May 17, 1943 BRUSA agreement (Britain–USA)	1942
International	BRUSA agreement (Britain–USA) May 17, 1943	1943
United States	Development of Project X under the aegis of Signal Corp, also known as Sigsaly or Ciphony-one code to set up an encrypted link between Washington and London, in which Claude Shannon and Alan Turing took part	1943
United States	Operation SHAMROCK, initiated by the military intelligence services, in which the American suppliers of international communications (ITT, Western Union International, RCA) transmitted copies of diplomatic messages passing through their networks to the intelligence services. The NSA took over the project when it was created in 1952. This program is an example of the cooperation (sometimes forced, not without industry reluctance) between the state and companies in the field of intelligence. Their cooperation is required and considered of the utmost importance for national security	1945

Country	Event	Year
United States	Creation of the NSA (by the directive "Communications Intelligence Activities" of President Harry S. Truman, October 24, 1952). The directive puts an end to the AFSA (*Armed Forces Security Agency*), whose resources and prerogatives are transferred to the new agency	1952
United States	ARPA creation	1958
France	GIC (*Groupement interministériel de contrôle*) creation (in charge of telephone interceptions over the national territory)	1960
United States	Launch of the ARPANET network, which will become the INTERNET	1962
United States/Cuba/USSR	Cuban Missile Crisis of 1962 that led to the establishment of the "red telephone" between Washington and Moscow from August 30, 1963	1962
United States	Creation of the *National Commission for the Review of Federal and State Laws Relating to Wiretapping and Electronic Surveillance*	1968
United States	NSA Minaret Operation relies on interceptions of international communications to carry out intelligence actions on foreign powers, organizations and individuals who seek to influence or control American organizations or individuals; and any individuals likely to carry out actions that threaten national security [DOJ 76][75]. In the 1970s, the actions expanded and included the fight against drug trafficking. Under this program, the NSA, which acts at the request of various American agencies (its "clients", such as the FBI, the CIA, etc.), ensures that it intercepts only international communications (i.e. they have at least one point abroad)	1969
International	UK–USA transforms into Echelon[76]	1971
United States	Watergate scandal	1972
United States	*The Vinh wiretap*. American espionage operation conducted during the Vietnam War. CIA interceptions of North Vietnamese[77] military telephone communications (1972–1973)	1972
United States	The NSA starts gathering intelligence on terrorism [DOJ 76][78]	1972
France	*Canard enchaîné* planted bugs	1973

75 See: www.nsarchive2.gwu.edu/NSAEBB/NSAEBB178/surv09a.pdf.

76 The project consists of a division of surveillance tasks among the five member countries of the project, each with a region of the world.

77 See: www.en.wikipedia.org/wiki/The_Vinh_wiretap.

78 See: www.nsarchive2.gwu.edu/NSAEBB/NSAEBB178/surv09a.pdf.

Country	Event	Year
United States	Publication of the report by the *National Commission for the Review of Federal and State Laws Relating to Wiretapping and Electronic Surveillance*[79] (in accordance with the 1968 Omnibus Law)	1976
France	Schmelck Commission on wiretaps	1981
France	The Élysée wiretapping affair. A scandal that would result in trials and amendments to the law to counter abuse of power practices (1983–1985)	1983
United Kingdom	Echelon network revelations	1988
United States	Revelation of the existence of the Omnivore Program (FBI – USA)	1997
Germany	German Foreign Intelligence (BND) had been wiretapping political figures and international institutions, European and American[80] companies (1998–2006)	1998
United States	Carnivore, Packeteer and CoolMiner (*DragonWare Suite*) programs replace the Omnivore program (FBI – USA)	1999
United States	New York Times article reveals that the federal government has monitored the international phone calls and emails of thousands of individuals in the United States territory without authorization	2005
United States	Carnivore program is replaced by Naru Insight commercial tools (FBI – USA)	2005
France	Trial for the Élysée wiretapping affair (November 9, 2005)	2005
Greece	Discovery of spyware that could listen to the mobile phones of politicians and the government	2005
Italy	Discovery of an illegal wiretapping system in Telecom Italia	2005
United States	*Wall Street Journal* article reporting bulk data collection [GOR 13]	2013
United States	Apple CEO Tim Cook refuses to comply with court order to unlock iPhone as part of FBI investigation	2016
United States	Edward Snowden published numerous documents attesting to the scope of the NSA's global Internet communications cyber surveillance programs	2012
Israel	Scandal related to the sale of Pegasus interception software	2021

---

79 See: www.hsdl.org/?view&did=728874.

80 These revelations were made by the public German radio Berlin-Brandenburg (rbb).

A.4. Reports on the interception of communications

Country	Document title	Years, period covered
Australia	Report of the Royal Commission of inquiry into alleged telephone interception[81]	1986
Australia	Surveillance Devices Act[82]. Annual Report. Report by Attorney General's Department	Reports from 2006 to 2019
Australia	TIA Annual Report (Act[83])	Annual Report from 2000 to 2018
California	California Electronic Interceptions Report. California Department of Justice. Office of the Attorney General. Division of Criminal Law	Annual Report from 2009 to 2018
Canada	Annual Report on the use of electronic surveillance. Public Safety Canada	Reports from 2000 to 2018
France	Annual activity report CNCIS, then CNCTR	The first issue of the CNCIS report series covers the period 1991–1992. Annual reports published from 1991 to 2015. The latest CNCIS report is for 2014–2015. It is report No. 23 The first CNCTR report covers the period 2015–2016. The CNCTR reports have been published on the Commission's[84] website since then
Hong Kong	Annual report to the chief executive. CIOCS. Commissioner on Interception of communications and surveillance	Period 2006–2019[85]

81 See: www.parliament.vic.gov.au/papers/govpub/VPARL1985-87No96.pdf.
82 Law from 2004.
83 Law from 1979.
84 See: www.cnctr.fr/8_relations.html.
85 See: www.sciocs.gov.hk/en/reports.htm.

Country	Document title	Years, period covered
Hong Kong	Transparency Report. JMSC	2016 and 2018 reports
Guernsey	Report of the Investigatory Powers Commissioner	Report 2017
International	HIPCAR (ITU)	Report 2013
United Kingdom	IOCCO/IPCO Annual Reports[86]	Reports from 2000 to 2016 New series of reports from 2017 to 2019
United Kingdom	Becket Report	1957
United Kingdom	Dip Lock Report	1981
United States	FBI Report on Wiretap Capacity	1996
United States	Statistical transparency report regarding the use of national security authorities	DNI reports from 2013 to 2918
United States	Electronic Privacy Information Center	EPIC Letter on FBI Wiretap Report 12/95
United States	Wiretap Report. Administrative Office of the United States Courts	Reports covering the period 1997–2020[87]
United States	FISA Annual Report to Congress	Reports from 2015 to 2018[88]

A.5. The international market of lawful interceptions

The importance of the lawful interception market is difficult to assess accurately.

Below are the figures that have been published by various organizations in recent years.

---

86 IOCCO (*Interception Of Communications Commissioner's Office*) was replaced in 2017 by the *Investigative Powers Commissioner's Office* (IPCO).

87 See: www.uscourts.gov/statistics-reports/analysis-reports/wiretap-reports.

88 See: www.uscourts.gov/statistics-reports/analysis-reports/directors-report-foreign-intelligence-surveillance-courts.

	Low amount	High amount
2019	US$2.58 billion[89]	
2020	US$1.3 billion[90]	US$2.58 billion[91]
2021	US$2.58 billion[92]	
2025	US$4.53 billion[93]	US$8.8 billion[94]
2026	US$6.96 billion[95]	US$9.2 billion[96]

A.6. The international cryptography market

The summary table below shows some figures that have been published in company reports over the last few years and months. It offers an assessment of the revenue generated in the global cryptography market.

	Encryption software	Encryption hardware	Email encryption
2018	US$2.98 billion[97]		
2019	US$6.82 billion[98]; US$8.82 billion[99]	US$131.77 billion[100]	

89 See: www.imarcgroup.com/lawful-interception-market [Accessed October 6, 2021].

90 See: www.pdf.marketpublishers.com/bisreport/global-lawful-interception-market-report-2018_bisreport.pdf [Accessed October 6, 2021].

91 See: www.aws.amazon.com/marketplace/pp/prodview-v62bpwhotdhye [Accessed October 6, 2021].

92 See: www.researchandmarkets.com/reports/5317117/global-lawful-interception-market-2021-2026-by [Accessed 6 October 2021].

93 See: www.industryarc.com/Research/Lawful-Interception-Market-Research-500821 [Accessed October 6, 2021].

94 See: www.aws.amazon.com/marketplace/pp/prodview-v62bpwhotdhye [Accessed October 6, 2021].

95 See: www.imarcgroup.com/lawful-interception-market [Accessed October 6, 2021].

96 See: www.researchandmarkets.com/reports/5317117/global-lawful-interception-market-2021-2026-by [Accessed 6 October 2021].

97 See: www.grandviewresearch.com/industry-analysis/encryption-software-market [Accessed October 6, 2021].

98 See: www.alliedmarketresearch.com/world-encryption-software-market [Accessed October 6, 2021].

99 See: www.fortunebusinessinsights.com/industry-reports/encryption-software-market-101058 [Accessed October 6, 2021].

100 See: www.alliedmarketresearch.com/hardware-encryption-market [Accessed October 6, 2021].

	Encryption software	Encryption hardware	Email encryption
2020	US$9.8 billion[101]		
2025	US$14.32 billion[102] US$20.1 billion[103]		
2027	US$22.7 billion[104]; US$24.9 billion[105]	US$1239 billion[106]	US$12.9 billion[107]

101 See: www.marketsandmarkets.com/Market-Reports/encryption-software-market-227254588.html#:~:text=The%20global%20encryption%20software%20market%20size%20is%20expected%20to%20grow,post%2DCOVID%2D19%20scenario. [Accessed October 6, 2021].

102 See: www.industryarc.com/Research/Encryption-Software-Market-Research-500800 [Accessed October 6, 2021].

103 See: www.marketsandmarkets.com/Market-Reports/encryption-software-market-227254588.html#:~:text=The%20global%20encryption%20software%20market%20size%20is%20expected%20to%20grow,post%2DCOVID%2D19%20scenario [Accessed October 6, 2021].

104 See: www.alliedmarketresearch.com/world-encryption-software-market [Accessed October 6, 2021].

105 See: www.fortunebusinessinsights.com/industry-reports/encryption-software-market-101058 [Accessed October 6, 2021].

106 See: www.alliedmarketresearch.com/hardware-encryption-market [Accessed October 6, 2021].

107 See: www.businesswire.com/news/home/20210825005563/en/Global-Email-Encryption-Market-2021-to-2027---by-Component-Organization-Size-Deployment-Mode-End-user-and-Region---ResearchAndMarkets.com [Accessed October 6, 2021].

References

[ADK 19] ADKENS S., "Le FBI a essayé d'installer une porte dérobée dans Phantom Secure, un réseau téléphonique chiffré axé sur la protection de la vie privée", *Developpez.com*, available at: https://securite.developpez.com/actu/277847/Le-FBI-a-essaye-d-installer-une-porte-derobee-dans-Phantom-Secure-un-reseau-telephonique-chiffre-axe-sur-la-protection-de-la-vie-privee-mais-qui-approvisionnait-le-marche-criminel/ [Accessed September 19, 2019], 2019.

[AGE 20] AGENCE FRANCE-PRESSE, "Une centaine de pays espionnés par les États-Unis et l'Allemagne via une société de cryptage", *Le Point*, available at: https://www.lepoint.fr/monde/une-centaine-de-pays-espionnes-par-les-etats-unis-et-l-allemagne-via-une-societe-de-cryptage-11-02-2020-2362174_24.php [Accessed February 11, 2020], 2020.

[AHM 21] AHMED S., Dark Web: A haven for fake digital certificates, available at: https://securityboulevard.com/2021/08/dark-web-a-haven-for-fake-digital-certificates/ [Accessed August 17, 2021], 2021.

[ALE 18] ALEGRE S., Interception of communications acts 1988 and 2001, Report, available at: https://www.gov.im/media/1367579/ioc-commissioners-report-for-the-year-ended-31122018-gd2019-0020.pdf, 2018.

[AMS 21] AMSILI S., "Vaste coup de filet mondial dans le crime organisé grâce à des téléphones cryptés du FBI", *Les Echos*, available at: https://www.lesechos.fr/monde/enjeux-internationaux/vaste-coup-de-filet-mondial-dans-le-crime-organise-grace-a-des-telephones-cryptes-du-fbi-1321768 [Accessed June 9, 2021], 2021.

[ASS 12] ASSANGE J., *Freedom and the Future of the Internet*, OR Books, New York/London, 2012.

[ATH 28] ATHANASE G., "Du secret des lettres et de la nécessité de mettre en accusation M. de Vaulchier, directeur-général des postes; par M. Germain, avocat à la Cour Royale de Paris", *Gallica*, available at: https://gallica.bnf.fr/ark:/12148/bpt6k54484280, 1828.

[ATK 13] ATKINS L., How the NSA reportedly intercepted BlackBerry communications, available at: http://n4bb.com/nsa-reportedly-intercepted-blackberry-communications/ [Accessed September 9, 2013], 2013.

[AUD 10] AUDENARD J.F., Interceptions légales : retour aux bases, available at: http://www.orange-business.com/fr/blogs/securite/lois-reglementations-standards-et-certifications/interceptions-legales-retour-aux-bases [Accessed November 2, 2010], 2010.

[BAR 01] BARNEY S.M., Innocent Packets? Applying navigational regimes from the law of the sea convention by analogy to the realm of cyberspace, Report, Naval War College, available at: https://apps.dtic.mil/sti/pdfs/ADA389473.pdf, 2001.

[BAT 07] BATES D.H., *Lincoln in the Telegraph Office*, The Century Company, New York, available at: https://ia802706.us.archive.org/28/items/lincolnintelegra00bates/lincolnintele gra00bates.pdf, 1907.

[BEC 99] BECKER P., Development of surveillance technology and risk of abuse of economic information, Report, European Parliament, Scientific and Technological Options Assessment, available at: https://www.europarl.europa.eu/RegData/etudes/etudes/join/1999/168184/DG-4-JOIN_ET%281999%29168184_EN.pdf, 1999.

[BEI 21] BEIERLE C., DERBEZ P., LEANDER P., et al. "Cryptanalysis of the GPRS encryption algorithms GEA-1 and GEA-2", in CANTEAUT A., STANDAERT F.X. (eds), *Advances in Cryptology – EUROCRYPT 2021*, Springer, Cham, doi: 10.1007/978-3-030-77886-6_6, 2021.

[BEL 14] BELL P., CONGRAM M., "Communication interception technology (CIT) and its use in the fight against transnational organised crime (TOC) in Australia: A review of the literature", *International Journal of Social Science Research*, available at: https://eprints.qut.edu.au/64998/1/IJSSRCITFinal_Accepted_Version-4089.pdf, 2014.

[BEN 97] BENSON R.L., A history of U.S. communications intelligence during world war II: Policy and administration, Center for Cryptologic History, National Security Agency, available at: https://www.nsa.gov/Portals/70/documents/about/cryptologic-heritage/historical-figures-publications/publications/wwii/history_us_comms.pdf, 1997.

[BER 16] BERTHILLOT É., "Le Château de Dublin de 1880 à 1922 : repaire de traîtres ou d'agents doubles ?", *Études d'Histoire et de Civilisation*, no. 41, pp. 9–34, available at: https://doi.org/10.4000/etudesirlandaises.4785, 2016.

[BER 18] BERNSTEIN S., "Interaction of technology and organization: Case study of US military COMINT in world war II", in KOSAL M. (ed.), *Technology and the Intelligence Community*, Springer, Cham, doi: 10.1007/978-3-319-75232-7_2, 2018.

[BIA 92] BIANCHI TUPPER A., *La guerra civil de Chile en 1891*, available at: https://ia800200.us.archive.org/6/items/laguerracivildec00bian/laguerracivildec00bian.pdf, 1892.

[BIE 20] BIERMANN F., RAKHYUN E.K. (eds), *Architectures of Earth System Governance*, Cambridge University Press, Cambridge, 2020.

[BIG 19] BIGO D., BONELLI L., "Digital data & transnational intelligence", in BIGO, D., ISIN E., RUPPERT E. (eds), *Data Politics*, Routledge, London, 2019.

[BOH 17] BOHNENBERGER F., "The proliferation of cybersurveillance technologies: Challenges and prospects for strengthened export controls", *Strategic Trade Review*, no. 2, pp. 81–102, 2017.

[BON 14] BONELLI L., RAGAZZI F., "Low-tech security: Files, notes, and memos as technologies of anticipation", *Security Dialogue*, no. 45, pp. 476–493, 2014.

[BOU 20] BOUDOT F., GAUDRY P., GUILLEVIC A. et al., "Nouveaux records de factorisation et de calcul du logarithme discret", *Techniques de l'Ingénieur*, p. 17, 2020.

[BRA 18] BRAVERMAN A., United States of America versus Vincent Ramos, United States District Court, Southern District of California, San Diego, available at: https://www. courthousenews.com/wp-content/uploads/2018/10/Ramos.Plea_.pdf, 2018.

[BRE 82] BRENNAN B., "Investigating the puzzle palace", *The Fletcher Forum*, vol. 7, Boston, 1982.

[BUC 16] BUCHANAN B., *The Cybersecurity Dilemma*, Oxford University Press, Oxford, 2016.

[BUR 16] BURZSTEIN E., How email in transit can be intercepted using dns hijacking, available at: https://elie.net/blog/security/how-email-in-transit-can-be-intercepted-using-dns-hijacking/, 2016.

[BUT 12] BUTTIGIEG DEBONO H., Interception of communication technologies: A privacy assessment, available at: https://www.um.edu.mt/library/oar/handle/123456789/6645, 2012.

[CAM 99] CAMPBELL D., Interception Capabilities 2000, Report, Director General for Research of the European Parliament (Scientific and Technical Options Assessment programme office) on the development of surveillance technology and risk of abuse of economic information, Edinburgh, 1999.

[CAM 00] CAMPBELL D., *Surveillance électronique planétaire*, Allia, Paris, 2000.

[CAY 19] CAYRE H., *The Godmother*, ECW Press, Toronto, 2019.

[CEN 13] CENTRAL SECURITY SERVICE, Intelligence Oversight Board on NSA activities, Report, NSA, available at: https://www.nsa.gov/Portals/70/documents/news-features/ declassified-documents/intelligence-oversight-board/FY2013_2Q_IOB_Report.pdf, 2013.

[CHA 13] CHATTERJEE P., Glimmerglass intercepts undersea cable traffic for spy agencies, available at: https://corpwatch.org/article/glimmerglass-intercepts-undersea-cable-traffic-spy-agencies, 2013.

[CHE 16] CHESTNUT GREITENS S., *Dictators and their Secret Police: Coercive Institutions and State Violence*, Cambridge University Press, Cambridge, doi: 10.1017/CBO978131 6489031, 2016.

[CIM 19] CIMPANU C., Over 100,000 GitHubrepos have leaked API or crypto-graphic keys, available at: https://www.zdnet.com/article/over-100000-github-repos-have-leaked-api-or-cryptographic-keys/ [Accessed September 1, 2021], 2019.

[CLE 14] CLEMENT A., NSA surveillance: Exploring the geographies of internet interception, available at: https://core.ac.uk/download/pdf/19961071.pdf, 2014.

[CLE 20] CLEARSKY, FOX KITTEN CAMPAIGN, Widespread Iranian espionage-offensive campaign, available at: https://www.clearskysec.com/wp-content/uploads/2020/02/ClearSky-Fox-Kitten-Campaign-v1.pdf, 2020.

[COC 21] COCHRANE P., Red Sea cables: How UK and US spy agencies listen to the Middle East, available at: https://www.middleeasteye.net/news/red-sea-cables-how-us-uk-spy-agencies-listen-middle-east, 2021.

[COL 31] COLLECTIF, *Manuel du Grade du Génie (partie militaire)*, Charles-Lavauzelle & Cie, Paris, available at: https://gallica.bnf.fr/ark:/12148/bpt6k96236247/f998.image.r=%22poste%20d'interception%, 1931.

[COM 14] COMEY J., "Going dark: Are technology, privacy, and public safety on a collision course?", *Brookings Institution*, Washington, available at: https://www.fbi.gov/news/speeches/going-dark-are-technology-privacy-and-public-safety-on-a-collision-course, 2014.

[CON 67] CONGRESSIONAL RECORD, First Session, *Proceedings and Debates of the 90th Congress*, Washington, available at: https://www.fordlibrarymuseum.gov/library/document/0054/12144653.pdf, 1967.

[CON 13] CONGRAM M., BELL P., LAUCHS M., "Integrating communication interception technology within investigations", *Policing Transnational Organized Crime and Corruption: Exploring the Role of Communication Interception Technology*, Palgrave Pivot, London, 2013.

[COO 11] COOPER A., "Doing the DPI dance. Assessing the privacy impact of Deep Packet Inspection", in ASPRAY W., DOTY P. (eds), *Privacy in America. Interdisciplinary Perspectives*, Scarecrow Press, Plymouth, 2011.

[COO 16] COOK T., A message to our customers, available at: https://www.apple.com/customer-letter/, 2016.

[CRY 86] CRYPTOLOG, Revue of the national security agency, available at: https://ia802503.us.archive.org/5/items/cryptolog_105/cryptolog_105.pdf, 1986.

[DAS 59] DASH S., SCHWARTZ R.F., KNOWLTON R.E., *The Eavesdroppers*, Rutgers University Press, New Brunswick, 1959.

[DAV 96] DAVIS L.E., "The Wassenaar arrangement", *The DISAM Journal*, available at: https://ia801008.us.archive.org/2/items/DTIC_ADA496568/DTIC_ADA496568.pdf, 1996.

[DEA 10] DEAN G., BELL P., CONGRAM M., "Knowledge-managed policing framework for communication interception technologies (CIT) in criminal justice system", *Pakistan Journal of Criminology*, no. 4, pp. 25–41, available at: http://www.pjcriminology.com/wp-content/uploads/2019/01/3-25.pdf, 2010.

[DEL 93] DELASTELLE F., *Cryptographie nouvelle assurant l'inviolabilité totale des correspondances chiffrées*, Dubreuil, Paris, 1893.

[DEL 17] DELOITTE, Tapping of fibre networks, available at: https://zybersafe.com/wordpress/wp-content/uploads/2017/04/Deloitte_Fiber_tapping_Q1_2017_English.pdf, 2017.

[DEP 18] DEPARTMENT OF THE ARMY, "Interception of wire and oral communications for law enforcement purposes", *Army Regulation*, Washington, available at: https://armypubs.army.mil/epubs/DR_pubs/DR_a/pdf/web/ARN6972_R190_53_FINAL.pdf, 2018.

[DEP 20] DEPARTMENT OF JUSTICE, Definition – Intercept, Report, United States, available at: https://www.justice.gov/jm/criminal-resource-manual-1046-definition-intercept, 2020.

[DES 21] DE SOMBRE W., Surveillance technology at the fair: Proliferation of cyber capabilities in international arms market, Report, Atlantic Council, 2021.

[DES 58] DESPLACES E., L'Isthme de Suez : journal de l'union des deux mers, available at: https://gallica.bnf.fr/ark:/12148/bpt6k6203087j, 1858.

[DIF 76] DIFFIE W., HELLMAN M.E., "New directions in cryptography", *IEEE Transactions on Information Theory*, no. 22, pp. 644–654, 1976.

[DOU 22] DOUIN G., *Un épisode de la guerre mondiale. L'attaque du Canal de Suez*, Librairie Delagrave, Paris, 1922.

[DUB 11] DUBOIS J.A., "Scandales sécuritaires et violence sociopolitique dans la Colombie d'Alvaro Uribe – Bilan et perspectives", *La Chronique des Amériques, Observatoire des Amériques*, Montreal, available at: http://www.ieim.uqam.ca/IMG/pdf/oct2011.pdf, 2011.

[DUR 15] DURUMERIC Z., ADRIAN D., MIRIAN A. et al., "Neither snow nor rain nor MITM… An empirical analysis of email delivery security", *Proceedings of the IMC'15*, Tokyo, available at: http://dx.doi.org/10.1145/2815675.2815695, 2015.

[EIJ 18] EIJKMAN A.M.Q., "Access to justice for communications surveillance and interception: Scrutinising intelligence-gathering reform legislation", *Utrecht Law Review*, no. 14, pp. 116–127, available at: http://doi.org/10.18352/ulr.419, 2018.

[ELE 05] ELECTRONIC FRONTIER FOUNDATION, 20150626-Intercept-(U) CI-030-05 Close Out for "Bush Lets U.S. Spy on callers without courts" – Action Memorandum, Report, EFF, available at: https://www.eff.org/fr/document/20150626-intercept-u-ci-030-03-close-out-bush-lets-us-spy-callers-without-courts-action, 2005.

[ETS 01] ETSI, Telecommunications security; Lawful Interception (LI); Concepts of Interception in a Generic Network Architecture, Technical report, ETSI TR 101 943 V1.1.1, available at: https://www.etsi.org/deliver/etsi_tr/101900_101999/101943/01.01.01_60/tr_101943v010101p.pdf, 2001.

[FAC 15] FACTSHEET BULK INTERCEPTION, Investigatory powers bill, available at: https://www.gov.uk/government/uploads/system/uploads/attachment_data/file/473751/Factsheet-Bulk_Interception.pdf, 2015.

[FAV 93] FAVIER J.L, DE VERGENNES C., TURGOT J. et al., *Politique de tous les cabinets de l'Europe, pendant les règnes de Louis XV et de Louis XVI*, Buisson, Paris, available at: https://gallica.bnf.fr/ark:/12148/bpt6k432080t, 1793.

[FBI 12] FBI, Stingray agreements: Declassified 31 October 2012, Report, FBI, available at: https://archive.org/details/StingrayAgreements/page/n1/mode/2up, 2012.

[FIS 11] FISC, Memorandum Opinion, Report, available at: https://www.dni.gov/files/documents/0716/October-2011-Bates-Opinion-and%20Order-20140716.pdf, 2011.

[FLÉ 13] FLÉCHAUX R., NSA : les matériels CISCO, Juniper et Huawei transformés en passoires, available at: https://www.silicon.fr/nsa-les-materiels-cisco-juniper-et-huawei-transformes-en-passoire-91760.html, 2013.

[FLI 53] FLICKE W.F., War secrets in the ether, National Security Agency, Washington, available at: https://ia801308.us.archive.org/7/items/41761019080017/41761019080017.pdf, 1953.

[FOG 06] FOGEL R., Ori Cohen, Private Eye, available at: https://www.haaretz.com/1.4856925 [Accessed July 26, 2021], 2006.

[FOL 16] FOLLOROU J., "American and British spy agencies targeted in-flight mobile phone use", *The Intercept* in partnership with *Le Monde*, available at: https://theintercept.com/2016/12/07/american-and-british-spy-agencies-targeted-in-flight-mobile-phone-use/, 2016.

[FOR 05] FORCADE O., LAURENT S., *Secrets d'État. Pouvoirs et renseignement dans le monde contemporain*, Colin, Paris, 2005.

[FOR 11] FORERO J., Wiretapping scandal shakes Colombia, available at: https://www.npr.org/2011/08/29/140043175/wiretaping-scandal-shakes-colombia?t=1586865618866, 2011.

[FUE 12] FUECHLE M., MIWA J.A., MAHAPATRA S., et al., "A single-atom transistor", *Nature Nanotechnology*, no. 7, pp. 242–246, 2012.

[GAL 16a] GALLI F., "The interception of communication in France and Italy – What relevance for the development of English law?", *The International Journal of Human Rights*, no. 5, pp. 666–683, doi: 10.1080/13642987.2016.1162412, 2016.

[GAL 16b] GALLAGHER R., "Inside Menwith Hill", *The Intercept*, available at: https://theintercept.com/2016/09/06/nsa-menwith-hill-targeted-killing-surveillance/, 2016.

[GAÜ 16] GAÜZERE D., "La bataille du renseignement en Kirghizie : un enjeu global aux conséquences imprévisibles", *Bulletin de documentation*, no. 18, available at: https://cf2r.org/documentation/la-bataille-du-renseignement-en-kirghizie-un-enjeu-global-aux-consequences-imprevisibles/, 2016.

[GEL 14] GELLMAN B., TATE J., SOLTANI A., "In NSA-intercepted data, those not targeted far outnumber the foreigners who are", *The Washington Post*, available at: https://www.washingtonpost.com/world/national-security/in-nsa-intercepted-data-those-not-targeted-far-outnumber-the-foreigners-who-are/2014/07/05/8139adf8-045a-11e4-8572-4b1b969b6322_story.html, 2014.

[GEN 93] GENERAL ACCOUNTING OFFICE, Communications privacy, Report, Federal policy and action, available at: https://www.gao.gov/assets/220/218755.pdf, 1993.

[GIL 93] GILBERT J.L., FINNEGAN J.P., *U.S. Army Signals Intelligence in World War II: A Documentary History*, Center of Military History, Washington, D.C., available at: https://archive.org/details/CMHPub70-43/page/n1/mode/2up, 1993.

[GOE 81] GOETSCHY J., "Les théories du pouvoir", *Sociologie du travail*, no. 4, pp. 447–467, available at: https://doi.org/10.3406/sotra.1981.1699, 1981.

[GOO 16] GOODWIN C.F., Microsoft Corporation, oversight and government reform subcommittee on information technology, Report, Homeland Security Subcommittee on Cybersecurity, Infrastructure Protection, and Security Technologies, Joint Subcommittee on Wassenaar: Cybersecurity & Export Control, 2016.

[GOO 19] GOODIN D., Hackers steal secret crypto keys for NordVPN. Here's what we know so far, available at: https://arstechnica.com/information-technology/2019/10/hackers-steal-secret-crypto-keys-for-nordvpn-heres-what-we-know-so-far/, 2019.

[GOR 09] GORMAN S., DREAZEN Y.J., COLE A., "Insurgents hack U.S. drones", *The Wall Street Journal*, available at: https://www.wsj.com/articles/SB126102247889095011, 2009.

[GOR 13] GORMAN D., PEREZ E., HOOK J., "U.S. collects vast data trove", *The Wall Street Journal*, available at: https://www.wsj.com/articles/SB10001424127887324299104578 529112289298922,2013.

[GUI 19] GUILLOT P., VENTRE D., Capacités d'interception et de surveillance. L'évolution des systèmes techniques, Report, Projet UTIC, ANR, available at: https://forum.arn-fai.net/uploads/short-url/86JXLbMkx8b1q4d6w4S5y9KIp9U.pdf, 2019.

[HAT 00] HATCH D.A., BENSON R.L., The SIGINT background, Declassified document, NSA, available at: https://www.nsa.gov/News-Features/Declassified-Documents/Korean-War/Sigint-BG/#7, 2000.

[HER 75] HERSH S.M., "Submarines of U.S. stage spy missions inside Soviet waters", *The New York Times*, available at: https://www.nytimes.com/1975/05/25/archives/submarines-of-us-stage-spy-missions-inside-soviet-waters-submarines.html, 1975.

[HER 02] HERBIG K.L., WISKOFF M.F., Espionage against the United States by American Citizens 1947–2001, Report, Perserec Technical, Monterey, available at: https://www.dni.gov/files/NCSC/documents/archives/espionageAgainstUSbyCitizens.pdf, 2002.

[HIN 01] HINSLEY F.H., STRIPP A., *Codebreakers: The Inside Story of Bletchley Park*, Oxford University Press, 2001.

[HOF 05] HOFFMANN P., *Intelligence Support Systems: Technologies for Lawful Intercepts*, Auerbach Publications, Boca Raton, 2005.

[HOM 17] HOME OFFICE, Interception of communications, pursuant to schedule 7 to the investigatory powers act 2016, Draft Code of Practice, available at: https://assets.publishing.service.gov.uk/government/uploads/system/uploads/attachment_data/file/593748/IP_Act_-_Draft_Interception_code_of_practice_Feb2017_FINAL_WEB.pdf, 2017.

[HOR 76] HORROCK N.M., "Nixon testifies Kissinger picked wiretap targets", *The New York Times*, available at: https://www.nytimes.com/1976/03/11/archives/nixon-testifies-kissinger-picked-wiretap-targets-says-he-ordered.html, 1976.

[HOU 44] HOUSE OF COMMONS, Report from the secret committee on the post-office, Report, UK Parliament, 1844.

[IMP 95] IMPAGLIAZZO R., A personal view of average-case complexity, *Proceedings of the 30th Annual IEEE Conference, Structure in Complexity Theory*, 1995.

[INT 12] INTERNATIONAL TELECOMMUNICATION UNION, Interception of Communications: Assessment, Report, Geneva, 2012.

[JEN 08] JENNER L., Backdoor: How a metaphor turns into a weapon, available at: https://www.hiig.de/en/backdoor-how-a-metaphor-turns-into-a-weapon/, 2008.

[JOH 06] JOHN D., Negroponte, Report, C-06-0672-VRW, available at: https://www.clearinghouse.net/chDocs/public/NS-CA-0004-0009.pdf, 2006.

[JOI 13] JOINT CHIEFS OF STAFF, Joint Intelligence, available at: https://fas.org/irp/doddir/dod/jp2_0.pdf, 2013.

[JOI 18] JOINT CHIEFS OF STAFF, Cyberspace operations, available at: https://www.jcs.mil/Portals/36/Documents/Doctrine/pubs/jp3_12.pdf, 2018.

[JUS 06] JUSTICE, Intercept evidence: Lifting the Ban, Report, JUSTICE available at: https://files.justice.org.uk/wp-content/uploads/2015/07/06170838/Intercept-Evidence-1-October-2006.pdf, 2006.

[KAT 94] KATHY R., COKER K.R., CAROL E. et al., "A concise history of the U.S. Army Signal Corps", *DTIC*, Virginia, 1994.

[KEE 16] KEENAN B., "A very brief history of interception", *Media Policy Project Blog*, available at: http://blogs.lse.ac.uk/mediapolicyproject/2016/02/15/a-very-brief-history-of-interception/, 2016.

[KEE 17] KEENAN B., Interception: Law, media, and techniques, PhD thesis, LSE Law School, London, available at: http://etheses.lse.ac.uk/3640/1/Keenan_Interception_Law.pdf, 2017.

[KER 89] KERBEY J.O., *The Boy Spy, Belford*, Clarke & Co, New York, 1889.

[KHA 13] KHAZAN O., "The creepy, long-standing practice of undersea cable tapping", *The Atlantic*, available at: https://www.theatlantic.com/international/archive/2013/07/the-creepy-long-standing-practice-of-undersea-cable-tapping/277855/, 2013.

[KHA 14] KHANDELWAL S., 90 percent of the information intercepted by NSA belongs to ordinary internet users, available at: https://thehackernews.com/2014/07/90-percent-of-information-intercepted.html [Accessed October 28, 2021], 2014.

[KLE 09] KLEIN M., *Wiring Up the Big Brother Machine... And Fighting It*, Book Surge, Charleston, 2009.

[KOB 07] KOBLITZ N., "The uneasy relationship between mathematics and cryptography", *Notices of the AMS*, no. 8, pp. 972–979, 2007.

[KOS 17] KOSSEFF J., *Cybersecurity Law*, Wiley, Hoboken, 2017.

[LAR 13] LA RUE F., Report of the special Rapporteur on the promotion and protection of the right to freedom of opinion and expression, Report, United Nations, General Assembly, available at: http://www.ohchr.org/Documents/HRBodies/HRCouncil/RegularSession/Session23/A.HRC.23.40_EN.pdf, 2013.

[LAU 09] LAURENT S.Y., *Politiques de l'ombre. État, renseignement et surveillance en France*, Fayard, Paris, 2009.

[LAU 14] LAURENT S.Y., *Atlas du renseignement : géopolitique du pouvoir*, Presses de Sciences-Po, Paris, 2014.

[LAU 15] LAURENT S.Y. (ed.), *Le secret de l'État – Surveiller, protéger, informer XVIIe-XXe siècle*, Nouveau monde éditions, Paris, 2015.

[LAU 18] LAURENT S.Y., KHELOUFI M., "Les normes juridiques internationales applicables aux communications individuelles : les enjeux du 'secret des correspondances' et des 'données personnelles'", *Programme UTIC*, no. 7, 2018.

[LAU 19] LAURENT S.Y., "Les gouvernances mondiales fragmentées de l'Internet", *Projet UTIC*, no. 8, 2019.

[LEE 12] LEE M., Microsemi denies it put a backdoor in chips, available at: https://www.zdnet.com/article/microsemi-denies-it-put-a-backdoor-in-chips/, 2012.

[LEG 16] LEGER T., Introduction à la cyber intelligence, available at: https://www.darkstrategic.com/news/2018/2/2/introduction-la-cyber-intelligence, 2016.

[LEU 16] LEUNG C., "Hong Kong surveillance watchdog eyes fair play", *South China Morning Post*, available at: https://www.scmp.com/news/hong-kong/law-crime/article/2052284/hong-kong-surveillance-watchdog-eyes-fair-play, 2016.

[LEU 18] LEUNG C., "Law enforcement officers need more training on interception and surveillance, says watchdog, after rise in reported irregularities", *South China Morning Post*, available at: https://www.scmp.com/news/hong-kong/law-and-crime/article/2176336/law-enforcement-officers-need-more-training, 2018.

[LIN 76] LINDEN T.A., Security analysis and enhancements of computer operating systems, Report, NBSIR 76-1041, The RISOS Project, Institute for Computer Sciences and Technology, National Bureau of Standards, U.S. Department of Commerce, Washington, available at: https://nvlpubs.nist.gov/nistpubs/Legacy/IR/nbsir76-1041.pdf, 1976.

[MAH 13] MAHLINGER A., "Le 'Cabinet Noir' à travers le monde", *La semaine politique et littéraire de Paris*, available at: https://gallica.bnf.fr/ark:/12148/bpt6k5717293g, 2013.

[MAI 19] MAIMON D., WU Y., MCGUIRE M., et al., SSL/TLS certificates and their prevalence on the dark web (first report), Report, ENCS, University of Georgia, available at: https://scholarworks.gsu.edu/cgi/viewcontent.cgi?article=1000&context=ebcs_reports, 2019.

[MAK 11] MAKARIM E., "Indonesia: The controversy over the bill concerning lawful interception", *Digital Evidence and Electronic Signature Law Review*, no. 8, pp. 130–138, available at: https://sas-space.sas.ac.uk/5592/1/1962-2787-1-SM.pdf, 2011.

[MAR 73] MARCILHACY P., MONORY R., Rapport fait au nom de la Commission de contrôle des services administratifs procédant aux écoutes téléphoniques, Report, Sénat, Première session ordinaire de 1973–1974, Paris, available at: https://www.senat.fr/rap/r73-030/r73-0301.pdf, 1973.

[MAY 01] MAYER J.D., "The racial politics of the 1964 presidential campaign", *Prologue Magazine*, no. 1, available at: https://www.archives.gov/publications/prologue/2001/spring/lbj-and-white-backlash-1.html, 2001.

[MEH 09] MEHTA I., India joins the idiotic global alliance calling for encryption backdoors, available at: https://thenextweb.com/news/india-joins-the-idiotic-global-alliance-calling-for-encyption-backdoors, 2009.

[MIC 17] MIC P., POTTER C., Poverty in the U.S.? Yes – and it's a digital rights issue, available at: https://www.accessnow.org/poverty-u-s-yes-digital-rights-issue/, 2017.

[NAT 05] NATIONAL SECURITY AGENCY, Report to the intelligence oversight board on NSA activities, fourth quarter FY0, Report, NSA, available at: https://www.nsa.gov/Portals/70/documents/news-features/declassified-documents/intelli-gence-oversight-board/FY2005_4Q_IOB_Report.pdf, 2005.

[NAT 15] NATIONAL SECURITY AGENCY, Report to the intelligence oversight board on NSA Activities, Report, NSA, available at: https://www.nsa.gov/Portals/70/documents/news-features/declassified-documents/intelligence-oversight-board/IOB%202Q%20CY 2015.pdf, 2015.

[NGW 17] NGWENDE O.F., "The interception of communication laws in Zimbabwe: Assessing the impact on the fundamental right to privacy", *Imperial Journal of Interdisciplinary Research*, no. 1, pp. 819–827, available at: http://www.onlinejournal.in/IJIRV3I1/145.pdf, 2017.

[NOH 11] NOHL K., MELETTE L., GPRS intercept: Wardriving your country. Chaos Communication Camp, available at: http://events.ccc.de/camp/2011/Fahrplan/attachments/1868_110810.SRLabs-Camp-GRPS_Intercept.pdf, 2011.

[NSA 53] NSA, The potentialities of COMINT as a source of warning of the eminence of hostilities, available at: https://www.nsa.gov/Portals/70/documents/news-features/declassified-documents/friedman-documents/reports-research/FOLDER_138/41712209075151.pdf, 1953.

[NSA 88] NSA, "Operation regal: The Berlin tunnel", *United States Cryptologic History Social Series*, no. 4, available at: https://archive.org/details/operation_regal-nsa/mode/2up, 1988.

[NYE 96] NYE J.S., WILLIAM A., "Owens, America's information edge", *Foreign Affairs*, no. 2, pp. 20–36, 1996.

[OFF 85] OFFICE OF TECHNOLOGY ASSESSMENT, Electronic surveillance and civil liberties federal government information technology, Report, Washington Congress, OTACIT-293, available at: https://ota.fas.org/reports/8509.pdf, 1985.

[OFF 87] OFFICE OF TECHNOLOGY ASSESSMENT, The electronic supervisor: New technology, Report, New Tensions, U.S. Congress, OTA-CIT-333, Government Printing Office, available at: https://ota.fas.org/reports/8708.pdf, 1987.

[OFF 19] OFFICE OF THE DIRECTOR OF NATIONAL INTELLIGENCE, Legal reference book, available at: https://www.dni.gov/files/documents/OGC/LegalRefBook2019.pdf, 2019.

[OSB 16] OSBORNE C., "Dutch police close Ennetcom encrypted communications network", *ZDNet*, available at: https://www.zdnet.com/article/dutch-police-arrest-owner-of-ennetcom-encryption-network/, 2016.

[OSU 16] O'SULLIVAN A., DOURADO E., "Going dark? Federal wiretap data show scant encryption problems", *Mercatus Center*, available at: https://www.mercatus.org/publications/technology-and-innovation/going-dark-federal-wiretap-data-show-scant-encryption, 2016.

[PAG 16] PAGANINI P., An investigation conducted by the motherboard demonstrates that is *(sic)* quite easy to buy Surveillance Equipment avoiding export restrictions, available at: http://securityaffairs.co/wordpress/43711/security/tactical-surveillance-technology-investigation.html, 2016.

[PAN 20] PANDIELLA L.M., Vuelven las "chuzadas" a Colombia: El Ejército espió magistrados, congresistas y periodistas según investigación, available at: https://www.france24.com/es/20200113-vuelven-las-chuzadas-a-colombia-el-ej%C3%A9rcito-espi%C3%B3-magistrados-congresistas-y-periodistas-seg%C3%BAn-investigaci%C3%B3n, 2020.

[PEA 16] PEARSON J., LIN J., Exclusive: How Canadian police intercept and read encrypted BlackBerry messages, available at: https://motherboard.vice.com/en_us/article/rcmp-blackberry-project-clemenza-global-encryption-key-canada, 2016.

[PEC 72] PECK W., U.S. Electronic espionage: A memoir, *Ramparts*, vol. 11, no, 1972.

[PER 11] PERDERSEN J., Le secret dans les communications radiotélégraphiques, Annales des postes, télégraphes et téléphones : recueil de documents français et étrangers concernant les services techniques et l'exploitation des postes, télégraphes et téléphones, available at: https://gallica.bnf.fr/ark:/12148/bpt6k9679966v, 1911.

[PIN 84] PINKERTON A., *The Spy of the Rebellion*, Rose Publishing Company, Toronto, available at: https://www.parismuseescollections.paris.fr/sites/default/files/styles/pm_notice/public/atoms/images/CAR/aze_carg021974-49_rec_001.jpg?itok=sGZbwTrI, 1884.

[PLU 82] PLUM W.R., *The Military Telegraph During the Civil War in the United States*, Jansen, Mac Lurg & Company Publishers, Chicago, available at: https://ia800202.us.archive.org/0/items/cu31924092908742/cu31924092908742.pdf, 1882.

[POL 16] POLČÁK R., PAVEL L., JAKUB M., *Interception of Electronic Communications in the Czech Republic and Slovakia*, Masaryk University Press, Brno, available at: https://science.law.muni.cz/knihy/monografie/Polcak_Interception_of_EC.pdf, 2016.

[PRI 18] PRIVACY INTERNATIONAL, Communications surveillance, available at: https://privacyinternational.org/explainer/1309/communications-surveillance, 2018.

[PRI 21] PRIVACY INTERNATIONAL, Communications surveillance: Distinctions and definitions, available at: https://privacyinternational.org/course-section/2088/communications-surveillance-distinctions-and-definitions [Accessed May 12, 2021], 2021.

[PRO 18] PROVOST A., LEVILLAIN O., "Analyses des configurations SSL/TLS de serveurs SMTP", *MISC*, no. 96, 2018.

[RAJ 16] RAJAGOPALAN R.P., BISWAS A., Wassenaar arrangement: The case of India's membership, ORF Occasional Paper, no. 92, 2016.

[RAT 64] RAT M., *La guerre des Gaules, traduction du texte de Jules César*, Garnier-Flammarion, Paris, available at: http://classiques.uqac.ca/classiques/cesar_jules/guerre_des_gaules/guerre_des_gaules.doc, 1964.

[REE 16] REES M., Chiffrement : l'Intérieur veut obliger Skype "à procéder à des interceptions", available at: http://www.nextinpact.com/news/101236-chiffrement-l-interieur-veut-obliger-skype-a-proceder-a-interceptions.htm, 2016.

[REE 20] REES M., Face au chiffrement de bout en bout, Christophe Castaner rêve de backdoors, available at: https://www.nextinpact.com/article/30053/108718-face-au-chiffrement-bout-en-bout-christophe-castaner-reve-backdoors, 2020.

[REU 62] REUTERS, "Cosmonauts begin new orbit 'feeling fine'", *The Age*, available at: https://news.google.com/newspapers?nid=1300&dat=19620814&id=SXFVAAAAIBAJ&sjid=jJYDAAAAIBAJ&pg=3675,2084761, 1962.

[ROB 77] ROBINET J.B.R., *Dictionnaire universel des sciences morale, économique, politique et diplomatique, ou bibliothèque de l'Homme d'État et du Citoyen*, Libraires associés, London, available at: https://gallica.bnf.fr/ark:/12148/bpt6k940792, 1977.

[SAN 12] SANDERS R., "Israeli spy companies: Verint and Narus", *Spring*, no. 66, pp. 43–48, available at: https://fr.scribd.com/document/161872498/Israeli-Spy-Companies-Verint-and-Narus, 2012.

[SCA 15] SCAHILL J., BEGLEY J., "How spies stole the keys to the encryption castle", *The Intercept*, available at: https://theintercept.com/2015/02/19/great-sim-heist/, 2015.

[SCH 01] SCHMID G., Projet de rapport sur l'existence d'un système d'interceptionmondial des communications privées et économiques (système d'interception ECHELON), Commission temporaire sur le système d'interception ECHELON, Report, European Parliament, Brussels, available at: http://strategique.free.fr/analyses/echelon_projet_rapport_final_180501.pdf, 2001.

[SCH 16] SCHNEIER B., Why you should side with Apple, not the FBI, in the San Bernardino iPhone case, available at: https://www.schneier.com/essays/archives/2016/02/why_you_should_side_.html, 2016.

[SCH 17] SCHAAKE M., Draft opinion of the Committee on Foreign Affairs for the Committee on International Trade on the proposal for a regulation of the European Parliament and of the Council setting up a Union regime for the control of exports, transfer, brokering, technical assistance and transit of dual-use items, Report, European Parliament, available at: https://www.europarl.europa.eu/doceo/document/AFET-PA-602925_EN.pdf?redirect, 2017.

[SEE 18] SEEDYK C., "Characterizing cyber intelligence as an all-source intelligence product", *DSIAC Journal*, no. 3, available at: https://www.dsiac.org/resources/articles/characterizing-cyber-intelligence-as-an-all-source-intelligence-product/, 2018.

[SEE 20] SEEKS F., Drone-mounted device to intercept battlefield radio communications, available at: https://www.thedefensepost.com/2020/11/19/france-seeks-drone-device/, 2020.

[SHE 16] SHERMAN D., *The First Americans: The 1941 US Codebreaking Mission to Bletchley Park*, National Security Agency, Center for Cryptologic History, Washington, available at: https://www.nsa.gov/Portals/70/documents/about/cryptologic-heritage/historical-figures-publications/publications/wwii/sherman-the-first-americans.pdf, 2016.

[SHE 21] SHERMAN J., Cyber defense across the ocean floor. The geopolitics of submarine cable security, Report, Atlantic Council, available at: https://www.atlanticcouncil.org/wp-content/uploads/2021/09/Cyber-defense-across-the-ocean-floor-The-geopolitics-of-submarine-cable-security.pdf, 2021.

[SIL 18] SILL E., PÉTIN P.O., Techniques et contre-mesures techniques, Report, Projet UTIC, 2018.

[SIU 13] SIU P., "Surveillance watchdog seeks power to listen to intercepted material", *South China Morning Post*, available at: https://www.scmp.com/news/hong-kong/article/1372142/surveillance-watchdog-seeks-power-listen-intercepted-material, 2013.

[SKO 12] SKOROBOGATOV S., WOODS C., "Breakthrough silicon scanning discovers backdoor in military chip", *Cryptographic Hardware and Embedded Systems Workshop (CHES 2012)*, Louvain, available at: https://www.cl.cam.ac.uk/~sps32/ches2012-backdoor.pdf, 2012.

[SLO 33] SLOCOMBE G., "La bataille de la Sarre, Evening Standard, Royaume-Uni", *Bulletin quotidien de la presse étrangère*, available at: https://gallica.bnf.fr/ark:/12148/bpt6k6266 7790, 1933.

[SMI 00] SMITH GROUP, Technical and cost issues associated with interception of communications at certain communication service providers, Report, The Smith Group Limited, 2000.

[SNO 19] SNOWDEN E., *Permanent Record*, Macmillan, New York, 2019.

[SOO 14] SOOD A.K., ENBODY R., *Targeted Cyber Attacks*, Elsevier, Amsterdam, 2014.

[STE 76] STERN L., "Nixon defends plots in Chile", *The Victoria Advocate*, available at: https://news.google.com/newspapers?nid=861&dat=19760312&id=LhRZAAAAIBAJ&sjid=WE YNAAAAIBAJ&pg=1747,2067202, 1976.

[STR 46] STRATEGIC SERVICES UNIT, Japanese Intelligence Organizations in China, Declassified report from the CIA files, Langley, 1946.

[THE 06] THE STRAITS TIMES, Untitled article, available at: https://eresources.nlb.gov.sg/newspapers/Digitised/Article/straitstimes19060820-1.2.31?ST=1&AT=search&k=interception%20of%20telegraph&QT=interception,of,telegraph&oref=article, 1906.

[THI 13] THINKERVIEW, Eric Filiol (hacker, cryptanalyste, ancien de la DGSE), available at: https://www.youtube.com/watch?v=Fn_dcljvPuY, 2013.

[THO 15] THOMAS T., VALLI C., Mapping the laws which apply to intercepting wireless communications in a Western Australian legal context, *13th Australian Digital Forensics Conference, Held from the 30 November – 2 December*, Edith Cowan University, Perth, available at: https://ro.ecu.edu.au/cgi/viewcontent.cgi?article=1145&context=adf, 2015.

[THO 18] THOMAS S., FRANCILLON A., Backdoors: Definition, deniability and detection, *Proceedings of the 21st International Symposium on Research in Attacks, Intrusions, and Defenses (RAID 2018)*, Heraklion, Crete, available at: https://hal.inria.fr/hal-01889981/document, 2018.

[TIL 20] TILOUINE J., "Comment le Togo a utilisé le logiciel israélien Pegasus pour espionner des religieux catholiques et des opposants", *Le Monde*, available at: https://www.lemonde.fr/afrique/article/2020/08/03/au-togo-un-espion-dans-les-smartphones_6048023_3212.html, 2020.

[TIN 19] TING V., "Breaches in Hong Kong police surveillance operations 'shocking', says lawmaker James To, warning trust in force is already at rock bottom", *South China Morning Post*, available at: https://www.scmp.com/news/hong-kong/politics/article/3040290/breaches-hong-kong-police-surveillance-operations-shocking, 2019.

[TRÉ 17] TRÉGUER F., "Renseignement : derrière le brouillard juridique, la légalisation du Deep Packet Inspection", *La Quadrature du Net*, available at: https://halshs.archives-ouvertes.fr/halshs-01649986/document, 2017.

[TRÉ 19] TRÉGUER F., "Seeing like big tech: Security assemblages, technology, and the future of state bureaucracy", in BIGO D., ISIN E., RUPPERT E. (eds), *Data Politics*, Routledge, London, 2019.

[UNV 18] UNVER A., Politics of digital surveillance, national security and privacy, available at: https://edam.org.tr/en/politics-of-digital-surveillance-national-security-and-privacy/, 2018.

[VAN 18] VAN NOORT A.E.F., Interception of electronic communications. The (dis)approval of backdoors in an increasingly encrypted digital world, Master's thesis, Tilburg University, 2018.

[VED 19] VEDOYA S., Operación Topógrafo: Quiénes son los jueces que autorizaron las escuchas y que podrían declarar ante la fiscalía, available at: https://www.msn.com/es-cl/noticias/chile/operaci%C3%B3n-top%C3%B3grafo-qui%C3%A9nes-son-los-jueces-que-autorizaron-las-escuchas-y-que-podr%C3%ADan-declarar-ante-la-fiscal%C3%ADa/ar-AAFO6ei, 2019.

[VEN 20] VENTRE D., *Artificial Intelligence, Cybersecurity and Cyber Defense*, ISTE Ltd, London, and John Wiley & Sons, New York, 2020.

[VIT 20] VITARD A., "Chiffrement des données : la NSA refuse de révéler sa doctrine en matière de backdoors", *L'Usine Digitale*, available at: https://www.usine-digitale.fr/article/chiffrement-des-donnees-la-nsa-refuse-de-reveler-sa-doctrine-en-matiere-de-backdoor.N1021989, 2020.

[WAR 76] WARE W.H., Security controls for computer systems: Report of defense science board task force on computer security, R-609-1, RAND Corporation, available at: https://www.rand.org/pubs/reports/R609-1.html, 1976.

[WAR 01] WARNER M., "Web warriors looking for a good software firm", *CNN Money*, available at: https://money.cnn.com/magazines/fortune/fortune_archive/2001/10/15/311567/index.htm [Accessed July 26, 2021], 2001.

[WEB 47] WEBER M., *The Theory of Social and Economic Organization*, Free Press, Chicago, 1947.

[WIN 01] WINCHESTER R.S., Constitutional conflicts with encryption regulation, Master's thesis, Purdue University, West Lafayette, 2001.

[WIN 15] WINKLER R.J., Silencing the enemy: Cable-cutting in the Spanish-American War, War on the Rocks, available at: https://warontherocks.com/2015/11/silencing-the-enemy-cable-cutting-in-the-spanish-american-war/, 2015.

[WOL 01] WOLF P. (ed.), Cointelpro: The untold American story, available at: https://cldc.org/wp-content/uploads/2011/12/COINTELPRO.pdf, 2001.

[WOO 06] WOOLLEY P.L., Defining cyberspace as a United States Air Force Mission, Master's thesis, Air Force Institute of Technology, Wright-Patterson, 2006.

[WRI 87] WRIGHT P., GREENGRASS P., *Spycatcher*, Robert Lafond, Paris, 1987.

[WRI 98] WRIGHT S., An appraisal of the technologies of political control, Report, Omega Foundation, European Parliament (STOA), 1998.

[YAA 20] YAACOUB J.P., NOURA H., SALMAN O., et al., "Security analysis of drones systems: Attacks, limitations, and recommendations", *Internet of Things*, vol. 11, doi: 10.1016/j.iot.2020.100218, 2020.

[YAR 31] YARDLEY H.O., *The American Black Chamber*, The Bobbs-Merrill Company Publishers, Indianapolis, 1931.

[YEN 15] YEN A., Why banning secure email won't stop terror, available at: https://protonmail.com/blog/privacy-encryption-and-terrorism/ [Accessed June 23, 2021], 2015.

[ZET 15] ZETTER K., After Paris attacks, here's what the CIA director gets wrong about encryption, available at: https://www.wired.com/2015/11/paris-attacks-cia-director-john-brennan-what-he-gets-wrong-about-encryption-backdoors/ [Accessed June 23, 2021], 2015.

[ZIO 13] ZIOLKOWSKI K. (ed.), Peacetime Regime for state activities in cyberspace, Report, International Law, International Relations and Diplomacy, NATO CCD COE, available at: https://www.ilsa.org/Jessup/Jessup16/Batch%202/Peacetime-Regime.pdf, 2013.

Index

U, W

Other titles from

in

Science, Society and New Technologies

2023

ELAMÉ Esoh
*The Sustainable City in Africa Facing the Challenge of Liquid Sanitation
(Territory Development Set – Volume 2)*

JURCZENKO Emmanuel
Climate Investing: New Strategies and Implementation Challenges

2022

AIT HADDOU Hassan, TOUBANOS Dimitri, VILLIEN Philippe
Ecological Transition in Education and Research

CARDON Alain
*Information Organization of The Universe and Living Things: Generation of
Space, Quantum and Molecular Elements, Coactive Generation of Living
Organisms and Multiagent Model
(Digital Science Set – Volume 3)*

CAULI Marie, FAVIER Laurence, JEANNAS Jean-Yves
Digital Dictionary

DAVERNE-BAILLY Carole, WITTORSKI Richard
Research Methodology in Education and Training: Postures, Practices and Forms
(Education Set – Volume 12)

ELAMÉ Esoh
Sustainable Intercultural Urbanism at the Service of the African City of Tomorrow
(Territory Development Set – Volume 1)

FLEURET Sébastien
A Back and Forth Between Tourism and Health: From Medical Tourism to Global Health
(Tourism and Mobility Systems Set – Volume 5)

KAMPELIS Nikos, KOLOKOTSA Denia
Smart Zero-energy Buildings and Communities for Smart Grids
(Engineering, Energy and Architecture Set – Volume 9)

2021

BARDIOT Clarisse
Performing Arts and Digital Humanities: From Traces to Data
(Traces Set – Volume 5)

BENSRHAIR Abdelaziz, BAPIN Thierry
From AI to Autonomous and Connected Vehicles: Advanced Driver-Assistance Systems (ADAS)
(Digital Science Set – Volume 2)

BÉRANGER Jérôme
Towards an Ethical and Eco-responsible AI
Technological Prospects and Social Applications Set – Volume 4)

CORDELIER Benoit, GALIBERT Oliver
Digital Health Communications
Technological Prospective and Social Applications Set – Volume 5)

DOUAY Nicolas, MINJA Michael
Urban Planning for Transitions

GALINON-MÉLÉNEC Béatrice
The Trace Odyssey 1: A Journey Beyond Appearances
(Traces Set – Volume 4)

HENRY Antoine
Platform and Collective Intelligence: Digital Ecosystem of Organizations

LE LAY Stéphane, SAVIGNAC Emmanuelle, LÉNEL Pierre, FRANCES Jean
The Gamification of Society
(Research, Innovative Theories and Methods in SSH Set – Volume 2)

RADI Bouchaïb, EL HAMI Abdelkhalak
Optimizations and Programming: Linear, Non-linear, Dynamic, Stochastic and Applications with Matlab
(Digital Science Set – Volume 1)

2020

ALAKTIF Jamila, CALLENS Stéphane
Migration and Climate Change: From the Emergence of Human Cultures to Contemporary Management in Organizations

BARNOUIN Jacques
The World's Construction Mechanism: Trajectories, Imbalances and the Future of Societies
(Interdisciplinarity between Biological Sciences and Social Sciences Set – Volume 4)

ÇAĞLAR Nur, CURULLI Irene G., SIPAHIOĞLU Işıl Ruhi, MAVROMATIDIS Lazaros
Thresholds in Architectural Education (Engineering, Energy and Architecture Set – Volume 7)

DUBOIS Michel J.F.
Humans in the Making: In the Beginning was Technique
(Social Interdisciplinarity Set – Volume 4)

2019

BRIANÇON Muriel
The Meaning of Otherness in Education: Stakes, Forms, Process, Thoughts and Transfers
(Education Set – Volume 3)

DESCHAMPS Jacqueline
Mediation: A Concept for Information and Communication Sciences
(Concepts to Conceive 21ˢᵗ Century Society Set – Volume 1)

DOUSSET Laurent, PARK Sejin, GUILLE-ESCURET Georges
Kinship, Ecology and History: Renewal of Conjunctures
(Interdisciplinarity between Biological Sciences and Social Sciences Set – Volume 3)

DUPONT Olivier
Power
(Concepts to Conceive 21ˢᵗ Century Society Set – Volume 2)

FERRARATO Coline
Prospective Philosophy of Software: A Simondonian Study

GUAAYBESS Tourya
The Media in Arab Countries: From Development Theories to Cooperation Policies

HAGÈGE Hélène
Education for Responsibility
(Education Set – Volume 4)

LARDELLIER Pascal
The Ritual Institution of Society
(Traces Set – Volume 2)

LARROCHE Valérie
The Dispositif
(Concepts to Conceive 21ˢᵗ Century Society Set – Volume 3)

LATERRASSE Jean
Transport and Town Planning: The City in Search of Sustainable Development

LELEU-MERVIEL Sylvie, SCHMITT Daniel, USEILLE Philippe
From UXD to LivXD: Living eXperience Design

LENOIR Virgil Cristian
Ethically Structured Processes
(Innovation and Responsibility Set – Volume 4)

LOPEZ Fanny, PELLEGRINO Margot, COUTARD Olivier
Local Energy Autonomy: Spaces, Scales, Politics
(Urban Engineering Set – Volume 1)

METZGER Jean-Paul
Discourse: A Concept for Information and Communication Sciences
(Concepts to Conceive 21st Century Society Set – Volume 4)

MICHA Irini, VAIOU Dina
Alternative Takes to the City
(Engineering, Energy and Architecture Set – Volume 5)

PÉLISSIER Chrysta
Learner Support in Online Learning Environments

PIETTE Albert
Theoretical Anthropology or How to Observe a Human Being
(Research, Innovative Theories and Methods in SSH Set – Volume 1)

PIRIOU Jérôme
The Tourist Region: A Co-Construction of Tourism Stakeholders
(Tourism and Mobility Systems Set – Volume 1)

PUMAIN Denise
Geographical Modeling: Cities and Territories
(Modeling Methodologies in Social Sciences Set – Volume 2)

WALDECK Roger
Methods and Interdisciplinarity
(Modeling Methodologies in Social Sciences Set – Volume 1)

2018

BARTHES Angela, CHAMPOLLION Pierre, ALPE Yves
Evolutions of the Complex Relationship Between Education and Territories
(Education Set – Volume 1)

BÉRANGER Jérôme
The Algorithmic Code of Ethics: Ethics at the Bedside of the Digital Revolution
(Technological Prospects and Social Applications Set – Volume 2)

DUGUÉ Bernard
Time, Emergences and Communications
(Engineering, Energy and Architecture Set – Volume 4)

GEORGANTOPOULOU Christina G., GEORGANTOPOULOS George A.
Fluid Mechanics in Channel, Pipe and Aerodynamic Design Geometries 1
(Engineering, Energy and Architecture Set – Volume 2)

GEORGANTOPOULOU Christina G., GEORGANTOPOULOS George A.
Fluid Mechanics in Channel, Pipe and Aerodynamic Design Geometries 2
(Engineering, Energy and Architecture Set – Volume 3)

GUILLE-ESCURET Georges
Social Structures and Natural Systems: Is a Scientific Assemblage Workable?
(Social Interdisciplinarity Set – Volume 2)

LARINI Michel, BARTHES Angela
Quantitative and Statistical Data in Education: From Data Collection to Data Processing
(Education Set – Volume 2)

LELEU-MERVIEL Sylvie
Informational Tracking
(Traces Set – Volume 1)

SALGUES Bruno
Society 5.0: Industry of the Future, Technologies, Methods and Tools
(Technological Prospects and Social Applications Set – Volume 1)

TRESTINI Marc
Modeling of Next Generation Digital Learning Environments: Complex Systems Theory

2017

ANICHINI Giulia, CARRARO Flavia, GESLIN Philippe, GUILLE-ESCURET Georges
Technicity vs Scientificity – Complementarities and Rivalries (Interdisciplinarity between Biological Sciences and Social Sciences Set – Volume 2)

DUGUÉ Bernard
Information and the World Stage – From Philosophy to Science, the World of Forms and Communications (Engineering, Energy and Architecture Set – Volume 1)

GESLIN Philippe
Inside Anthropotechnology – User and Culture Centered Experience (Social Interdisciplinarity Set – Volume 1)

GORIA Stéphane
Methods and Tools for Creative Competitive Intelligence

KEMBELLEC Gérald, BROUDOUS EVELYNE
Reading and Writing Knowledge in Scientific Communities: Digital Humanities and Knowledge Construction

MAESSCHALCK Marc
Reflexive Governance for Research and Innovative Knowledge (Responsible Research and Innovation Set - Volume 6)

PARK Sejin, GUILLE-ESCURET Georges
Sociobiology vs Socioecology: Consequences of an Unraveling Debate (Interdisciplinarity between Biological Sciences and Social Sciences Set – Volume 1)

PELLÉ Sophie
Business, Innovation and Responsibility (Responsible Research and Innovation Set – Volume 7)

2016

ANDRÉ Michel, SAMARAS Zissis
Energy and Environment
(Research for Innovative Transports Set – Volume 1)

BLANQUART Corinne, CLAUSEN Uwe, JACOB Bernard
Towards Innovative Freight and Logistics
(Research for Innovative Transports Set – Volume 2)

BRONNER Gérald
Belief and Misbelief Asymmetry on the Internet

COHEN Simon, YANNIS George
Traffic Management
(Research for Innovative Transports Set – Volume 3)

EL FALLAH SEGHROUCHNI Amal, ISHIKAWA Fuyuki, HÉRAULT Laurent,
TOKUDA Hideyuki
Enablers for Smart Cities

GIANNI Robert
Responsibility and Freedom
(Responsible Research and Innovation Set – Volume 2)

GRUNWALD Armin
The Hermeneutic Side of Responsible Research and Innovation
(Responsible Research and Innovation Set – Volume 5)

LAGRAÑA Fernando
E-mail and Behavioral Changes: Uses and Misuses of Electronic
Communications

LENOIR Virgil Cristian
Ethical Efficiency: Responsibility and Contingency
(Responsible Research and Innovation Set – Volume 1)

MAESSCHALCK Marc
Reflexive Governance for Research and Innovative Knowledge
(Responsible Research and Innovation Set – Volume 6)

PELLÉ Sophie, REBER Bernard
From Ethical Review to Responsible Research and Innovation
(Responsible Research and Innovation Set – Volume 3)

REBER Bernard
Precautionary Principle, Pluralism and Deliberation: Sciences and Ethics
(Responsible Research and Innovation Set – Volume 4)

TORRENTI Jean-Michel, LA TORRE Francesca
Materials and Infrastructures 1
(Research for Innovative Transports Set – Volume 5A

TORRENTI Jean-Michel, LA TORRE Francesca
Materials and Infrastructures 2
(Research for Innovative Transports Set – Volume 5B)

VENTRE Daniel
Information Warfare – 2nd edition

YANNIS George, COHEN Simon
Traffic Safety
(Research for Innovative Transports Set – Volume 4)